OBJECTIVITY AND ITS OTHER

Multidisciplinary Studies in Social Theory

A collectively edited Guilford Series devoted to transdisciplinary understandings on key issues in contemporary social thought.

Editors

John Paul Jones III   **Wolfgang Natter**   **Theodore R. Schatzki**
Committee on Social Theory, University of Kentucky

POSTMODERN CONTENTIONS: EPOCHS, POLITICS, SPACE
John Paul Jones III, Wolfgang Natter, and Theodore R. Schatzki, Editors
(originally published in the Mappings: Society/Theory/Space series)

OBJECTIVITY AND ITS OTHER
Wolfgang Natter, Theodore R. Schatzki, and John Paul Jones III, Editors

Forthcoming

THE SOCIAL AND POLITICAL BODY
Theodore R. Schatzki and Wolfgang Natter, Editors

FROM DEMOCRATIC THEORY TO DEMOCRACY
John Paul Jones III, Wolfgang Natter, and Theodore R. Schatzki, Editors

DISCIPLINING BOUNDARIES
Wolfgang Natter, Theodore R. Schatzki, and John Paul Jones III, Editors

OBJECTIVITY AND ITS OTHER

Edited by
Wolfgang Natter
Theodore R. Schatzki
John Paul Jones III

The Guilford Press
New York   London

© 1995 The Guilford Press
A Division of Guilford Publications, Inc.
72 Spring Street, New York, NY 10012

Printed in the United States of America

This book is printed on acid-free paper.

Last digit is print number: 9 8 7 6 5 4 3 2 1

Library of Congress Cataloging-in-Publication Data

Objectivity and its other / edited by Wolfgang Natter, Theodore
Schatzki, John Paul Jones III.
    p.   cm.
 Includes bibliographical references and index.
 ISBN 0-89862-542-4—ISBN 0-89862-545-9 (pbk.)
 1. Objectivity. I. Natter, Wolfgang. II. Jones, John
Paul, 1955– . III. Schatzki, Theodore R.
 BD220.023 1995
 121'.4—dc20   94-38112
                                                        CIP

Preface

Objectivity and Its Other is the first book in a series of collected volumes entitled "Multidisciplinary Studies in Social Theory." Each volume will contain chapters from humanists and social scientists that focus on a key area of inquiry in contemporary social thought. The aim of the series is avowedly multidisciplinary. By collecting together chapters in each book from a range of social disciplines, we aspire not only to demonstrate the breadth of disciplinary perspectives that bear on central theoretical issues, but also to further cross-disciplinary exchange. The greater the number of forums in which scholars from different social fields gather to examine common theoretical concerns, the quicker social theory will establish itself as a distinct, non-disciplinary-specific field of inquiry. The envisioned series seeks to help realize this goal.

The series of volumes arises out of the activities of the Committee on Social Theory at the University of Kentucky (UK). Each spring semester, the Committee sponsors a public lecture series/graduate seminar combination that is focused on a problem area of broad critical import in contemporary social thought. Each of the books in the series contains the lectures delivered by the visiting scholars participating in a given spring's lecture series, together with chapters written by the UK faculty who have cotaught that semester's graduate seminar. The visitors' contributions are generally revisions of their public lectures that reflect discussions held with UK faculty and students during their stay in Lexington. The UK contributions, on the other hand, grow out of the lengthy discussions conducted among these faculty and students in the weekly graduate seminar. The volumes in the series, consequently, will differ from standard anthologies, which publish commissioned works and/or compile conference proceedings.

A first such collection, *Postmodern Contentions: Epochs, Politics, Space,* was published by The Guilford Press in 1993 in its "Mappings: Society/Theory/Space" series. *Objectivity and Its Other* is thus the second multidisciplinary volume arising from the Committee's activities, and the inaugural book in the new series. The series' next volumes, bespeaking the topic foci of ensuing Committee seminars, will address "The Social and Political Body," "From Democratic Theory to Democracy," and "Disciplining Boundaries."

We would like to take this opportunity to thank the people and programs who have made the Committee's endeavors, and thus the planned series, possible. First and foremost, we thank fellow members of the UK Committee on Social Theory and the students who have participated in our activities. Their enthusiasm and support makes all this possible and worthwhile. The Committee's activities have received support from several university offices. Initial financial support for the Committee came from the University of Kentucky's College of Arts and Sciences and its Graduate School. During the period that produced the chapters in the current volume, support came from the University's Multidisciplinary Feasibility Assessment Program. More recently, contributions have been provided by the College of Arts and Sciences, the Graduate School, the office of the Vice President of Research and Graduate Studies, and the Chancellor of the University of Kentucky's Lexington campus. We would like to thank the former Vice Presidents for Research and Graduate Studies, Len Peters and Lee Magid; the Chancellor of the Lexington campus, Robert Hemenway; the Dean of the College of Arts and Sciences, Richard Edwards, and former Associate Dean Kathy Blee. It is our pleasure to acknowledge the Director of the Gaines Center for the Humanities, Ray Betts, for offering the Center's elegant hospitality for so many memorable Social Theory conversations; research assistant Michael Dorn; and never last nor least, Dan Reedy, the Dean of the Graduate School.

Contributors

JAMES A. BOON is Professor of Anthropology, Princeton University, Princeton, New Jersey.

ANDREW J. GRIMES is Professor of Management and member of the Committee on Social Theory, University of Kentucky, Lexington.

DAVID COUZENS HOY is Professor of Philosophy, University of California, Santa Cruz.

JOHN PAUL JONES III is Associate Professor of Geography and member of the Committee on Social Theory, University of Kentucky, Lexington.

WOLFGANG NATTER is Associate Professor of Germanic Languages and Literatures and member of the Committee on Social Theory, University of Kentucky, Lexington.

GUNNAR OLSSON is Professor of Planning, NORDPLAN, Stockholm, Sweden.

JEREMY D. POPKIN is Professor of History and member of the Committee on Social Theory, University of Kentucky, Lexington.

DEBORAH L. ROOD is Assistant Professor of Management, Pacific Region Program of Troy State University, Troy, Alabama.

THEODORE R. SCHATZKI is Associate Professor of Philosophy and member of the Committee on Social Theory, University of Kentucky, Lexington.

BONNIE G. SMITH is Professor of History, Rutgers University, New Brunswick, New Jersey.

SAMUEL WEBER is Professor of English, University of California, Los Angeles, and Director of the Paris Program in Critical Theory, Paris, France.

Contents

III. RECONCEPTUALIZING OBJECTIVITY

1

Contexts of Objectivity

WOLFGANG NATTER
THEODORE R. SCHATZKI
JOHN PAUL JONES III

Objectivity, like many ends embedded within teleological hierarchies, is not what it used to be. During its reign over the greater part of the last two centuries, the concept has served as both practice and ambition. As practice, it delineated the procedures insuring valid research findings. As ambition, it drew an epistemological trajectory by which the social and humanistic disciplines might prove worthy in comparison to the physical sciences. To become some 200 years ago the prescriber of rules and aspirations, objectivity needed to overcome the criticisms of Romantic thinkers and the defenders of religion who charged that it was reductionist, conceptually impoverished, and spiritually barren. Two centuries later, it has been subjected to criticisms that are far more comprehensive and effective than these early ones. It has been challenged, first, by claims that real knowledge can be attained subjectively (e.g., some strands of phenomenology and standpoint theory); second, by the uncovering of submerged contexts formative of belief and cognition (e.g., language, gender, ethnicity, disciplines, culture); and third, through the breakdown of foundational thinking widely cognized under the banner of postmodernism. Today, as a result, the capacity of objectivity to specify proper research procedures and disciplinary ambitions has been severely compromised.

Despite these developments, the concept refuses to rest in the dustbin of social investigation. Indeed, it continues to inform contemporary reflections on methodology, theory construction, and praxis. Moreover, such contemporary challenges as subjectivism, contextualism, and postmodernism need not be seen as overthrowing objectivity, as it is typically understood, but instead as implicating different and potentially contradictory stances on its possibility and character. It is this premise, and the promise it holds for reconceptualizing objectivity, that animates the current volume. In it, the authors demonstrate that the resources of contemporary movements such as these lend themselves not only to disciplinary critiques of sovereign conceptions of objectivity, but equally propitiously to reformulations of it.

To understand what is at stake in these critiques and reformulations, it is first necessary to trace the recent history of the "question of objectivity." During the past two centuries, discussions of this question have typically focused on two major subquestions. The first is a question about conduct: Can investigators examine their subject matter in a rational, dispassionate, unprejudiced, and evenhanded manner, and if so, should they? The opposite of objectivity in this first sense is at best subjectivity, and at worst willfulness and arbitrariness. The second question addresses results: Can the products of research be true descriptions of a reality that is independent of investigators? The opposite of objective research in this second sense is false descriptions of reality or investigations that construct reality. These two historically important questions, although related, are distinct. This is shown by the fact that, under the above formulations, it is possible that the most rational and dispassionate researcher will fail to provide true accounts (in whatever sense of "true"), while an irrational and prejudiced colleague gets the facts right.

During the course of the 19th century, the increasingly spectacular discoveries and results of the natural sciences made these disciplines paradigms of objectivity in the two senses of objective conduct and objectively true results. Scientists and observers of science believed, moreover, that the natural sciences achieved true results in part because of their objective conduct. The idea of scientific method, adherence to which guaranteed truth, became widespread. As a result, 19th- and early 20th-century humanists and social scientists, in the hope of obtaining objective results and in their rush to professionalize and legitimate their status in the academy and in society, emulated the natural sciences and embraced objective conduct as their proper *modus operandi*. It became commonplace to argue that the "inferior state" of these fields was due to their incomplete adoption of scientific method. As J. S. Mill wrote, "The backward state of the moral sciences can only be remedied by applying to them the methods of physical science, duly extended and generalized."[1]

Among most scholars there was little doubt that the social and human disciplines could adopt the objective methods of natural science and thereby leave behind religion and metaphysics to join the ranks of true science. This optimism underlay the millennial enthusiasm of August Comte, who in conceiving of a "social physics" wrote,

> Now that the human mind has founded celestial physics, terrestrial physics (mechanical and chemical), and organic physics (vegetable and animal), it only remains to complete the system of observational sciences by the foundation of social physics.[2]

Comte's enthusiasm was not only scholarly. He also envisioned that social physics would constitute the intellectual apparatus with which an elite of scientific sages would run society and establish unanimous agreement "with regard to all [political–ethical] maxims whose fixity is the first condition of a true social order." The promise of political stability underwrites such scientism, for otherwise, Comte argued, "We cannot disguise the fact that the nations will necessarily remain in an essentially revolutionary state, in spite of all the political palliatives that may be adopted."[3]

From the middle to the end of the 19th century and continuing into the first half of the 20th, a cadre of scientists and philosophers attempted to codify objective method and thereby provide an epistemological and methodological blueprint for the social and humanistic disciplines. This effort reached a highpoint in the 1930s in the epistemological treatises of the Vienna school theorists (e.g., Karl Popper, Rudolf Carnap, and Otto Neurath), whose formulation of the "nomological–deductive" method served as a benchmark in epistemological discussion well into the 1970s. During the greater part of the 20th century, accordingly, the objectivity enshrined in the by now sovereign conception of "scientific method" reigned widely in scholarly work.

Of course, over these same 150 years there has been no shortage of critics who attacked objectivity by identifying a variety of contexts of thought and research that seem to undermine this norm. An example is emotions and passions and their impact on research. Not long after historians had begun to enforce objective conduct and results (i.e., dispassionate inquiry conforming to Leopold von Ranke's injunction to describe things "as they actually were"[4]), weighty critics of scientism like Friedrich Nietzsche argued that this ideal was naive and unattainable and that it was desirable for emotions and passions to animate historical accounts, for works devoid of them were cold, dead objects of value only to "declining" life:

> [History] requires above all a great artistic faculty, a creative vision from a height, the loving study of the data of experience, the free elaborating of a given type. . . . Objectivity is so often merely a phrase. Instead of the quiet gaze of the artist that is lit by an inward flame, we have an affection of tranquillity. . . . Everything is favored that does not arouse emotion, and the driest phrase is the correct one. [Historians] go so far as to accept a man who is *not affected at all* by some particular moment in the past as the right man to describe it.[5]

A second impediment to objectivity is the deep-seated psychological factors unearthed by Freud. Freud's conception of the unconscious as a representation without a represented breaks down any sharp differentiation between subject and object, thus problematizing their presumed boundaries along with the process of boundary formation itself.[6] This challenges an assumption underlying the ideal of objectivity, namely, the clean separation between subject and object. That unconscious factors are forever withdrawing from or censored before consciousness only compounds the problem, since this undermines apprehension of the ways they thwart rational and judicious research. Freud's theory of the mind further challenges the very possibility of such research by implying that the conscious ego is not the master of its own house.

A third prominent context undermining the reigning concept of objectivity has been political–ethical positionality. Theorists such as Karl Marx, Karl Mannheim, and members of the Frankfurt School all claimed that social scientific results are bound to political and economic contexts. Marx, for example, unearthed the ideological connections between the discipline of political economy and the bourgeois social order it served to legitimate, while Mannheim argued that different historical ontologies and models of causality reflect different political perspectives.[7] Max Horkheimer extended this idea by arguing that it is impossible to produce even a metatheory that would transcend the limitations of particular world views.[8] These thinkers further concurred that all apprehension of (social) reality is mediated by material and social contexts.

The scholarly establishment resisted these insights, however, withdrawing Marx's credentials as political economist by painting him as a mere ideologue and largely ignoring Mannheim and the Frankfurt School theorists. The politicization of research did not resurface in a threatening way, at least in the United States, until the 1960s when the antiwar, civil rights, and women's movements prompted some social scientists to question the model of scientific objectivity (i.e., neutrality) that had for so long reigned in their disciplines. Following the political turmoil of the 1960s, both the social sciences and the humanities largely lost any illusion of recapturing the consensual politics of the early post-World War II period that had veiled the ideological dimensions of research[9]. Bourgeois apologists for the status quo were set against liberals out to make the system more humane, who in turn were castigated by radicals for whom knowledge and social transformation went hand in hand.

In the meantime, language, discipline(s), and power expanded the list of factors thought to bear upon objectivity. Based on studies of traditional communities, the anthropologist Benjamin Whorff[10] claimed that linguistic communities in effect construct their own realities through the languages they speak. His theories raised general issues of linguistic idealism and caused some scholars to maintain that research communities construct the objects they study through specialized languages. Shortly thereafter, scholars such as Thomas Kuhn and Michel Foucault began to marshall impressive evidence demonstrating the dependence of the conduct and products of research upon "disciplinary matrices" or "discursive practices."[11] Both thinkers argued that norms of proper conduct are relative to disciplinary practices, that truth is indistinguishable from what counts as true, and that the possibilities of what can count as truth are laid down by disciplinary practices. In their work, examples of academic forms of disciplining included the perpetuation of intellectual norms via graduate training, the delineation and constitution of objects of analysis, accepted procedures for apprehending objects, and rules for speaking the truth. Foucault also highlighted how discursive practices are embedded in wider systems of power to whose propagation they contribute, as can be seen, for example, in the formation of criminology and demography in the early 19th century as part of the growing "disciplining" of social life.[12]

Among the most significant questions to be addressed in more recent years is whether and how gender affects research conduct and results. The claim that both the world and our ways of studying it are thoroughly gendered suggests to some that gender biases skew many if not most dimensions of research. For such "feminist empiricists," as Sandra Harding summarizes,

> sexist and androcentric claims . . . are caused by social biases. Social biases are . . . prejudices that . . . enter research particularly at the stage when scientific problems are being identified and defined, but they can also appear in the design of research and in the collection and interpretation of data.[13]

In the eyes of other feminists, however, the gendering of world and conduct implies far more strongly that rationality, logic, and research methods are inherently gendered, and that the received norms of objectivity are therefore androcentric constructions.[14]

More recently, feminist critiques have been supplemented by African-American and third world postcolonial claims that social scientific and humanistic research remains predominantly white, Anglo-Saxon, and first world.[15] Writers making these claims often maintain that traditional research does not uncover absolute truth, but only what can be seen from and what serves a restricted set of viewpoints:

> Western social and political thought . . . has long claimed that absolute truths exist and that the task of scholarship is to develop objective, unbiased tools of science to measure these truths. But Afrocentric, feminist, and other bodies of critical theory have unmasked the concepts and epistemology of this version of science as representing the vested interests of elite white men and therefore as being less valid when applied to the experiences of other groups.[16]

To many Afrocentric and feminist scholars, the task is to expose the biases inherent in traditional understandings of objectivity while retaining an ability to pronounce truths, however limited in scope:

> Those ideas that are validated as true by African-American women, African-American men, Latina lesbians, Asian-American women, Puerto-Rican men, and other groups with distinctive standpoints, with each group using the epistemological approaches growing from its unique standpoint, thus become the most "objective" truths. Each group speaks from its own standpoint and shares its own partial, situated knowledge.[17]

These scholars have been further joined by a growing contingent of gay and lesbian scholars who denounce mainstream scholarship as inextricably heterosexual.[18] Some scholars, moreover, argue that the subordinated social positions of all the above groups privilege their standpoints as forms of "subjugated knowledges." For such scholars, the positions of the subjugated are not innocent but nonetheless preferred because they "promise more adequate, sustained, objective, transforming accounts of the world."[19]

Finally, the above lines of critique are brought together in the now widely disseminated recognition of a "crisis of representation," the contention that no system of signification is able to re-present the world in its full presence. This central moment in poststructuralist thought has been focused by Jacques Derrida upon speech acts, undermining the ostensible transparency of mutual understanding fueling a communicative desire now seen as "logocentric."[20] Some theorists understand this debate as the denial of the possibility of meaning "in itself," and thus argue for relativism and subjectivism as the only intellectually honest norms. Others contend that the central task is to unveil the operative conditions of power (e.g., class, race, and gender) that ceaselessly intervene in the representation and dissemination of communication.

As the above discussion suggests, the "question of objectivity" has today become quite complex. The proliferation of critiques of the traditional notion prompts the question: Should the humanities and social sciences abandon the concept of objectivity altogether? Past and present defenders of the traditional conception typically insist that the only alternatives are arbitrariness, relativism, nihilism—in short, chaos. In doing so, they clutch one horn of a rigid either/or dichotomy: *either* traditional objectivity *or* their conception of objectivity's other, namely, nihilism, irrationality, and the like. In their eyes, a thinker who rejects objectivity must defend the latter.[21] Theorists challenging the ideal are painted accordingly as defenders or celebrants of decadence and irrationality. Charges of this nature have been leveled at thinkers as widely divergent in their sensibilities as Friedrich Nietzsche, Thomas Kuhn, Hans-Georg Gadamer, Jacques Derrida, and Jean-François Lyotard.

The persistence of traditionalists among practitioners in the contemporary humanities and social sciences demonstrates in part the power of this either/or logic. It also reveals a capacity to deny, shrug off, or explain away the manifold and overwhelming conceptual arguments and empirical evidence demonstrating the theoretical and practical impossibility of achieving the ideal. The continuing reign of objectivity thus bespeaks a preference for venerable utopias in lieu of confrontation with and reflection about the unavoidable conditioning of thought and inquiry by social, historical, disciplinary, biographical, and gender contexts.

If, by contrast, we accept these critical arguments and evidence, must we follow the traditional logic and conclude that anything goes? Some critics of the traditional ideal have replied in the affirmative, and celebrated various combinations of playfulness and nihilism as a means of preserving freedom.[22] Others—for example, many hermeneutically oriented thinkers—have denied that the conditionality of inquiry forces an embrace of arbitrariness and nihilism. These thinkers believe that the traditional ideal rightly defended a way of being that rescued us from this abyss. For them, consequently, the conditionality of inquiry signals the need to conceptualize a *new* objectivity that does not simply reinstate the traditional other of relativism and willfulness.[23] Poststructuralist thinkers, meanwhile, reach a similar position by a different route. By rigorously demonstrating the dynamic at work in the "ceaseless recontextualization of context,"[24] they inquire as to how the force marshalled by the either/or logic has been stabilized over time and context. In doing so they, like other contextualists, posit the possibility of rigorous thought that avoids the fallacy of either embracing relativism or celebrating traditional objectivity.

For both strands of contemporary thought, the fact that the human epistemological condition renders traditional objectivity impossible raises the challenge of how to fashion a successor to the received ideal that is both consistent with this condition and yet able to constitute a meaningful and practical alternative to willfulness and nihilism. Building upon the efforts of thinkers in these and other traditions, the current volume seeks to continue the exploration of the disciplinary effects of the traditional ideal while further mapping the contours of a reconceptualized objectivity. Only with a clear understanding of these effects and an alternative, well-developed conception of objectivity in hand, can the remaining defenders of the traditional ideal be weaned from their utopias and fears, and scholars in general learn to practice their trade in an objective manner.

The organization of *Objectivity and Its Other* reflects the narrative just related. The volume opens in Part I with two pieces that outline some of the large-scale concerns connected with the question of objectivity. Gunnar Olsson begins by tying together the contemporary, widespread crises of representation, intentionality, and credibility under the mantle of power and signification. Samuel Weber then uncovers the profound reference to subjectivity and the subject present in both the concept of objectivity and the metaphysical "objectifying" order of the contemporary world.

Part II documents the continuing timeliness and vitality of disciplinary critiques of the traditional ideal of objectivity in contemporary humanistic and social scientistic scholarship. These chapters examine two disciplines, one social scientific and one humanistic, in which this critique has belatedly arrived. Bonnie Smith and Jeremy Popkin explore the impact of gender and national culture, respectively, on the writing of history, while John Paul Jones III examines objectivity's effects on the delimitation of geography's objects of inquiry and their representation.

In Part III, the volume turns its attention to the crucial and unfinished task of reconceptualizing an objectivity that (1) is consistent with the ineliminable sociohistorical, disciplinary, psychological, and gender conditionality of thought and inquiry and yet (2) constitutes an alternative to arbitrariness and nihilism. David Hoy and Ted Schatzki start the discussion by extending insights of Hans-Georg Gadamer into the reflexivity, self-knowledge, and self-overcoming characteristic of such an objectivity. Andrew Grimes and Debra Rood continue by developing the idea of descriptive epistemologies, which are theoretical devices for linking epistemological perspectives that allegedly are at odds with one another. James Boon concludes this section by exploring the descriptive/interpretive nominalism that characterizes a renewed objectivity. The reader will come away from the book as a whole not only with a heightened awareness of both the wealth of issues and concerns associated with objectivity and the difficulties attending the traditional ideal, but also with a concrete sense of the ways of being and operating that will qualify his or her activity as objective.

COMPLEX TERRAIN

In "Signs of Persuasion" (Chapter 2) Gunnar Olsson sets the stage for the volume's examination of objectivity in a brief but fertile chapter focusing on three related crises widely discussed in the humanities and social sciences today: representation, intentionality, and credibility. Together, these crises are brought to bear upon his central question, "What does it mean to make sense?" The point of reference for his discussion is Saussure's bar, which separates the signifier from the signified. In the impossibility of joining the two, of capturing the latter with the former, lies the crisis of representation, which Olsson illustrates via the Homeric fable of Odysseus, the Cyclops, and the cave. The second crisis is underscored by Olsson's claim that "making sense" is detached from intentionality; that is, our intentions as authors/readers to faithfully communicate/interpret meaning may bear no relation to the end results of communication. The final crisis is that of credibility: " . . . it is not enough to tell the truth. I must also be trusted" (Chapter 2, p. 23).

Underpinning all three crises is power—the power to represent, to determine meaning, and to be believed. Rhetoric, to Olsson, is pure power, and it is through the incessant exercise of power that we become obedient to rhetoric. Thus, the answer to the question, "What does it mean to make sense?," is not so simple as might be suggested from traditional notions of objectivity—for example, mutual understanding and agreement concerning reality. For lurking behind the question are three unresolvable crises, and with them the power of persuasion.

The title of the second chapter in Part I, Samuel Weber's "Objectivity Otherwise" (Chapter 3) conjoins two distinct but perhaps complicitous notions. "Objectivity otherwise" may mean objectivity examined in a manner different from the familiar or, divergently, it may signify objectivity or else!

Weber's reading of Webster's *New Collegiate Dictionary* and Martin Heidegger's *The Overcoming of Metaphysics* reveals an instructive relation between the two texts where the question of "objectivity and its others" is concerned. By offering a careful analysis of the relations among objectivity, objects, subjectivity, and objectives, Weber shows how the internal tensions and ambiguities in the dictionary definition of objectivity undercut the radical demarcation of objective and subjective it seeks to affirm. Its nonsubjective description of objectivity proves to be one in which divergent and possibly conflicting points of view can be reduced, or at least measured and managed, by appealing to the authority of an object that is held to be unified and self-identical precisely to the extent that it is independent of the subject. Hence, this other of objectivity proves to be the desire for conflict resolution, or at least control.

Turning to Heidegger, Weber first explains how Heidegger's overcoming of metaphysics has the character of a "winding up." Far from simply coming to an end (like an opinion), metaphysics is today consolidating and establishing its "unconditional domination" all the more thoroughly and extensively, leaving little room for alterity. Weber's reading of Heidegger's conceptualization of the status of objectivity in the contemporary world finds in the concept of technics the metaphysical other of objectivity. Parallel to the dictionary's invocation of a subject seeking to stabilize itself, the ultimate objective of technics is the establishment of a certitude and security that is unwilling, and perhaps unable, to make room for the incalculability of the other. Against the danger poised by the metaphysical foreclosure of incalculability, whose tendencies Heidegger had come to find most clearly embodied in Nazism, Weber closes with the question of whether such incalculability may not in fact be inseparable from a notion of liberty that would allow for what in the other resists objectification and hence for subjectification.

DISCIPLINARY CRITIQUES

In "Gender, Objectivity, and the Rise of Scientific History" (Chapter 4) Bonnie Smith kicks off the volume's engagement with disciplinary critique by considering the value of objectivity and its seemingly absent but determinate relationship to gender within the disciplinary practices of 19th- and 20th-century history. Nineteenth-century historians built a modern "scientific" profession whose practices seemed untroubled by the gender considerations then shaping society. Smith's chapter looks at these practices within the new institutional setting of the university in order to show how they in fact relied on gender to constitute a "gender-neutral" community of scholars that could persuade the public of its objectivity.

Using examples taken from the profession's founding father, Ranke, as well as from Acton and Doellinger, she argues that the process of basing "objective" historical writing on data and factuality implicates masculinity, femininity, and sexual difference. Hardly neuter, the metaphors of professionalization—most directly expressed in the desire attached to "penetrating" the "virgin archive" and carrying away its treasures—exuded the quest of a heroic male heterosexuality. As a contrast, Smith examines both the alternative "archives" and the linguistic strategies developed by women such as Lucy Maynord Salmon, Eileen Power, Jane Ellen Harrison, and Mary Beard in their pioneering studies. Backyard and kitchen factualities, in generating studies of a social reality not contained in diplomatic or state archives, fostered an alternative conception of the object(s) of history.

As revealing as an analysis of these women's writings may be in situating the relationship between objectivity, women, and gender as part of the discipline's professionalization, Smith cautions against monumentalizing these women. Doing so, she maintains, may serve ultimately dangerous fantasies, just as the monumentalization of great men and great historians has perpetuated the kind of professional writing about masters, authorities, and the like that heretofore served to exclude women.

John Paul Jones's "Making Geography Objectively: Ocularity, Representation, and *The Nature of Geography*" (Chapter 5) examines the role of objectivity in constructing prevalent notions about geography and its proper practice in the mid-20th century. He begins his account with the analogy of a scaffold, an assemblage of scientific discourses (e.g., rationality, the determinancy of reality) on which the concept of objectivity is perched. As such, objectivity is much more than merely the opposite of subjectivity: It is an instrument of disciplinary power that can distinguish science from art and professional knowledge from preprofessional opinion.

Jones then examines objectivity's role in disciplining geography's objects of inquiry and their representation in Richard Hartshorne's highly influential methodological opus, *The Nature of Geography*. Hartshorne, Jones offers, used the concept of objectivity to widen the discipline's scope by detaching objectivity *per se* from the ocularcentric constraints that had previously determined geography's proper objects of inquiry. While Hartshorne argued for geography's liberation from ocularcentrism, his understanding of objectivity nevertheless remained loyal to the division between knowledge and opinion and science and art. As

Jones argues it, Hartshorne viewed objectivity as a performance, that is, as a form of narration that masks the subjectivities of the author.

In the concluding section of his chapter Jones presents an encounter between objectivity and the ontology of social space developed by the French Marxist Henri Lefebvre. The dialectical sublation of social relations and space in Lefebvre's concept of "social space" provides the grounds for Jones' engagement with two critiques of objectivity: the double hermeneutic and the problem of representation. The former analysis suggests that attention be directed to the sociospatial contingencies of subjects, objects, and interpretive contexts. The latter analysis deploys the idea of "space-as-representation" to critique forms of representation based on mimesis and verisimilitude.

In "The American Historian of France and the 'Other'" (Chapter 6), the collection's final disciplinary critique of objectivity, Jeremy Popkin examines his field's recent encounter with the issue of objectivity. Through a case study of the way American historians have approached the history of France, the chapter deals with the problem of objectivity in intercultural historical research. It begins by examining how American historians of foreign cultures have been less preoccupied than colleagues in other disciplines such as anthropology with the problematic nature of their relationship with their subject matters. This is due in part to differences in the nature of the discipline, Popkin argues, but also to the way in which the study of history in the United States has evolved over the past 100 years. The case of American historians working on French history is instructive in this regard because of the disproportionate interest Americans have shown in that country and because of the exceptional status of the historical profession in France itself. American historians have struggled to overcome a sense of inferiority in relation to their French colleagues, articulated most forcefully in the late David Pinkney's several reflections on their "dilemma." Popkin suggests, however, that in the process of acquiring increased technical expertise and abandoning overt assumptions about French cultural backwardness, younger American scholars have often lost sight of the differences between the two cultures that can add real value to an outsider's perspective. By reflecting on this state of affairs Popkin contributes to the discipline's understanding of its construction and navigation of objectivity.

RECONCEPTUALIZING OBJECTIVITY

In the opening exploration of the contours of a reconceptualized objectivity, "Significant Others: Objectivity and Ethnocentrism" (Chapter 7),

David Hoy pairs objectivity with ethnocentrism. He suggests that we view these notions not as simple opposites, but instead as "significant others"—meaning that each is what it is in part through its contrast with the other. Hoy opens by arguing against the modernist picture of simple opposition, exposing an aporia in arguments of Allan Bloom, a recent champion of objectivity against ethnocentrism. He then suggests that it is from within the perspective of a postmodern hermeneutics that we can best understand ethnocentrism and objectivity as significant others. Ethnocentrism, he writes, is the fact that all understanding is bound to sociohistorical contexts. So construed, ethnocentrism undercuts the traditional notion of objectivity as the achievement of a transcultural viewpoint. But it recognizes a successor: the Gadamerian notion of objectivity as the continual reattainment, through self-criticism and conversation with others, of ever more comprehensive viewpoints that transcend previous understandings. Unlike the sort of ethnocentrism that maintains that our way is better than any other, there is nothing "pernicious" about this type because the paths of self-overcoming followed by different cultures need not converge on any single viewpoint—for instance, that of the modern West. So Hoy's "postmodern" ethnocentrism rejects simple relativism in conjoining ineliminable plurality with the possibility of criticism, improvement, and tolerance. Hoy elaborates this position through appropriative readings of Hans-Georg Gadamer and Clifford Geertz and criticisms of models of convergence found in Jürgen Habermas and Charles Taylor.

Ted Schatzki's "Objectivity and Rationality" (Chapter 8) explores the connections between objectivity and rationality, with special attention to social science. He begins by suggesting that a posttraditional conception of objectivity would treat it as a cluster of intellectual virtues. A summary of the views of Hans-Georg Gadamer identifies four such virtues: knowledge of one's prejudgments, willingness to revise them, openness to learning from others, and dialoguing in an evenhanded and sincere manner with the people one studies. A short discussion of Thomas Kuhn then suggests that this conception of objectivity is widespread in contemporary humanistic thought. The remainder of the chapter analyzes the relations between objectivity so construed and rationality. Defining a rational action or practice as one that it makes sense to perform, and arguing that judging an action or practice to make sense involves endorsing it, Schatzki concludes that rationality is relative to culture and person. This cultural and personal relativity in turn entails that, in social investigation as well as everyday life, people's differing senses of rationality are among the most crucial objects upon which to focus the cluster of virtues constituting objectivity. Schatzki then defends the cultural and personal relativity of rationality against a long list of putative universal criteria for the rationality of actions or practices. He maintains, however, that two such criteria, instrumentality and objectivity, do hold of the practices called social science. Thus, he concludes, rationality and objectivity entail one another in social investigation.

In "Beyond Objectivism and Relativism: Descriptive Epistemologies" (Chapter 9) Andrew Grimes and Debra Rood begin from the fact that although most organizational studies researchers now agree that values affect research, disagreement reigns about how to respond to this situation. Their chapter aims to transcend the traditional either/or of objectivist versus relativist epistemology through the idea of descriptive epistemologies. Descriptive epistemologies are theoretical bridges that link epistemological perspectives that are thought to be in conflict. In recounting the aims, methodologies, modes of knowledge validation, and notions of observer, observation, and observed advocated by different normative local epistemologies, they reveal affinities among these epistemologies and show how they can be reconciled.

Grimes and Rood outline five devices through which descriptive epistemologies that bridge epistemological perspectives can be generated: limiting notions, oppositional science, synthesis of partial truths, switching rules, and conversation. These bridging devices are extracted from the work of Peter Winch, Helen Longino, Karl Mannheim, Jürgen Habermas, and Richard Bernstein, all theorists concerned with different types of knowledge and strategies for attaining them. The conclusion of the chapter summarizes the consequences of descriptive epistemologies for theory and research: Theorizing will be epistemological from the ground up; the reflexivity this requires means that theory and research will be more complex; research will be self-consciously driven by the interests of practitioners or of the people studied; and research will be recognized as a community process.

In the volume's closing chapter, "Ultraobjectivity: Reading Cross-Culturally" (Chapter 10), James Boon stages a reconceptualization of objectivity within the traditional battle lines of interpretive versus positivistic social science. He rejects a "reductive objectivity" that relegates the plurality of differences in human life to a set of fixed, normalizing categories. His alternative notion of ultraobjectivity is a form of descriptive nominalism that aims to recover these differences, to resist their homogenization under static indices, and to abjure zealotry in interpreting those differences that separate the interpreter from his or her subjects. Boon gives more specific content to this notion by arguing that social scientists—indeed, all of us—are enmeshed in tissues of readings: of experience, of others, of others' readings of experience and others, and of one's own past readings of all these things. Through an extended analysis of the reception of Ruth Benedict's *The Patterns of Culture*, however, he shows that the myriad specifics encountered in the tissue of readings are typically screened out in memory through the imposition of simplifying oppositions and organizing schemas, the "*ex post facto* 'correction' into exaggerated order of irregular experience" (Chapter 10, p. 185). Recovering these specifics requires a repeated and "spiraling art of rereading" (p. 196). This art has special pertinence in cultural anthropology, Boon suggests, for all cross-cultural evidence is intertextual. It also warrants the label "ultraobjectivity," since it entails transcending the order imposed on a ragged reality by the mind's processing of it, and literally means going beyond something defined in relation to a subject.

In conclusion, we wish to emphasize that the project of rethinking objectivity must finally remain an open one, cognizant not only of the dangers that accompany a rigid formulation of objectivity, but also of those which lurk in its facile rejection. As we hope this volume demonstrates, one precondition for such openness is multidisciplinarity. Objectivity is always contextually sutured to disciplinary imperatives that not only appropriate the concept for their own purposes, but also contribute to its ongoing redefinition. Thus it is only through engaging in a multidisciplinary dialogue that researchers can grasp and contextualize their own situatedness vis-à-vis the objectivity question.

NOTES

1. J. S. Mill, *The Logic of the Moral Sciences* (part VI of *The Science of Logic*) (La Salle, IL: Open Court, 1988), 19.
2. August Comte, "Introduction to Positive Philosophy," in *The Positive Philosophy*, Frederick Ferré, ed. (Indianapolis: Bobbs-Merrill, 1970), 13.
3. Ibid., 28.
4. Leopold von Ranke, *The Theory and Practice of History*, Georg Iggers and Konrad von Moltke, eds. (New York: Irvington, 1973).
5. Friedrich Nietzsche, *The Use and Abuse of History* (2nd rev. ed.), Adrian Collins, trans. (Indianapolis: Bobbs-Merrill, 1957), 39.
6. See Sigmund Freud, *"The Interpretation of Dreams,"* in *Standard Edition of the Works of Sigmund Freud*, vol. 4, James Strachey, ed. and trans. (London: Hogarth, 1953–1974). On Jacques Lacan's extension of Freud's questioning of boundary formation, see Samuel Weber, *Return to Freud* (Cambridge: Cambridge University Press, 1991).
7. See, for example, Karl Marx and Frederick Engels, "Feuerbach. Opposition of the Materialist and Idealist Outlook," in *The German Ideology* (Moscow: Progress Publishers, 1970), 27–98; and Karl Mannheim, *Ideology and Utopia*,

Louis Wirth and Edward Shils, trans. (New York: Harcourt, Brace, and World Inc., 1936), 97–171.

8. Max Horkheimer, "A New Concept of Ideology," in *Max Horkeimer. Between Philosophy and Social Science: Selected Early Writings.* G. Frederick Hunter, Mathew Kramer, and John Tarpey, trans. (Cambridge: MIT Press, 1993), 129–149. For a discussion of this point and its connections to Mannheim, see Douglas Kellner *Critical Theory, Marxism, and Modernity* (Baltimore: Johns Hopkins University Press, 1989), 22–50.

9. See, for example, Peter Novick, *That Noble Dream: The "Objectivity Question" in the American Historical Profession* (Cambridge: Cambridge University Press, 1988), 415–629; and Derek Gregory, *Ideology, Science and Human Geography* (London: Hutchinson, 1978).

10. Benjamin Whorff, *Language Thought and Reality* (Cambridge: MIT Press, 1956); see also Paul Feyerabend, *Against Method: Outline of an Anarchistic Theory of Knowledge* (Atlantic Highlands: Humanities Press, 1975).

11. See, for example, Thomas Kuhn, *The Structure of Scientific Revolutions* (Chicago: University of Chicago Press, 1962); Michel Foucault, *The Archaeology of Knowledge*, A. M. Sheridan Smith, trans. (New York: Harper and Row, 1972), and "Truth and Power," in *Power/Knowledge*, Colin Gordon, ed. (New York: Pantheon, 1980), 109–133.

12. Michel Foucault, *Discipline and Punish*, Alan Sheridan, trans. (New York: Vintage, 1979).

13. Sandra Harding, "Conclusion: Epistemological Questions," in *Feminism and Methodology* (Bloomington: Indiana University Press, 1987), 181–190; p. 182.

14. For feminist perspectives in epistemology, see, for example, Sandra Harding and Merill B. Hintikka, *Feminist Perspectives in Epistemology, Metaphysics, and Methodology* (Boston: D. Reidel, 1983); Evelyn Fox Keller, *Reflections on Gender and Science* (New Haven: Yale University Press, 1984); Sandra Harding, *Feminism and Methodology*, 1987; Joan Scott, *Gender and the Politics of History* (New York: Columbia University Press, 1988); Susan Bordo and Alison M. Jagger, eds., *Gender/Body/Knowledge: Feminist Reconstructions of Being and Knowledge* (New Brunswick: Rutgers University Press, 1989); and Linda Alcoff and Elizabeth Potter, eds., *Feminist Epistemologies* (New York: Routledge, 1993).

15. See bell hooks, *Talking Back: Thinking Feminist, Thinking Black* (Boston: South End Press, 1989); Patricia Hill Collins, *Black Feminist Thought: Knowledge, Consciousness, and the Politics of Empowerment* (Boston: Unwin Hyman, 1990); Gayatri Spivak, *The Post-Colonial Critic: Interviews, Strategies, Dialogues*, Sarah Harasym, ed. (New York: Routledge, 1990); and Rey Chow, *Woman and Chinese Modernity: The Politics of Reading between East and West* (Minneapolis: University of Minnesota Press, 1991).

16. Patricia Hill Collins, *Black Feminist Thought*, 235.

17. Ibid., 236.

18. See, for example, Eve Kosofsky Sedgwick, *Epistemology of the Closet* (Berkeley: University of California Press, 1990). For a recent and comprehensive guide

to this literature, see *The Lesbian and Gay Studies Reader*, Henry Abelove, Michèle Aina Barale, and David M. Halperin, eds. (New York: Routledge, 1993).

19. Donna Haraway, "Situated Knowledges: The Science Question in Feminism and the Privilege of Partial Perspective," *Feminist Studies* 14, No. 3 (1988): 575–599; p. 584.

20. Jacques Derrida, *Limited Inc.*, Samuel Weber, trans. (Evanston: Northwestern University Press, 1988).

21. As a recent and celebrated example, see Allan Bloom, *The Closing of the American Mind*. (New York: Simon & Schuster, 1987).

22. See, for example, André Breton, *Manifestos of Surrealism*, Richard Seaver and Helen R. Lane, trans. (Ann Arbor: University of Michigan Press, 1969); *Dada Berlin: Texte, Manfeste, Aktionen*, Karl Riha, ed. (Stuttgart: Reclam, 1977); Georges Bataille, *Visions of Excess: Selected Writings, 1927–1939* (Minneapolis: University of Minnesota, 1985); and Jean Baudrillard, *Simulations*, Paul Foss, Paul Patton, and Philip Beitchman, trans. (New York: Semiotext[e], 1983).

23. For example, Hans-Georg Gadamer, *Truth and Method* (2nd rev. ed.), Joel Weinsheimer and Donald G. Marshall, trans. (New York: Crossroad, 1989); Wolfgang Iser, *The Act of Reading: A Theory of Aesthetic Response* (Baltimore: Johns Hopkins University Press, 1978); Jürgen Habermas, *Communication and the Evolution of Society*, Thomas McCarthy, trans. (Boston: Beacon Press, 1979); Richard Bernstein, *Beyond Objectivism and Relativism: Science, Hermeneutics, and Praxis* (Philadelphia: University of Pennsylvania Press, 1983); and Richard Rorty, *Objectivity, Relativism, and Truth* (Cambridge: Cambridge University Press, 1991).

24. Derrida, *Limited Inc.*, 136.

I

Complex Terrain

2

Signs of Persuasion

GUNNAR OLSSON

A long the way. Like the earnest himself, across the waters and into the trees. In search of a his-story of thought-and-action, navigation and power. Such is the context of this chapter: What does it mean to make sense?

My question is at the same time dangerous and challenging. The reason is that to me the concept of thought-and-action plays the same role as the nucleus does to the physicist and the gene to the biologist. If the latter are trying to crack the code of the human body, then it is our distant belief that some day, some where, some one will do the same with the cultural code. In turn, this belief raises ethical problems of a magnitude that the physicists and the biologists do not even come close to; destroying people is bad business, destroying culture is beyond imagination.

As a consequence, culture has always defended itself against knowledge which cuts too deep. The best examples are in the Bible itself, especially in the story of how Eve picks the apple which later is to fall on Newton's head. In general, culture defends its secrets through the institution of the taboo; something is taboo because it is too important to understand. But why would I waste my own life on something that is not worthy of being taboo? Sacrifice in the making.

As if to prove its own point, the most powerful paradigm of human thought-and-action is in the myth of creation. With his physical strength God did nothing but talk. Let there be! And there was. Stones and trees,

fish and fowl, man and woman. All flowed with the baptizing words out
of his mouth. God did not build the world. He uttered it. We do likewise,
for man is a semiotic animal, a species whose individuals are kept together
and apart by their use of signs. It is through them that we constantly define
ourselves, well knowing that in our social being we are limited by two types
of silence. On the one hand is the silence of pure meaning, on the other
that of pure physicality. The former belongs to God, the latter to the
stones. The former is white, the latter is black.

The conception of man as a semiotic animal is well established.
Indeed both genetics and psychoanalysis are most properly understood
as disciplines of applied linguistics. This tradition has been best developed by Jacques Lacan, but its roots are in Ferdinand de Saussure.
According to these thinkers every language consists of a system of signs,
where every sign itself is a merger of the two ingredients called "signifier"
and "signified." Eventually, the sign has thus come to be expressed as

$$s = \frac{S}{s} = \frac{signifier}{signified}$$

Put differently, the Saussurean sign is constituted by the relation
between signifier and signified, just as the Marxian commodity is composed by the relation between use value and exchange value. Oversimpli-
fied, the signifier is in the physicality of the sign, the signified in its
meaning. Thus, when I now write the word "I," then it contains two parts.
One is in the lightwaves which fill the emptiness between my pen and
your eyes. The other is in the cultural meanings of our respective
unconscious. Likewise, when you now consider this sign "I" which is my
body, also that has two ingredients. One is in the biological fact that I *am*
a body, the other in the social fact that I *have* a body. But the I itself is
always constructed, never pre-existent.

*

The mystical and extremely interesting problem should now be
obvious. Which are the couplings between what my five senses can grasp
of the signifier, on the one hand, and the nonphysical meanings of my
sixth sense, on the other? Even though it was Freud who argued that
"castration bears the transmission of culture," it is equally true that
without shared symbols we would be literally nothing, lost in a noise
without meaning. There is no escape and that is what makes the situation
so challenging.

* * *

My story of thought-and-action has two starting points. The first comes from the conviction that it is not enough to tell the truth. I must also be trusted. To have knowledge is in fact to say that something is something else and be believed when you do it. In condensed form,

$$a = b$$

But everyone with eyes to see and ears to hear immediately recognizes that a equals a, not b. Every identity statement is by necessity a statement of difference. How small shall this discrepancy be and still be accepted as a truth? How big shall it be to be refused as a lie.

A tentative answer is in my second starting point. This says that our modes of reasoning have changed remarkably little since the times of the Greeks. And that is why I take seriously the rumor that above the entrance to Plato's Academy there was a message, simultaneously inviting and forbidding. It warned that

HERE NOBODY IS ADMITTED
WHO DOES NOT KNOW HIS GEOMETRY

It cannot be said more clearly: Our (Western) understanding is patterned on the principles of Euclidean geometry, itself perhaps patterned on sculpture. Statements which conform to this particular mode of thought-and-action carry a high degree of credibility. Thus it was that Paul Valéry could describe Descartes as a geometer, who took his self as the point of origin of the axes of his thought.

*

Be this as it may. What seems beyond doubt is that geometry is most properly read as a form of rhetoric so convincing that we have blessed it with a new name. Therefore, when I reach the three letters Q.E.D.—*Quod Erat Demonstrandum*, "which was to be demonstrated"—at the end of a proof, then I interpret them as a kind of approval stamp, an indication that the reasoning is beyond doubt. Put differently, the argument has been checked to see that it accords with the acceptable canon of axioms and inference rules. The Q.E.D. is itself a symbol of perfect submission, a verification of the taken-for-granted. No news, no surprise.

It is nevertheless worth stressing that Euclid signed some of his proofs not with the Q.E.D., but instead with the Q.E.F.—*Quod Erat Faciendum*, "which was to be done." Moreover, there is much to indicate that the proofs blessed with the Q.E.F. are somehow more fundamental than those stamped with the Q.E.D. To give an example: Euclid is on the beach teaching his geometry. He draws two lines and claims that they are equivalent. The student objects, because he cannot grasp how the teacher's conclusion ties in with the axioms and inference rules that he has been taught. "Oh, my dear friend," says Euclid, "I will show you. Take my hand and walk with me. Three steps in this direction, three steps in that! Do you now believe me?" "Yes, of course," says the student, "how can I doubt my own body." "Well then," says Euclid, "we agree. Let us stamp the argument as convincing: Q.E.F."

And so, with Euclid's help, I have illustrated that there are two drastically different ways to be believed. In the case approved by the Q.E.D., the conviction comes from shared ideas, in a sense from perfectly socialized minds. In the case of the Q.E.F., on the other hand, we agree because somehow we share the same body. In the vocabulary of the Saussurean sign, the Q.E.D. alludes primarily to the s, the Q.E.F. to the S.

Empirical positivism extends this rhetoric one step further, for it says that a statement is meaningful, when it meets the double requirement of being logically consistent and empirically true. Neither mind nor body can be trusted. To be really persuasive, the argument should therefore be doubly anchored, both in the Q.E.D. and in the Q.E.F.

Clear enough. Easy to follow. Knowledge is by definition an exercise in translation. The trouble is that no translation can be perfect. Every statement is open to doubt.

It is this problem of trust that the 20th century has brought to crisis proportions. After the hypermodernity of postmodernism it can no longer be ignored. The crisis is closely tied to the sign itself and to its paradoxical nature of trying to be what it cannot be. It is extremely significant that it was Sisyphus who was called the father of Odysseus. Hence it is not surprising that the problems of the sign were well known already to Homer. For me, it is helpful to distinguish three aspects of the current crisis; the first I call "representation," the second "intentionality," the third "credibility."

* * *

Where Homer treated the issue of *representation* was in the story of Polyphemos, the cyclops who was a beast somewhere between man and animal. Since he had only one eye, he had no perspective and could not detect difference. You remember the story.

Odysseus and his men were thrown ashore and they sought shelter in a cave. This turned out to be the cave of Polyphemos, who lived there with his sheep. When this creature got hungry, he started to eat, not of the sheep but of Odysseus's men, one after the other. The cyclops quickly became a threat to Odysseus's own authority, for how much could the men take, before they turned their fear against their leader? Something had to be done.

So Odysseus started to talk with the beast. In the course of the conversation Polyphemos began to like his prisoner so much that he promised that "Odysseus the last man will be that I eat." Upon this he fell asleep, full of wine and human meat. In his sleep he began to vomit. Half digested limps welled out of his mouth, the stench as horrible as the sight. It was then that Odysseus saw his opportunity, sharpened an olive pole, rammed it into the beast's eye and turned it as a shipwright's screw. And the eye hissed, when it burned into blindness.

The pain was unbearable, he screamed and he howled. Outside the cave gathered his likes, asking who had caused him the harm. To this he replied back; "Ovtis, has done it, Ovtis has ruined me." It is of course on this mispronunciation of the name "Odysseus" as "Ovtis" that the story of representation hinges, for in Greek the word "Ovtis" sounds like "Nohbdy." And to a cyclops, who could not detect difference, it was self-evident that if somebody is *called* "Nobody" then he *is* a nobody. To them there was no difference between word and object, signifier and signified. As a consequence, they replied to Polyphemos that "if nobody has done you harm there in your solitude, then it is the work of Zeus. About that we can do nothing." So they simply left, not knowing what to do or what to believe. But Odysseus himself he was filled with laughter to see how like a charm the name deceived them. It takes a cyclops not to understand that S and s never can be the same.

But the story continues. Polyphemos is determined not to give in. Therefore he places himself at the opening of the cave, blocking the exit. Odysseus then orders his men to escape by hanging themselves in the wool under the sheep's belly. And when the sheep want to get out, Polyphemos holds down his hands to check whether what is departing is a sheep or a man. Once again, however, he makes the same mistake as before, for now he touches only the backs of the sheep, not their underneaths. Already Homer knew the structure of the Saussurean sign.

*

Also the crisis of *intentionality* has deep roots. One of the best illustrations comes from the 5th century B.C., that century when most tragedies were written. During the mythological era which preceded this period, people believed that when a man did something, it was not he who acted on his own, but the gods who acted through him. For various reasons, this idea began to change and the suspicion arose that man may indeed have a will of his own. With this emerged new questions of responsibility, guilt, and punishment. The story moves on until two and a half millenia later, Nietzsche could announce that now, finally, God was dead. Instead of Man being created in the image of God, the relation is just the opposite; in defining himself, man has expanded his territory into that which earlier belonged to the gods. As Nietzsche himself put it, "Our salvation lies not in knowing but in creating."

Modernism and the political ideologies of the 20th century are all descendants of this same spirit of intervention. Nobody has captured it better than Marx in his eleventh Feuerbach thesis, which states that even though the philosophers have tried to understand the world, the point is to change it. Never was Marx more wrong than here, for it is more difficult to understand the world than to change it. In nazism, in communism, in social democracy, the power of will has become the will of power. This is why all three have died.

This is also why I continue to insist that any valid theory of action must contain the fundamental structure of classical tragedy: that in the beginning everything is beautifully right and that in the end everything is horribly wrong. But on the way between intention and result, nobody has acted wrongly, only been a good person true to his own principals. This is the crisis of intentionality: the emperor on his balcony waving the crowd to its foregone conclusions.

*

Are these foregone conclusions to be trusted? Of course not! Hence the crisis of *credibility*. For an historic example, consider the end of the 15th century. The Church was then issuing tickets to the heaven of the after-life. To obtain one of these treasures, you should be able to prove that you had been a good person travelling down the narrow road. But if you could not prove this—and if you had the right connections—then you could buy yourself a letter of indulgence: a black market ticket to eternity, a forged set of identity papers to keep you out of purgatory.

To the reformists and to ordinary people the lie was simply too obvious. As a consequence, the Church lost its credibility and the worldly powers took over. The parallels to periods of inflation are clear, for there we discover that the promises issued in the language of money are not to be trusted. Even more astonishing are the similarities with the current situation both in the former Soviet Union and in welfare states like

Sweden. Here politicians have been promising to take care of us, not after death, but whenever we get sick, old and mistreated. Now even they have stopped claiming that they can deliver the goods.

*

Where the three crises of representation, intentionality and credibility come together is in a crisis of *politics*, that is, in the relation between individual and society. My fear is in fact that democracy, as we have come to define it, may not survive.

* * *

What the three crises share in common is their inability to handle phenomena that are nonvisible and therefore untouchable. Advances in epistemology have thus brought us back to issues of ontology. How can we capture and make credible that which is beyond our five senses, that is, that which is contained in the small s of the Saussurean sign, that which alone makes us human?

It is with such questions that Kant is pushed to his own limits, for whereas his categorical net of time and space enables us to capture physical phenomena, meaning itself simply slips through. My prediction is that within a fairly short time somebody will have invented a third category to go along with Kant's time and space, a third category which will enable us to talk convincingly about phenomena beyond the five senses. Indeed I conceive of time and space as different forms of silence. How is it at all possible to express the limits of language, hence of what it is to be a semiotic animal? What is the ontology of an *a priori*?

As a way of approaching this question, let us return once again to the paradoxical nature of the sign itself, especially to the extreme and non- satisfiable desire it embodies. More pointedly, it is difficult to accept that even though S and s are obsessed by a desire to become the same, this desire can never be satisfied. In the apparent interest of communication, it is thus hard to resist the temptation of thingification, of not turning the signifier into a fetish. When I fall into this trap, my desire is operationalized into that which is desired. S comes to dominate s.

But relations must not be confused with what is related, love not with the lover, the words not with the said. To have power is in this perspective to be a magician skilled in the double art of turning things into relations and relations into things. To have power is indeed a tricky business: It is to build in the concrete that which is in thought, at the same time as it is to give meaningful interpretations to physical, legal and organizational structures. To have power is to be a master in the zen of ontological transformations.

It is a fundamental characteristic of this challenging world that it does not sit still. What makes it move around is that whenever I encounter the sign

$$\frac{S}{s}$$

then the s immediately ceases to be a pure signified and itself becomes a signifier. Pictured differently, signifier and signified form a kind of staircase like

$$\rightarrow \frac{S_1}{s_1} \rightarrow \frac{S_2}{s_2} \rightarrow \frac{S_3}{s_3} \rightarrow \frac{S_4}{s_4} \rightarrow$$

The move down this ladder is determined by the internal structure of the sign, the move to the right by its external structure. In the former case a concrete S searches for its abstract s, in the latter the absence of the s transforms itself into the presence of the S. The rhetorical success of the vertical move depends on the choice of metaphor, the success of the horizontal move on the metonymy. As a consequence, it makes sense to think of the master methaphor of metaphor as an anchor, and the master metaphor of metonymy as an arrow. And even though every metaphor contains a metonymy and every motonymy a metaphor, it is the metonymic that is more powerful. It is through the metaphoric condensations of the eye that I fool myself just as it is through the metonymic displacements of the ear that I fool others. It was as a protection against the power of metonymy that Odysseus ordered his men to put wax in their ears and himself to be bound to the mast.

* * *

Now before it disappears completely: What *is* a sign? What is it to be a semiotic animal? Perhaps it is a desire of desire. On the surface a desire of perfect translation. Deeper down a desire impossible to name, a name impossible to answer. But sliding under the bar you never find what you want.

And yet, I suspect I *do* know what is hidden in the secrecy of the cultural code. It is the mechanisms of power, themselves protected by the taboo against making for yourself a graven image. In my own search for images rich enough to contain these difficult issues, I mention only two.

The *first* comes from Kazimir Malevich, by many claimed as the original painter of abstract art. The reason is that his black square was an icon, a picture of the nonpicturable; that unmentionable, which I call "power" and he named "God," had for him four corners. In addition to the ordinary three of Father, Son, and Holy Spirit, was also the Rebel or perhaps the Devil himself. It is well established how it is this shifting figure who symbolizes change and movement, the other three who represent stability. It is also well established that Malevich's icon was deeply influenced by Walt Whitman's poem "Square Deific."

Indeed I have gradually come to suspect that it is the habit of thinking in threes that now has reached its limits. This may even go so far, that if Euclid had based his geometry not on the triangle but on the square, then perhaps Columbus would have gone not to America but to the moon; everybody knows what non-Euclidean geometry has meant to modern physics. And we are well advised to remember that it was not Plato, but Descartes, who said that "the whole of physics is nothing other than geometry."

The *second* example of a graven image comes from the Bible, especially from the architectural description of Solomon's Temple in the First Book of the Kings. Thus in the rear of the house which Solomon built in honor of the Lord, there was an inner sanctuary, the holiest of the holy. This, the most Unnameable of all, was shaped as a cube, measuring $20 \times 20 \times 20$. But even within this cube there were gradations such that the holiest of the holy was the upper side of the cube, that is, that plane which could not be seen, merely be touched by the air above it. Such is the taboo of the taboo.

And once here I again encounter the name of Jacques Lacan, the surrealist who insisted that the unconscious is structured like a language. For to me, the upper side of Solomon's cube corresponds to Lacan's Imaginary, the air above it to the Real, the cube itself to the Symbolic. It is by dancing in the ceiling of the cube that we approach the taboo, itself unmentionable.

What is *there* to be discovered? Impossible to tell. Except I am once again reminded of Ludwig Wittgenstein, who argued that to create new meanings is to break the hitherto taken-for-granted. Herein lies temporary madness, for in Wittgenstein's own words (1967, p. 393), "If I were sometime to see quite new surroundings from my window instead of the long familiar ones, if things, humans, and animals were to behave as they never did before, then I should say something like 'I have gone mad'; but that would merely be an expression of giving up the attempt to know my way about."

And yet! Who knows? What I see when I look out of my window may indeed by something never seen before. If so, how do I then convince you of its reality, especially if what I see is a novel meaning, a small s not hitherto imagined?

The answer is that you come to believe me, only if I can give proper names to the points, lines, and planes of the appropriate geometry. And whereas to construct is to be a geometer, to name is to be a geographer. And if my story is convincing enough, then I am entitled to apply the third approval stamp of rhetoric. It consists of the three letters Q.E.I.—*Quod Erat Inveniendum,* "which was to be invented." And as we are now about to leave the Greek Academy, we discover that above the exit there is a new message. It reads

> HERE NOBODY IS LET OUT
> WHO DOES NOT KNOW HIS GEOGRAPHY

* * *

Thus it sounded, the beginning of the story I came this long way to tell. Fantastic. For what can now be glimpsed is a human science more beautiful and more frightening than anything ever imagined.

Paradox upon paradox. Self-reference upon self-reference. And yet. The remarkable is of course, that even though you have never read this his-story before, you have nevertheless been able to follow it. Via my use of language, you have made your own connections. What has been shown is that there is no power more powerful than the power of the example. And so it is that my performance has tried to be a kind of icon which is not *about* something but which *is* that something itself. An attempt to represent the nonrepresentable. A show of how it is that we become so obedient and so predictable.

When the verb appears in the perfect passive imperative, the indicative is extended into a command. Let there be, and there was:

> *Quod Erat Demonstrandum!*
> *Quod Erat Faciendum!*
> *Quod Erat Inveniendum!*

The difficulty is not to tell the truth. It is to be believed when you do it. *"Quod Erat . . .-dum"* expresses it clearly. The extreme challenge is to be abstract enough. Not so easy, for it is in our intellectual heritage to say that truth is in concrete exhibition, in reason's desire to objectify itself, in the impossibility of keeping s from becoming S.

Man's desire is by necessity impossible to satisfy, for it is a desire of the Other. Rhetoric is the expressive mode of ethics.

ACKNOWLEDGMENTS

This chapter draws heavily on two lectures from April 1991. The first was delivered at the University of Kentucky as part of a series arranged by its Committee on Social Theory. The other was read to the Swedish Society for Anthropology and Geography at a seminar in conjunction with Allan Pred's receipt of the Retzius Medal. I am grateful for both invitations.

SUGGESTED READINGS

Derrida, J. (1989). *Edmund Husserl's origin of geometry: An introduction.* Lincoln: University of Nebraska Press. (French original published 1962)

de Saussure, F. (1986). *Course in general linguistics* (R. Harris, Ed.). Peru, IL: Open Court. (French notes 1907–1911)

Dufour, D.-R. (1990). *Les mystères de la trinité.* Paris: Gallimard.

Focillon, H. (1989). *The life of forms in art.* New York: Zone Books. (French original published 1934)

Freud, S. (1950). *Totem and taboo.* London: Routledge & Kegan Paul. (German original published 1913)

Homer. (1963). *The odyssey* (R. Fitzgerald, Trans.). New York: Doubleday.

Kandinsky, W. (1979). *Point and line to plane.* New York: Dover. (German original published 1926)

Lacan, J. (1977). *Écrits: A selection.* London: Tavistock. (French original published 1966)

Lacan, J. (1978). *The four fundamental concepts of psychoanalysis.* New York: Norton. (French original published 1964)

Lachterman, D. R. (1989). *The ethics of geometry: A genealogy of modernity.* New York: Routledge.

Malevich, K. (1968). *Essays on art.* Copenhagen: Borgen. (Russian originals published 1915–1933)

Nietzsche, F. (1968). *The will to power.* New York: Vintage. (German original published 1883–1888)

Olsson, G. (1980). *Birds in egg/eggs in bird.* London: Pion.

Olsson, G. (1991). *Lines of power/limits of language.* Minneapolis: University of Minnesota Press.

Vernant, J.-P., & Pierre, V.-N. (1988). *Myth and tragedy in ancient Greece.* New York: Zone Books. (French originals published 1972–1986)

Whitman, W. (1955). *Leaves of grass.* New York: New American Library. (Originals published 1855–1892)

Wittgenstein, L. (1967). *Zettel.* Oxford: Basil Blackwell. (Original fragments published 1929–1948)

3

Objectivity Otherwise

SAMUEL WEBER

The title of the volume to which this chapter contributes, is both sugges-tive and enigmatic. We are called upon to consider *Objectivity and Its Other,* but this title leaves open just what that "other" might be, or even why it is in the singular. Is there only *one* other that counts, one might wish to object? Does this preference for the singular noun reflect an attempt to render the other powerful enough, unified enough, so as to be able to hold its own over against *its other:* which in this case is, of course, "objectivity"? Since objectivity, for its part, must presumably also be understood in the singular, as an instance that is identical with itself if not indeed as the enabling condition of all such self-identity, it would stand to reason that *its* other would have to be no less unified, no less substantial. By determining the other through the genitive *its,* to be the other *of* objectivity, that other is construed as being the property of the same: that is, as the other that properly belongs to objectivity.

In short, in addressing objectivity in this way, the title linking the contributions it assembles is anything but simply objective. Objectivity itself, it suggests, is not enough: It must be considered in relation to something else. The question that thereby emerges, however, at least implicitly, between the lines or words of the title, is this: If objectivity itself is not enough, and if it therefore must be considered in relation to something else—to its other—are there any grounds for thinking that this other, particularly once it has been determined as the *singular property of objectivity*, will be any more capable of providing us with whatever it is we are seeking, which is to say, with whatever it is that has called us to this title and to each other?

Since I very much doubt that the thinking that produced this enigmatically suggestive title was in itself entirely homogeneous or unified, I will bracket the question of the intentions that may or may not have led to the choice of this title—a title that I find very felicitous, precisely in its enigmatic and provocative suggestibility. Instead then of trying to delve into the motivations of the title, I propose to respond to its provocation by offering a suspicion, and a question, of my own: What if there were not *one single, proper* other of objectivity, but rather *several?* And what if it were precisely this singular excess, this "more than one," that is at issue or at stake in the enigmatically suggestive, eminently questionable title, *Objectivity and Its Other?* What if the other of objectivity turned out to be not just one (and the same), but rather one and another? What if, for instance, *the* other of objectivity were precisely there so that we might forget that there is a difference between other as a pronoun and other as an adjective, and that this difference might not be simply reducible to one single, self-identical concept of the other?

The word "other" is of course a relational term par excellence: It cannot be understood apart from its relation to what it is not: to the non-other, which is to say, to the same. In the title we are considering, the "same" is "objectivity." Taken as a pronoun, the other of objectivity mirrors—that is, *repeats* and *reflects*—the structure of the object. It opposes it, stands apart from it, takes its stand over/against it. Taken as an *adjective*, however, the other loses much of its ostensible fixity. It no longer mirrors the object in a symmetrical inversion by opposing it: Rather, as adjective, it is neither objective in this sense, nor simply nonobjective. As adjective, "other" no longer stands firmly in place, over/against the object, but rather sidles up to the object and contaminates it, as it were, or diverts it from being simply itself to being *otherwise.* Being otherwise, however, is quite different from being *the* other, much less being *its other.* We can see this at once if we choose to reformulate our title so that instead of *Objectivity and Its Other,* it reads: *Objectivity Otherwise.* This can be understood in at least two ways, which are not clearly compatible with one another, but which are also not necessarily mutually exclusive. Objectivity otherwise can mean "objectivity conceived in a different manner," and it is clear that to an extent, some such hope underlies any event such as this one, which brings people together in part at least in the hope of hearing something a bit different from what one already knows. But if objectivity otherwise can mean objectivity examined differently from the way that is familiar, it can have a quite divergent meaning. Objectivity otherwise can signify: Objectivity or else! It can be a command, warning us that we had better keep our objectivity, for otherwise who knows what might happen. Although at first sight these two readings do not appear to be very compatible with one another, we should keep open the possibility that they might just turn out to be complementary or complicitous. It is the possibility of such a complementarity or complicity, at any rate, that will guide my reflections in approaching "Objectivity and Its Other."

In order to explore "Objectivity and Its Other," or what I have called "objectivity—otherwise," I will take two texts as my guides: two texts as different in form and content, in purpose and provenance as one could imagine. The first text is one we share in common, even if many of us may never have opened the book in which it is contained: It is *Webster's New Collegiate Dictionary*, originally published in 1916.[1] The second text, less a part of our shared experience, is by Martin Heidegger and is entitled in English *The Overcoming of Metaphysics*; written over a period dating from 1936 to 1946, it was first published in 1954. As far apart conceptually and chronologically as these two works are, where the question of "objectivity and its others" is concerned, they turn out to stand in a quite instructive relation to one another. Let us begin with *Webster's New Collegiate Dictionary*: Since it defines "objectivity" simply as the "state, quality, or relation of being objective," I ask you to bear with me as I quote the entry for "objective" in its entirety. To abbreviate it, especially here at the outset, would be to run the risk of treating objectivity unobjectively by truncating the richness and complexity of the object with which we are concerned:

> ob-jec'tive adj. 1. Of or pertaining to an object, esp. to the object, or end; as to reach our *objective* point. 2. Exhibiting or characterized by emphasis upon or the tendency to view events, phenomena, ideas, etc. as external and apart from self-consciousness; not subjective; hence, detached, impersonal, unprejudiced; as an *objective* discussion; *objective* criteria. 3. *Gram.* Pertaining to or designating the case of the object of a verb or preposition. 4. *Med.* Perceptible to persons other than the patient;—of symptoms. 5. *Perspective.* Belonging or relating to the object to be delineated; as, an *objective* line, plane, or point. 6. a. *Philos.* Contained in, or having the nature or status of, an object, or something cognized or cognizable; as, to render an abstraction *objective.* b. Existing independent of mind, pertaining to an object as it is in itself or as distinguished from consciousness or the subject; as, to deny the *objective* reality of things. Cf. SUBJECTIVE—Syn. See FAIR, MATERIAL. (p. 579)

I interrupt this definition in order to underscore just how much it tells us about "objectivity and its others." The first "other" of objectivity is, of course, the "object" itself: There can be no objectivity that is not "of or pertaining to an object." But what is an object? The first point of the definition is suggestive in the example it gives: "pertaining to an object, esp. to the object, or end; as, to reach our *objective point*." An object is thus something that can be aimed at and even reached. An object, *qua* objective, both opens and *ends* the space of a *reach*. To sum up the implications of this initial definition: If the object is manifestly the other of objectivity, the other of the object, *qua* objective, is the *reach* of which it is the enabling limit.

The second point in the definition differs from the first in a number of ways. First of all, whereas the initial definition determines the other of "objective" positively, as the object, the second designates that other negatively as the subject, from which it demarcates the "objective." What is objective is thus designated as that which is "not subjective," as the negative other of subjectivity. Subjectivity, in turn, is determined above all as *self-consciousness*. Thus, objectivity is described as "the tendency to view events, phenomena, ideas as external and apart from self-consciousness." This second definition, largely negative, already suffices to suggest that the notion of objectivity is not without its internal tensions and ambiguities. In the first place, the very phrase that seeks to define objectivity by demarcating it from subjectivity *qua* self-consciousness, is itself already formulated in terms that strongly suggest a certain subjectivity. Thus, objectivity is described as "the tendency to view events, phenomena, ideas as external" to self-consciousness. But just how external to self-consciousness, or at least to subjectivity, can something like a "tendency to view" be? In short, the very attempt to define objectivity through its independence with respect to a subject does so only by resorting to a subjective "tendency to view." The fact that the very definition that seeks to represent objectivity as something radically distinct from subjectivity must recur to notions of "tendency" and of "perspective" undercuts the radical demarcation of objective and subjective it is seeking to affirm. The end of this definition indicates what may be at stake in such a contradiction. The nonsubjective description of objectivity, which emphasizes its "detached, impersonal, unprejudiced" quality, concludes by adducing two examples in which such qualities are invoked: "as an *objective* discussion" and "*objective* criteria." An objective discussion, in this sense, is one in which the plurality and diversity of divergent and possibly conflicting points of view can presumably be reduced, or at least measured and managed, by appealing to the authority of an object that is held to be unified and self-identical precisely to the extent that it is independent of the subject. The authority of the object would thus depend upon its distance from the subject. The second example, "objective criteria," confirms that what is at stake in this definition of objectivity—its "other" if you will—is nothing other than the desire for conflict resolution, or at least control. Disputes, which are inevitable as long as there is only subjectivity, can be decided, settled, and judged insofar as they can be measured by an object that is clearly separable from all subjectivity.

Summing up, then, the "others" in this second definition of "objective" can be divided into two sorts: negative and positive. The negative others of objectivity include first of all the subject as self-consciousness, and second the subjective as personal, prejudicial, and hence partial. The positive other emerges as the negation of these negatives: namely, as that which allows conflicts arising from the partiality of subjective self-interest to be resolved or at least adjudicated by appeal to an object that presumably transcends such partiality, and that therefore can serve as the basis both of "objective discussion" and of "objective criteria"—that is, of conflict-resolving communication.

But as I mentioned above, the status of this second definition is undercut by the fact that it is attributed to what is called a "tendency to view," something that it is difficult to conceive as being entirely separable from a subject. As it turns out, the next three definitions reinforce this aspect of "objective": Its meanings entail less an absolute separation from or negation of subjectivity than a complex relationship to it. The third definition, which addresses the grammatical meaning of the word, the "objective case," describes this case as "designating ... the object of a verb or preposition," and thereby relates the term once again to a grammatical "subject." The fact that the antecedent of the "objective case" can be either a "verb" or a "preposition" suggests two further aspects or possibilities of this relation: The object can be tied to the subject either through an action or process (through the verb), or through its positioning (through the preposition). This third definition thereby adds two further "others" to objectivity: *process* and *position*.

The fourth and fifth definitions, referring to the medical and perspectival uses of the word, both formulate its meaning in terms of perception: negatively, in regard to medical usage, where the word designates that which is "perceptible to persons other than the patient," and positively, in regard to perspective, where it can refer to an "objective line, plane or point," held to belong or relate "to the object to be delineated." As the reader will probably have noticed, however, the subjective reference recurs in both of these two definitions: In the case of perspective, it is in the naming of the object itself as that which is "to be delineated" (by whom?); and in the medical usage, it is explicit as those "persons other than the patient" to whom the latter's "symptoms," for instance, are "perceptible." In the medical use of the term, then, the "other of objectivity" is the active, nonpatient medical observer and clinician, who sees what the patient cannot: the objective meaning of the latter's symptoms. In the case of perspective, the other of objectivity is the "object to be delineated," and hence, the subjective instance that determines just *what is to be delineated* as an object, and *how such* delineation is to be executed.

But all of these others come together, it would seem, in the sixth and final definition of the term, which turns to its use in philosophical discourse, where once again, the other of the objective is determined initially as the "object," this time, however, as that which "contains" or determines what may be called objective. This initial and rather tautological definition—objective being that which is contained in an object—is then fleshed out, as it were, by being given a second and significant dimension: "Objective" is now said to refer not just to an object, to its container or to something having its nature or status, but moreover to "something cognized or cognizable; as to render an abstraction *cognizable*." In this definition, then, the objective is equated with the known or the knowable, and thereby made a function of knowledge. This has already been implied in the preceding definitions, but in being made explicit here, it is also rendered problematic. For what, then, is the status of knowledge? Once again, the examples chosen to illustrate this usage of the word seem to intensify the problem rather than to resolve it. The example given, I remind you once again, is: "something cognized or cognizable; as, to render an abstraction *objective*." An abstraction, even one that is "rendered *objective*," remains something that is difficult to construe independently of a subject. The question or problem that is thus broached, implicitly at least, is whether or not the definition of the object as something known or knowable must not inevitably wind up reaffirming that the other of the objective is the subjective. Can there be an abstraction, however "objective" it may be, without reference to a subject? Perhaps this is why the second part of Webster's discussion of the philosophical uses of the word returns to the connotation of "objective" as the property of "existing independent of mind, pertaining to an object as it is in itself or distinguished from the consciousness of the subject." That this declaration of independence is not entirely unproblematical, however, is once again confirmed by the example given as illustration: "as to deny the *objective* reality of things. Cf. SUBJECTIVE." And so, at the end of this passage, we are returned, by way of the *denial* of "the objective reality of things," to the "subjective." Whatever else it might include, the other of objectivity seems definitively, or at least definitionally, to include the subjective.

This impression is both confirmed and elaborated in the final section of the dictionary definition, which deals with the word "objective" not as adjective, but as noun. This final definition makes explicit what was implicit in the initial definition of object as a "point" that was to be "reached." "Objective" as noun is defined as "an aim or end of action; point to be hit, reached, etc." An object is that which gives direction to an action, just as it gives movement a determinate end. But an objective, in this sense, is not just the exclusive property of an object: It once again implies the participation of those performing the action. At the same time, in order to give direction to a movement or striving, an objective—as a "point to be hit, reached, etc.," must in some way encounter and exclude other possibilities. Perhaps this is why it is not entirely fortuitous if the chain of words we have been examining—objectivity, object, objective—also includes another element, which at the same time brings to light a very different dimension of this semantic group: namely, the word "objection." This is in turn related to the word *object*, not as noun but as verb: To object is literally to cast something in front of, before, over against something else, thus producing an encounter or even a shock that can be more or less violent, more or less conflictual.

In summing up this discussion of the dictionary definition of "objective" I offer the following suspicions or speculations. First, the firm guidance that the object, as the other of the subject, is called upon to provide presupposes a stability that is achieved only at the cost of excluding, fending off, or fencing out others—that is, other possibilities, other ways, other encounters. Second, such exclusions serve the interest of that privileged other of objectivity that turns out to be the subject seeking to stabilize itself. And finally, this stability is not exempt from the tension and tendencies that it seeks to harness, and that our brief discussion of the definitions in *Webster's New Collegiate Dictionary* has brought to light.

Curiously enough, the questions of *stability* and *tension* are very much at the heart of the interpretation of objectivity in the second of the two texts that I wish to discuss: Heidegger's *Overcoming of Metaphysics*.[2] Under this title are gathered a series of meditations, 28 in all, that despite their fragmentary and extremely condensed character, attempt nothing less ambitious than to sketch out the main tendencies of the history of Western philosophy, which Heidegger construes and designates as "metaphysics," as well as to derive from them certain consequences concerning the political tendencies that were working themselves out during the fateful decade in which the text was written (1936-1946). The title of these remarks, Heidegger begins by acknowledging, is somewhat misleading, since "metaphysics" as he understands it is not something that can be

simply "overcome," if by overcoming is meant leaving behind, once and
for all. For metaphysics is neither an "opinion" that might be "abolished,"
nor "a doctrine" that is "no longer believed" (85/64). Rather, for Heidegger the term designates a historical "destination" (a *Geschick*) in which the
irreducible distinction between Being and beings—that is, the difference
between being as verb and being as noun—has been progressively effaced
and forgotten as the conception of *being qua* entity has come to dominate
the way in which *Being as such* is construed. This historical destiny
Heidegger traces back to the origins of Western philosophy itself, in the
thought of the Presocratics and in its ensuing systematization at the hands
of Plato and Aristotle. Although "metaphysics" thus turns out to be as old
as Western philosophy itself, Heidegger's focus in this text is far more
specific: It has to do with what might be described as the *wind-up* of
Metaphysics, which entails both its consummation and its conclusion
(*Verendung*). In winding up, however, metaphysics, far from simply coming
to an end, consolidates and establishes its "unconditional domination"
all the more thoroughly and extensively. Being winds up both as something that has exhausted its possibilities, and as a boxer winds up for a
punch. Winding up, metaphysics is both at the end of its rope and at the
beginning of its hegemony.

Heidegger describes this domination as "unconditional" (*un-
bedingt*), inasmuch as the effacement of the difference between beings
and Being—or what one could designate (although Heidegger does
not) as the *hypostasis of being*—leaves little room for alterity and in this
sense is both uncompromising and unconditional. Being *qua* verb,
which can be thought of both as the *other* of beings *qua* noun and as
their *condition*, is rendered progressively inaccessible, and with it the
"truth" of beings is as well.

Thus, the wind-up of metaphysics entails the "going under" of the
truth of beings, insofar as this truth requires a heterogeneity—a difference
and an other, that is effaced and forgotten in the hypostasis of being as
entity: "The consequences of this occurrence (*Ereignis*) are the events
(*Begebenheiten*) of world history in this century" (86/65). The overall
process by which "the truth of beings" goes under is described in general
terms by Heidegger as both "the collapse of the world shaped by metaphysics" and as "the desolation of the earth," which also "stems from
metaphysics" (86/64). This, then, sets the scene in which Heidegger will
attempt to outline both the apocalyptical dangers attendant upon the
wind-up (*Verendung*) of metaphysics, as well as briefly suggesting the
possible perspective of its "winding down."

What does all this have to do with our theme: objectivity and its
other? Quite simply this: The distinctively modern form in which meta-

physics consolidates and consummates its "unconditional domination" entails nothing other than the hypostasis of beings precisely as *objects*. If metaphysics completes itself in part at least through the "collapse" of the very "world" it helped to shape, it is because that world has come to be defined in terms of what Heidegger calls the "truthless form of the real [*des Wirklichen*] and of objects" (85/63). The question that now must be addressed is: What is an object, what does it entail, and in what way is it, or does it become, "truthless"?

Heidegger's response to this question passes by a reflection on the historical emergence of modern metaphysical thinking with Descartes. Descartes sought to distinguish "the search for truth" from the more or less reliable "opinions" upon which one is customarily forced to rely in conducting most of one's affairs. As opposed to the uncertainty of such customary activity, Descartes writes, he decided to "reject as absolutely false everything in which I could imagine the slightest doubt, in order to see if there was not something left over, after that, something in my belief that would be entirely indubitable" (31).[3] Descartes' argument, of course, is that none of the contents of consciousness, no matter what their origin (the senses, reasoning, opinion) can be regarded as being immune to doubt, "considering that all of these same thoughts, which we have being awake, can also come when we sleep, without any of them therefore being true" (32). Descartes' response is to take the worst case as the norm, and therefore "to feign that all the things that had ever entered the mind were no more true than the illusions of my dreams." In so doing, he discovers that there is only one thing that might plausibly claim to be free of doubt:

> In thus seeking to think that everything was false, it was necessary that I who thought this should be something. And remarking that this truth: *I think, therefore I am*, was so firm and so secure (*assurée*) that all of the most extravagant suppositions of the Sceptics were incapable of shaking it (*l'ébranler*), I judged that I could admit it, without second thought, as the first principle of philosophy for which I was searching (32).

What precisely is Descartes doing in this celebrated passage from the Fourth Part of the *Discourse on Method*? First of all, in generalizing the possibility of doubting, he is, by implication and by inversion, defining the object of his search as the negative of doubt—as the "indubitable" or the doubtless. Truth, he is saying, should be beyond all doubt; it should be certain. Second, since truth is here construed as the correspondence of thought with that which is being thought, the question of truth as indubitable certitude involves the relation of thinking and being. That relationship, however, turns out to be less simple than it might appear at first glance. For the "being" of the cogito is precisely not that of material reality. Rather, it is the being of thinking itself; or more precisely, it is the being of a reflexive relationship of self-consciousness. This is why Heidegger will gloss Descartes' celebrated position in the following way: *Ego cogito* is *cogito*: *me cogitare*. I think is I think myself thinking. In the light of the cogito, then, being is only indubitable as the reflective relation of thinking to itself.

Up to this point, our review of Heidegger's response to the Cartesian *cogito* has nothing specifically Heideggerian about it. The emphasis upon reflexivity as constitutive of modern philosophical consciousness, and indeed, perhaps of modernity itself, is familiar and widespread. All that could be concluded from this is what is well known anyway: namely, that the Cartesian *cogito ergo sum* initiates a quintessentially modern form of thinking by determining it as subjective idealism. "In order to think, one must be," Descartes observes, but the "being" to which he thereby refers is truly accessible only in and as self-consciousness, as thought thinking itself, that is, as reflection. It is precisely in continuing on beyond this familiar point, however, that Heidegger's interpretation of the *cogito* begins to forge its own way, and it does so first of all by demonstrating how a certain notion of the object and of objectivity are very much at work in the Cartesian *cogito*:

> The *ego cogito* is for Descartes that which in all *cogitationes* is already represented and produced (*Vor- und Her-gestellte*), that which is present, unquestionable, which is indubitable and which has already taken its stand in knowing, as what is authentically known for certain, that which stands firm in advance of everything, namely as that which places everything in relation to itself and thus "against" everything else. (87/66)

What Heidegger is attempting to do here, and in the passages that follow, is to elicit the implications of the famous *cogito*, a notion whose very familiarity may well serve to hide the fact that its significance is anything but self-evident. A major difficulty in discussing Heidegger's arguments here proceeds from an aspect of German, and in particular of philosophical German, which tends to get lost in English. I am thinking here in particular of the spatial connotations of certain metaphors that are both central philosophical terms in German, and also household words. I am referring in particular to the verbs *stehen*, to stand; *stellen*, to place; and *setzen*, to set, but there are many others as well. When we speak in English of "objectivity" and of "object," for instance, we rarely think of the spatial aspect of those terms, since the Latin roots ob- and -ject (*jacere*) are generally associated with nontechnical uses. We require a particular etymological effort to recall that the word *object* is composed of words meaning "to throw against or before." Although the word "object" also is used in German, the more common, less technical word to which Heidegger recurs in his discussion of the *cogito* is *Gegenstand*—literally, standing against. Whereas the etymology of the English word "object" stresses the "throw," the German reminds us that the point of that throw, at least in the perspective of Descartes, is to take a stand against doubt, and thereby to establish a certain stability: the stability of certitude itself. What provides this stability, Heidegger observes, is not the contents of what is thought, but thinking itself inasmuch as it can enter into a reflective relation to itself, the *cogito: me cogitare*. From this perspective, thinking accedes to truth as certitude by recognizing itself over against itself, and it does this by recalling, as it were, that however dubious the contents of its representations may be, what is beyond all doubt is the fact that it is *representing*. In German, the word for "representation," *vorstellen*, means literally "placing-before." One can therefore sum up Heidegger's account of the *cogito* thus: For Descartes, thinking takes a stand against doubt by placing itself—*qua* the activity of placing before—before itself as something that stands and withstands: as an ob-ject (a Gegen-stand). "The original object," Heidegger thus observes, "is objectivity itself" and "the original objectivity is the 'I think' in the sense of 'I perceive'."

From this a number of related conclusions can be drawn. First of all, the essence of the object, in this context at least, is the structure and process of objectivity itself. Second, this structure is a process that entails both a movement and also the arresting of movement: a bringing to the fore and a bringing to a stand. Thirdly, what is at work in this process of setting up and taking a stand is nothing other than the subject itself, both in the familiar figurative sense of self-consciousness, and in the less familiar literal sense of that which is "thrown under" everything else—that is, everything that can be thought and said about reality. It is only in setting itself up *qua* object—as its own other, one might add—that the *cogito* becomes the model of truth and of certitude. By thus identifying the reflective recognition of thinking by itself to be the sole medium of truth, Descartes implicitly installs self-consciousness at the basis of all reality, including "objective" reality. From this Heidegger concludes: "In the order of the transcendental genesis of the object, the first object of ontological representation is the subject" itself (87–88/66).

What does this initial conclusion of Heidegger's tell us about the question of objectivity and its others? First of all, it confirms many of the points that emerged in our discussion of the dictionary definition: The other of objectivity is the object, the other of the object is the subject, the other of subject is self-consciousness; self-consciousness in turn has something to do with reaching an end, attaining an *objective*, at the same time, in order for such an objective to be reachable, it must ob-ject, in the sense of offering resistance to others, perhaps even excluding them, in order that it maintain anything like a stable and attainable position. By maintaining that position, the objective can function as a criterion, upon which judgment can be based. In this sense, judgment, knowledge, and truth also emerge as others of objectivity. But implicit in our discussion of the dictionary definitions of the word was the fact that this latter set of others-the adjudicatory, epistemological function of objectivity—was at least tendentially at odds with the former set, *qua* subjectivity. Indeed, one might argue that each of these two sets conditions the other: The fact that objectivity implies subjectivity makes it all the more necessary that objectivity also imply an other of its other—that is, the other of cognition, judgment, truth.

It is this tension that Heidegger retraces in Descartes, who seeks to determine an object that would be free of the "doubt" that arises precisely from the dependency of all objects upon subjective thought processes. Descartes attempts to resolve this problem in a way that for Heidegger is symptomatic of the history of modern metaphysics: By determining the true object—which is to say, the only one of which we can be certain—as the process of objectification itself, Descartes construes the truth of things, *qua* objects, to be a function of their ability to be to be *brought forward and fixed in place* (in German: *vorgestellt, hergestellt*, and *festgestellt*). This in turn is tantamount to saying that the truth of objectivity is determined in terms of its capacity to fix and secure the subject, and this is just the direction that metaphysics, according to Heidegger, will take after Descartes.

The question then becomes: How must this subject, which turns out to be the privileged other of objectivity, be conceived? For Heidegger, the Cartesian privileging of the notion of *certitude* indicates two things. First, that truth is now determined in terms of the reflective relation of the thinking subject to itself—that is, to its activity of representation, of bringing things before itself, of *Vorstellen*. And second, that what is involved in this privileging of certitude is the project of *self-securing*. The self is secured by means of the process of fixing into place, which is how Heidegger interprets objectification. Over against the object, the subject is to be secured: That, at least, is the project.

The problem, however, is that this project of securing can itself never be entirely secure or stabilized, since the only true—that is, certain—object is the process of objectification itself and not the product. What counts in this perspective is the bringing to the fore and setting into place, the representing and producing, but not what is represented and produced. Or rather, what is represented and produced counts only insofar as it supplies "raw materials" to this product of objectification, representation, and production.

This is why Heidegger is able to retrace the dominant tendency of modern metaphysics as extending from Descartes' determination of truth as certitude to Nietzsche's notion of the will to power. What is ultimately at work, and at stake, in the Cartesian theory of the reflexive *cogito* as the outcome of the struggle against doubt and for certitude, Heidegger argues, is the will to reduce the other to the self. Since, however, the essence of the self consists precisely in the process of bringing to the fore and setting into place—which is to say; in the project of *securing*—the ultimate outcome of the will to power can only be the *will to will*, since the will itself is precisely the effort to set things into place. In other words, the "power" that constitutes the objective of the will cannot be understood as being anything other than the will itself. What power in this sense does is precisely to reduce all others to raw material for the will, construed as the striving to set things into place, which is to say, to make things into objects and objects into objectives. It is this process, rather than any determinate aspect of it, that constitutes the movement of the will willing itself.

From this discussion of the will to will as the ultimate form of subjectivity Heidegger adduces a number of implications that were relevant to the political situation in which he was writing, and that remain quite pertinent today as well. I am thinking here in particular of the phenomenon of the Leader, whether one defines it with the German word, Führer, or with its apparently more anodyne English equivalent, "leadership." I mention only one other of these implications here, since it constitutes what is undoubtedly, for Heidegger at least, the ultimate metaphysical other of objectivity: technics.

Heidegger's word is *Technik*, which I prefer to translate as "technics" rather than as technology, since in German it can also mean "technique" and since in any case Heidegger is using it in a way that is anything but simply familiar to us. Hence, the very strangeness of the word "technics" is precisely an advantage over the all too familiar word, "technology." Like the Cartesian emphasis upon certitude, technics, according to Heidegger, is both "the highest form of rational consciousness" and at the same time profoundly associated with a certain form of insensitivity (*Besinnungslosigkeit*), which Heidegger describes as "the incapacity, organized so as to be opaque to itself, of entering into a relation with what is both questionable and worthy of being questioned" (99/79). Striving for certitude tends thus to exclude all others insofar as they cannot be brought before the subject and set into place over against it. The essence of technics, as Heidegger describes it, resides precisely in this ability to *place*, or rather, in the power of *emplacement*. As discussed above, however, the power to place is very different from any particular place or any particular object, and this is why one of the primary manifestations of technics, as Heidegger interprets it, is the production and stocking of *energy* (and of its "raw materials"). For disposable, available energy is what allows the process of emplacement to go on. What is distinctive, in Heidegger's determination of modern technics as emplacement (the German word is *Ge-stell* and it is usually translated as "framing," although it means "frame" as well), is that it is linked to the unfolding of subjectivity as the securing of self and ultimately as the will not just to power, but to will. In short, modern technics thus emerges as the other and the condition of the unconditional voluntarism that according to Heidegger marks the conclusion and consummation of modern metaphysics.

If we keep in mind the extremely dynamic nature of modern technics as emplacement, and if we remember that it pursues its project of self-securing as the will to will by what Heidegger calls, literally, the "placing of orders"—in German; *Bestellen*—then we can begin to see why the very notion of objectivity has perhaps begun to sound somewhat antiquated today. For the aspect of objectivity that objects to or resists the subjective project of self-securing is progressively reduced as the object is increasingly determined as the raw material of the *objective*, to be striven for and attained by the subject. A simple, and yet telling instance of this triumph of technics can be seen in the privilege assigned to the private automobile over mass transportation in the United States: Mass transport subordinates the will to will to instituted orders and arrangements of places, to networks and trajectories that cannot simply be rearranged at will. The lure of the private automobile consists in large part precisely in the promise of greater "freedom" it seems to afford with regard to such instituted circuits: The automobile promises the freedom of being able to displace oneself at will: of being truly *auto-mobile*. That this hoped-for *mobility* of the *self*, which perhaps is itself driven by the striving to secure oneself and by the fear of not being able to place oneself into total security, is progressively being revealed as rather a constraint than a liberation is symptomatic of the more general difficulties encountered by technics, as the metaphysical other of objectivity.

Such difficulties arise when the ultimate objective of technics becomes that of establishing a certitude and a security that is unwilling and perhaps unable to leave any place for the incalculability—that is, the insecurity—of the other. I leave open the question of whether or not such incalculability might not be inseparable from another notion of liberty that would entail not reducing of the other to a calculable object, but rather admitting and allowing for what in the other resists objectification (and hence subjectification). Perhaps this is one of the implications of the following observation of Heidegger, with which I close, and which sounds less antiquated today than it probably did when it was written, half a century ago:

> The fact that technological projects and measures succeed in yielding inventions and innovations, which replace each other at breakneck pace, in no way proves that even the conquests of technics can make the impossible possible. . . . Nature and spirit [have become] objects of self-consciousness; the latter's unconditional domination forces both in advance into a uniformity from which metaphysically there is no escape. It is one thing merely to use the earth, quite another to receive its blessings and to be at home in the law of this receiving . . . by watching over the mystery of being and over the inviolability of the possible. (109/91)

NOTES

1. The edition I will be referring to dates from 1961.
2. The page references to the Heidegger text in English translation follow Martin Heidegger, *The End of Philosophy*, Joan Strambaugh, trans. (New York: Harper & Row; 1973). The second of the two page numbers given references the German edition, *Vorträge und Aufsätze* (Pfullingen: Neske, 1954).
3. René Descartes, *Discours de la méthode*, IV (Paris: Partie, 1947).

II

Disciplinary Critiques

4

Gender, Objectivity, and the Rise of Scientific History

BONNIE G. SMITH

More than 20 years ago some historians in the West began asserting that women had a history; more practically, they started writing it. Bemoaning the ghettoization that the new field of women's history seemed to generate, historian Joan Scott by the mid-1980s was asking that the category "woman" be replaced by that of "gender." Scott maintained that "man" and "woman" were binary terms that had operated throughout history to produce differentials in power. "Woman" by itself was an insufficient category and one, moreover, that led to separatism. Recently the German historian Gisela Bok has interpreted the controversy over whether to use "gender" or "women" as itself a binary discourse in need of deconstruction. But now, several years after Scott's important article in the *American Historical Review*, the problem of ghettoization—or to put it another way, the failure of either women's history or gender history to attract a "mainstream" audience—suggests that the difficulty lies not in the categories themselves but in the construction of history over the past century and a half. This chapter proposes that history has operated in such a way as to constitute either women or gender as its negative. It also addresses the question that springs to all our minds: If both women and gender (or either one on its own) are historical categories, where have they been hiding all these years?

51

The question of sexual difference loomed increasingly large after the French Revolution. Suffragist and feminist movements developed mass constituencies, numbering in the millions during this time and bringing to the fore a concern for sex inequality. Labor unions and socialist organizations addressed the "woman question" in their theoretical debates and political activism, while mainstream bodies like scholarly academies, law schools, and newspapers argued in prize competitions, theses, and journalistic articles about male prerogatives, the status of women, and the fate of the family. Where did history situate itself as a scholarly discipline and profession in this intellectual and political ferment, and how was its generic shape affected by the use it made of sexual difference? If the categories of gender and women feature prominently in historical discussion today, what has been their relationship to historical study in the course of professionalization?

During the 19th century historians formed a modern, scientific profession whose practices were explicitly unconcerned with considerations of gender, class, or politics as they then were shaping society at large. These practices involved a commitment to objectivity above such categories as class and gender, the strict use of evidence, the taming of historical narrative to a less rhetorical style, the development of archives and professional libraries, the organization of university training in seminars and tutorials, and in the case of the United States, a commitment to democratic access to the profession based on ability. This chapter proposes to look at these practices in order to see how they in fact touched on gender while constituting a gender-neutral community of scholars.

History has long displayed all the ingredients that make for a successful scholarly field. As it was professionalized during the 19th century into the discipline we know today, its practitioners usually came from at least the respectable and more often the well-to-do classes. Its practices occurred in universities, libraries, and archives—places associated (falsely, as we know) with gentility and cleanliness. Moreover, professionalizing historians had a way of removing all sense of the personal or subjective from their work. As the great French historian, Fustel de Coulanges, put it, "Gentlemen, it is not I who speak, but History that speaks through me."[1] In this way the historian created a space inhabited by an invisible "I," one without politics, without an ego or persona, and certainly ungendered. I want to examine here first the discipline of history as it developed this ungendered, "objective" narrative in the course of its professionalization, and second what this meant for a few of the interesting women who entered the field, in order to foreground the politics and specifically the gendering of the historical enterprise.

The 19th-century professionalization of history, with its attendant focus on scientific models, constituted a momentous change in the genre. Proclaimed emphases on objectivity, on special skills like paleography or epigraphy, on the designation of archives and other repositories, as well as the creation of seminars and courses of advanced study, the conferral of advanced degrees, and the phenomena of professional meetings and journals all transformed the production of historical texts. The one inconstant in the mass of new standards and regulations was the status of women in the profession: At some universities, like Cambridge and Oxford, they could not obtain those coveted degrees; at professional meetings like those of the American Historical Association they could not attend social functions; major libraries like Widener at Harvard and the Bibliothèque nationale in Paris restricted hours for women more than those for men; some archives prohibited women from using their re-sources; and so on. In the drive to standardize and rationalize both profession and genre the place of women was always irregular. I address this further below.

The reconstruction or professionalization of history from the middle of the 19th century on also rested on an apparent shift in emphasis from historical writing itself to pretextual efforts. An endorsement of archives and uncovering the facts they contained—popularly attributed to a "found-ing father," Leopold von Ranke—gave rise to the modern discipline, with its authorized repositories, its credentialling of researchers, and its secret research methods passed down only after 20 or so years of schooling. Avoiding Romantic excess, the historical text itself was not to revolve around an exciting narrative (although Ranke initially was drawn to history in part because of its narrativistic possibilities); rather, the histori-cal text would unfold the results of investigations using documents in archives and employing a range of professional methods. It resulted, in the words of Lord Acton, from the "heroic study of records."[2] Profession-als denounced their predecessors' emphasis on rhetorical and literary skills and in so doing tried to shift attention to their efforts not as writers but as researchers.

This revolutionary move worked to undermine the truth claims of history's rivals, not only the closely related antiquarianism, but the more important and ever growing genres—the novel and the newspaper. The truth of so-called scientific history resided in its absolute factuality (unlike the novel) and (unlike the newspaper) in its evolution from secret, privi-leged sites like archives and libraries, from manuscripts hidden away and unearthed, from documents from centuries past looked at for the first time. The new historical knowledge was so recondite that the French historian Ernest Lavisse even locked the door of his classroom while his seminar was in session to protect its status. The newspaper, by contrast, counted on public, accessible, and current knowledge. Its greatest sin, however, stemmed from its literary nature, and this literariness the newspaper shared with the novel and with the heroic history of Carlyle, Macaulay, and that archenemy Sir Walter Scott. Trapped in fact within a whole circuit of sins, these unscientific challengers incited textual excitement, deployed larger-than-life heroes, and cast their net to entrap a wide audience.

Amidst the claims to "neutrality" and "objectivity" the reconstruction of history within the new institutional setting of the university and historical association left behind it traces of the metaphorical assignment of gender roles and the eroticization of the historical project. Even in the process of basing historical writing on data, factuality, and objectivity a lightly sketched path reveals an involvement with masculinity, femininity, and sexual difference. Leopold von Ranke, for instance, professed to have a "desire for the data." Hidden away in archives, the facts contained in ancient documents were "so many princesses, possibly beautiful, all under a curse and needing to be saved." Hardly neuter, the metaphors of professionalization exuded heterosexuality in which an adventurous historian rescued the beautiful princess. In another instance Ranke referred to a specific Venetian collection of documents, hitherto unexplored, as "the object of my love . . . a beautiful Italian, and I hope that together we shall produce a Romano–German prodigy." And, finally, still another unseen archive was "an absolute virgin. I long for the moment I shall have access to her . . . whether she is pretty or not."[3]

Ranke invested his fight against the idealist or romantic version of history with libidinal energy. In this he hardly differed from those who continued to seek the heroic past offered in Romantic history, where the knight in shining armor had his way with one and all. In particular one is reminded of all the important new work on masculinity that reveals how much it resided in reviving and acting out historical scenes and rituals such as duelling, medieval fairs and contests at universities, and so on. But even professional history in the 19th and 20th centuries formed a chivalric haven for the development and play of masculine desires and libidinal activities. As a site invested with aspects of masculine identity—a heroism, for instance, in discovering records or acquiring knowledge (embodied today in the "archive jock" who has visited every municipal archive in a given country)—historical study was and remains a properly important but hardly unproblematic place. Thus a first point is this: how dangerous it is to pretend that there is no masculine investment in the "heroic" act of research, in the creation of a this archive "jockery," or in the erotic relationship developed with facts by maintaining that history is neutral or "neuter."

Operating from this metaphoric space, scientific history, around which the profession constituted itself, proceeded to engage its literary enemy on a gendered terrain. The *English Historical Review* began with the promise not to offer "allurements of style" to its readers.[4] It praised works for their "utter want of tinsel embroidery" or their refusal to "adorn a tale."[5] Other periodicals pointed to the "tawdry trappings" of literary works.[6] Allurements, adornments, tawdry trappings, and tinsel embroidery in the 19th century constituted the materia of prostitution, of public women and their sexuality. Romantic history, like the whore, was all decked out. Historic imagery and heroic narratives paraded about like so many strumpets, leading the public to sin and infecting it. "Clio is going to be just a gal-about-town," wrote one American university historian to a colleague, "on whom anybody with two bits worth of inclination in his pocket can lay claims."[7] The course of professionalization followed the lure of sexualized language and the metaphors of whoredom.

At the same time amateurs began castigating professionals in a similarly sexual way. The *Atheneum* in discrete reviews found Gardiner a "Dryasdust," someone whose "pulse was slow." "Of Cecil's scandalous private life, of his sumptuous lodgings, of his secret orgies, of his intrigues with Lady Suffolk and other frail women, the writer has no conception."[8] In fact, whether amateur or professional, scientific or Romantic, the voice of history betrayed a dependence on heterosexual articulations and conventions. These conventions remain today not only in the charge that whole fields like black and women's history are "fashionable," "sexy," or "hot." In fact, historiographical works, like the recent and popular work of Peter Novick, revel in repeating gendered or sexual slurs, metaphors, and *bons mots* of previous historians to make their claims. Such sexualizing of the text, however, is excessive: The point could be made in a more forthright way. Marking the text with their own superfluity, gendered and sexual metaphors serve the end of indicating good history's essential necessity. As a consequence, the language of bad history was also the language of women.

Another historical metamorphosis in the 19th century involved history's renewal as a discourse of power through its attachment to the workings of power and the state. As the English historian E. A. Freeman so famously put it, "History is past politics." Although Ranke maintained that literature and the arts were appropriate to history, somehow his best energy was spent in political and institutional studies. The project of the Enlightenment and Romanticism to widen the historical lens, as seen in the works of Voltaire, Herder, or de Stael, abruptly ended (although there would be later history wars over whether historical science should include the study of culture and society), leaving the historical narrative to spin out a thick description, daily more intricate, of the state, its personalities, rituals, obsessions, and so on. When other aspects of history—such as concern for social groups or cultural life—revived, they did so guided by political chronology, the archival research methodology for political history, and so on.

Historical methodology reveled in this connection to the state. Ranke had noted the importance of reading secret ambassadorial reports as a way of knowing about the workings of power. Later in the century Lord Acton noted that after Ranke's insights about the importance of documents came the next stage in the development of scientific and professionalized history "when the war of 1859 laid open the spoils [i.e., the archives] of Italy."[9] From then on, he continues, every country was forced to open its records. Or, as Acton's teacher Ignaz von Doellinger put it in the 1860s, "Every library corner [in Europe] has been searched."[10] The forced openings of governmental sources, this unveiling and probing of high-level secrets, like articulations of historical methodology in general, were intertwined with the course of masculine politics. According to historians from Ranke to Acton and later, the ways of the historian, particularly his probing and assessing of the secrets of politics, were precisely those needed by the successful leader. History no longer involved the narrative celebration of knights in shining armor à la Walter Scott (one of Ranke's sworn enemies) but rather the feats of archival discovery and investigation followed by assessment of facts and their proper disciplining into a text. So too politics at the turn of the century (as Weber first suggested) had come to depend on the bureaucratic administrator and parliamentary politician. Historical work, like political rule, involved the methods of bureaucratic life. In doing research the historian struggled with "those passages that raised difficulties in his way"; he "set up masters (including people, facts, and principles) whom . . . he could obey."[11] Setting up masters and rulers as great men, historians constructed their scientific study of the past as a narrative of male authority in politics. This was an exercise in hierarchization in which other subfields were characterized as inferior. A discourse of male identity, history concerned great men and, as historiography advanced in importance, it was written by great men. Historiography's cast of great male historians, like that of political figures, was naturalized, masking the gender exclusivity of their ranks.

By the mid-19th century, what with the idea of searching out fairy princesses and assaulting the archives, the masculine identity of history was secure. If political power was for men, then so was professional history, its subject matter, methodology, and even its fantasies. Historians revived the call of the 2nd-century author Lucian for scholars whose professional qualities duplicated the masculinity of their subject matter:

> [Give us the historian with an] ability to understand and express himself, keen-sighted, one who could handle affairs if they were turned over to him, a man with the mind of a soldier combined with that of a good citizen, and a knowledge of generalship; yes, and one who has at some time been in a camp and has seen soldiers exercising and drilling and knows of arms and engines; again, let him know what 'in column,' what 'in line' mean, how the companies of infantry, how the cavalry, are maneuvered, the origin and meaning of lead out and lead around, in short not a stay-at-home or one who must rely on what people tell him.[12]

If powerful men from Napoleon to John F. Kennedy professed to love history, the lives of historians were intertwined with those of politicians. Lord Acton spent his fondest moments with Gladstone, Arthur Schlesinger with Kennedy, and in the late 20th century Francois Furet was hailed as one of the three most powerful men in France.

Could female leaders fit this political/historical paradigm? One female leader *was* the center of historical controversy, and the singular attention paid her also shaped the professionalizing process. This was Pope Joan, and on the surface she seemed to challenge the progress of gendering. According to the legend—repeated, rebutted, and refurbished over the centuries but looming large in the 19th—Pope Joan had been elected to the papacy in the middle of the 9th century for her great learning. A woman of disputed origin, she had gone to Athens (or some other center of learning) and became one of the most learned people of her day. For two years or so, she performed all the duties of Pope conscientiously, but then, in a procession through the streets of Rome, she suddenly gave birth to a child. In a single moment Joan had turned a religious display into a carnivalesque one, placing cross-dressing and the grotesquery of papal childbirth right on the papal throne. As a result Joan died on the spot (some said she was stoned to death, though Boccacio's version maintains that she quietly and peacefully took early retirement). From then on popes received the symbols of office sitting on a pierced chair, so that masculine nature of their genitals could be confirmed. Not a pretty story, but both Catholic and later Protestant historians and popular culture too reveled in it or confronted it.

The phenomenon of Pope Joan haunted the historical imagination, but never so much as in the 19th century. Distinguished Dutch, German, French, and Italian historians all had much to say about her in the 1840s and 1850s. Alfred Plummer of Trinity College, Oxford, called her story "monstrous" and "preposterous." Joan had transgressed the norms of knowledge, of political power, and of just about anything else one might think of; for these reasons historians and other intellectuals repeated her story nervously across those many centuries. But the newly opened archives of Europe were about to expunge her from the record. Early in the 1860s no less a historian than von Doellinger, teacher of Lord Acton and definitely his superior when it came to publishing, took on the embarrassment once and for all.

Doellinger professed to know every archival source in Europe; no authentic written account of Pope Joan, he maintained, existed before the mid-12th century. She existed before then merely "in the mouth of the people," of well-intentioned but guillible clergy, monks, and other "guileless" folk. Moreover, the props in her story lacked authenticity. For instance, the story that she had a Greek education that impressed the Romans could hardly be true. By the 9th century anybody who was anybody went to Paris. He found, in addition, that chroniclers gave her prepapal name variously as Agnes, Gilberta, Gerberta, Joanna, Margaret, Isabel, Dorothy, and Jutta—textual inconsistencies that threw her very being into question. Her fate was just as inconsistently reported, while the details of how the people protected themselves thereafter from another woman pope travestied historical logic. The pierced chair was not merely used to allow the crowd the chance to affirm for itself that the pope's genitals were male. For the serious and scientific Doellinger authorities introduced the pierced chairs into the service only because of their "beautiful color."[13] In sum, a woman of great learning and power could not have existed because of universal standards like the beauty of a chair or the truth of writing.

Doellinger's account of Pope Joan opens his book on other forgeries and fables, and thus served as the emblem for the progress of archival history. Joan's story stood beyond the boundaries of professional standards, and in so doing helped define the new scholarship. In this way, far from being beyond politics, it served as well Doellinger's own cause of showing that the universal Church could survive even in the face of inaccuracy and scandal. Fighting the secular power intrinsic to the new doctrine of papal infallibility, he was excommunicated in the 1870s. Yet the carnivalesque woman, who inverted the gendering of knowledge and power, was the sign of battle for him; by pushing her to the margins and outside the canon, Doellinger like other historians in the process of professionalization made history universal, not gendered. Such stories as that of Pope Joan or the other equally important controversy over the *droit de seigneur*—that is, the lord's right to intercourse with any bride connected with his dominion—continued to prove not just important, but constitutive of history. For one thing, they continued to infuse history with the tincture of sexuality and thus to channel libidinal energy into historical work. More importantly, scientific history did the ideological work for the system of separate spheres and modern forms of political and gender power. Using women as the sign of both gender in its entirety (i.e., both masculinity and femininity) and of all that was outside history, the new scholars created a fantasy world of the Real, that is, of history. It was a world purged of gender (as well as class), sufficient unto itself in charting and defining significant human experience in the past, and redolent of the power such claims generated. Those who sought to resurrect women ended up with foolishness, hypersexuality, or looking like advocates of one harebrained scheme or another.

In the midst of all of this some women in the 19th century—that is, in the middle of the professionalizing process—were also becoming professional historians. Did things look the same from their perspective? How did they themselves construct a professional identity and a set of historical questions within this particular gendering of the historical genre? Within a heterosexualized schema, they often drew admiring mentions, but these were hardly sustained. For when it came to writing up the story of historiography or the professionalization of the discipline, one ended up with such books as J. P. Kenyon's *History Men*, which focused on male historians and made female historians appear ephemeral. Seeing the many ways in which historians stamped their profession and its subject matter as male makes studying women historians problematic. A feminine list of historical greats to rival the Rankes, Actons, and Doellingers, only produces women dressed up in masculine garb. All the admiring stories of exemplary female researchers equaling the heights of masculine prowess merely replicates the (not unimportant) utopian vision of a genderless historical space. It still leaves most women on the outside, with no clear reason as to why this is the case.

Alongside the decorous accounts of unsexed female lives, of those who wrote exemplary history in the style of the masters, there exists another story of women in the professionalizing process. It too poses problems, but is worth trying to relate. At Cambridge there was "the wicked dangerous Jane Ellen Harrison, the perverter of youth." She smoked, wore daring clothes, especially featuring what were regarded as excessively low necklines. Hardly leading a cloistered scholarly life, Harrison had passionate loves and equally passionate break-ups with friends and colleagues.[14] At the London School of Economics in the 1920s and

1930s Eileen Power reportedly spent her evenings wildly dancing in nightclubs and "making eyes" at all the men. As a result of the spectacle she provided novelists loved to use her as a prototype of oversexed femininity.[15] At Saint Hugh's, Oxford, the Renaissance scholar Cecilia Ady led a legendary fight of the women tutors against the administration. Supported by women scholars elsewhere, the tutors walked off the job, while Ady herself was called "a menace" to the health of the university.[16] Caroline Skeel of Westfield College University of London, had many hysterical breakdowns and periodically retired under the weight of them.[17] In the United States the President of Vassar had to reprimand Lucy Maynard Salmon for being so loose as to ride a bicycle. Salmon, like many women historians, lived for most of her life with another woman.

Women amateur historians had similarly difficult public personae. The most shocking, Vernon Lee, sent mothers scurrying to hide their daughters from seduction whenever that notorious and charming lesbian announced a visit.[18] Her writing, according to Henry James, had "too great an implication of sexual motives." And to his brother William he wrote "a word of warning . . . she's a tiger cat."[19] The amateur art historian and wife of the sickly Mark Pattison decked herself out in seductive clothing, smoked French cigarettes, and to one young man, conveyed a distinct sense of "feminine fastness."[20] She lived apart from her husband for long stretches of time.

Was there a message in this frenzied madness, of which we could cite countless other examples? Virginia Woolf noted that for her to come to professionalism as a writer, she had to confront the 19th-century version of womanhood—the "angel of the house"—who counselled sympathy, flattery, and deception, especially when dealing with works written by men. In order to write, Woolf faced the "angel" violently: "I turned upon her and caught her by the throat. I did my best to kill her."[21] Confronting the image of the "angel," women scholars performed purgative rituals when undertaking to write professional history. Although many women entered the professions with a sense of bringing maternal values to the public sphere, in the case of writing and research something different was demanded. Killing the angel may have overcome many problems on the women's side of things, but it did put women at a disadvantage. No longer prim, they might look more like the fashioners of literary histories with all their adornments—that is, like whores. The sexualized metaphors of scientific and professional history perhaps did their cultural work by making the establishment of a professional persona a tricky undertaking.

The writing of history proved a more difficult matter. If the symbolic act of killing the angel seemed a prerequisite for presenting the professional female self, it also infiltrated writing. The work of Eileen Power and Lucy Maynard Salmon provide but two instances among many possibilities. Power's earliest work fulfilled all the professional requirements for archival research using unseen documents. She went the extra mile by looking in addition at secret places—nunneries. Unlike Ranke, Power hardly found "angels" or "princesses," but rather what she called "pandemonium—a place or gathering of demons."[22] Nuns behaved coyly, dishonestly, and in a thoroughly worldly manner. They went sleepily to early services and instead of having a sense of metier, devised a system of cutting syllables out of the litany in order to return to bed more quickly. On the other hand, whenever the rule of silence was in effect they found ways to subvert that as well. If the laws of liturgy encouraged them to slash away at words, the laws of silence found the nuns ingeniously creating them: "The sister who desired fish would 'wag her hands displayed sidelings in the manner of a fish tail'; she who wanted milk would 'draw her little finger in the manner of milking'; . . . and guilty sacristan, struck by the thought that she had not provided incense for the Mass, would 'put her two fingers into her nostrils.'"[23] Power's foray into the archives produced demons, tax cheats, transgressive talkers, and other miscreants. Moreover, her comic literary style made history appealing (as all of us know who continue to rely on it); perhaps she even prostituted it. F. W. Maitland eulogized another medievalist, Mary Bateson of Newnham College, with the greatest praise when he claimed that she refused to "attract the general reader," preferring instead "a few students of history."[24] Such was not the case with Power.

Lucy Maynard Salmon employed another strategy, though with similarly inappropriate results. Salmon had begun decorously in her prizewinning thesis on the appointing powers of the presidency. Fairly quickly, however, she abandoned properly restricted and professional sources. Far from interrogating the masters or diplomatic archives, her next book centered on the results of questionnaires answered by the commonest and lowest workers—domestic servants. Then, in her seminars at Vassar, she would fling down all sorts of ordinary artifacts for her students to scrutinize: cookbooks, railroad schedules, laundry lists, newspapers.[25] (Her classes were called "Miss Salmon's Laundry Lists."[26]) Not only did students write history from these widely available sources (nor did Salmon lock the seminar door); she also encouraged them after graduation to develop local repositories to make historical material widely available. No wonder young men coming to Vassar tried to overthrow her power in the history department.[27] Not that Salmon eschewed all of the new professionalism; to the contrary, she often merely had her students hand in note cards with sources and bits of information. She herself left the skeleton of a manuscript on fans; it is a series of cards—hundreds of them—each containing a single fact, tersely noted. Compelling narrative thus seemed of little importance. Nonetheless, Salmon's two works on the newspaper as a source for historians and as history itself displayed an amazing understanding of the importance of rhetoric and textuality. Newspapers as a source of factual information were not necessarily reliable, Salmon maintained. The amount of space devoted to advertisement, the items given attention, the size of type, the shape of features, or the physical make-up of the editorial page, told everything about an age. The judgment about Salmon's work—that she did, in the opinion of the *Nation*, a kind of history "unworthy" of her talents and of the profession itself—is easily understood.[28] Salmon, according to one of her students, constantly championed "the new, the unknown, the untried, and the dangerous."[29] Yet relegating her and Power's daring into models of resistance to the confines of the profession (or to its sexism or use of sexual metaphors) is problematic. Such a strategy risks finding a female version of the "masters," all female, where gender does not operate. Or it suggests a world of women that stands for gender as a whole, outside history's bounds, but that is in reality segregated.

Instead of posing this or any other strategy as a way out of the gendered model of the profession, I would like to look at the dead ends and blind alleys placed in the way of, but entered into by women's historical writing. These blind alleys particularly sprang up when women (or anyone, for that matter) ventured to write about women's pasts. As one example, Lucy Maynard Salmon, who proceeded from her work on the presidency to servants, ended up with such improbable works as "The Family Cookbook," "On Beds and Bedding," "History in a Backyard," and "Ode to a Kitchen Sink." Her writing left the realm of historical prose, as in this example from a history of the cookbook. Here Salmon displays images of cooking that recalled the family: "Aunt Hannah's loaf cake, Cousin Lizzie's waffles, Grandmother's cookies, Grandma Lyman's marble cake, Sister Sally's quince jelly, Mother's raspberry vinegar, Warren's cake, Jennie's gingerbread, Jack's oyster stew, Mercy's nasturtium pickles, johnny cake, brown betty, and carolines." Or she found place names of cooking: "Lady Baltimore cake, Philadelphia ice cream, Irving Park cake, Bangor pudding, Nuremberg cakes, Banbury tarts, Bavarian cream, Irish stew, Scotch broth, English muffins, and Hamburg steak."[30] Recounting the domestic—not the political—past, Salmon often ended up in the realm of sheer poetics. The poetic, Gaston Bachelard reminds us, leaves concern for cause and effect behind in favor of evocations, reverberations, and echoes.[31] Salmon, like the housewife who was "emancipated from time and space" into poetry, could become absorbed in reverie and invention but not, perhaps, history: "Birds on canapes, bird's-nest pudding, floating islands, apples in bloom, shadow potatoes, cheese aigrettes, apple snow, snowballs, gossamer gingerbread, fairy gingerbread, aurora sauce, moonlight cake, lily cake, lady fingers, and amber pudding."[32]

Mary Beard sometimes ended up in a similar place, such as in *On Understanding Women*, where for pages she employs an odd looking textual arrangement and an insistent summoning of women that resembles nothing so much as free verse:

> exotic entertainers firing young blood, circus performers, swan and
>   nose divers, rodeo strategists, parachutists, and high kickers
> domestic amusers with babies, one baby this year, another next,
>   possibly one free year, than twins, one's own, one's employer's
>   pushing carts, scolding, chattering, spanking, laughing, wheedling,
>   nursing, bottling, with nice babies, lovely babies, cross babies, sick
>   babies, babies learning to walk and babies that won't walk; anyway
>   babies
> dog fanciers and tenders
> actresses putting new wine into old bottles to tempt the uninitiated
>   and excite the jaded
> hostesses promoting trade, letters and philosophy, marrying off their
>   sons and daughters, allaying tedium.[33]

Beard also had another strategy, and that was laughter. Her coedited historical book, *Laughing Their Way: Women's Humor in America*, brings together a wide range of women's cartoons, satiric verse, humorous stories, and stand-up comic routines. A spinster aunt visits her nephew in boot camp and on the battlefield in World War I. Having first removed the body of her car and made it into a luxurious ambulance, she wreaks a havoc that puts the slaughter going on around her to shame. Witty poems on the poster girl, the married Romeo, old ladies, and so on provoke smiles, chuckles, and belly laughs. But the collection had a point: What would happen if men "could no longer fall back on the obscure divine mother for militant justification—if armored ladies symbolizing war, preparedness and patriotism or unarmed angels and Amazons leading on embattled hosts were removed from their minds."[34] What if, in other words, women were not angels or princesses but rather laughing, rollicking beings, always joking around? Although Beard and Bruere claimed to examine the "function" of humor in America—that is, it could get women through bad times at home or help them fight for a cause— eventually the book ended only with a short overgeneralization that women were always laughing. That laughter, indeed the overwhelming joking in the entire collection, subsumed any seriousness of purpose or of history.

Professional historical writing promoted ideology the way all cultural activity does. That ideology appeared in metaphors and historical heuristics, accompanying and even advancing the much celebrated objectivity and factuality. Women's writing of history displayed coordinate metaphorical markings that leave important traces of struggle, definition, and direction. Rather than disdain these discursive traces, we should at least begin to ponder their sense. Merely monumentalizing professional women may (as in the monumentalization of great men and great historians) serve fantasies that could ultimately be dangerous. For instance, bringing worthy women to the fore in a genealogical way as improvers or mothers perpetuates the kind of professional writing about masters, authorities, and the like that heretofore served to exclude women. On the other hand only praising their rebellions works a simple reversal in categories of analysis—a reversal that merely expresses our own wishes to kill angels in fanciful ways. Most women professionals were hardly rebels, but they often show that a consciously gendered subject matter did not fit professional historical procedures and categories. Writers like Lucy Maynard Salmon and Mary Beard tested the limits and reached the dead ends of those procedures. The remarkable or perhaps not so remarkable thing is that those metaphorical and literary bounds paralleled the lived experience of many women historians. Women never confronted a neutral profession but one heterosexualized, confined, and limited in the opportunities it offered them.

Salmon and Beard, reaching these limits of history, did so in periods of great ferment. Challenges to separate spheres offered by feminists, and to the clarity of sexual difference that became apparent during the depression, offered the possibility to change the particular gendered configuration of history as it had evolved during the 19th century. As practitioners like Beard and Salmon kept reaching history's confines and borderlands, they repeatedly drew attention to the discipline's limitations. But neither of them had a smooth time of it. Instead, Mary Beard herself became a continuously disappearing author of historical works (i.e., Charles Beard was usually cited as the sole author of their many joint works), while Salmon hardly got any of her 20th-century, modernist work on women published in book form or in any but Vassar publications until after her death. Then, her students actually paid for their publication.

In this chapter I try to show that understanding women's writing is only possible when seen in relationship to unfolding professional norms, that the institutional place of women is only pertinent when looked at in terms of the sociological practices and gendering of professionals. Likewise, professional norms like objectivity and professional practices like archival research can only be understood in relationship to what they have been defined against, in the most notably overt manner. Gender interests constitute one of the central categories of such definition.

NOTES

1. "Fustel de Coulanges," *Revue historique 41* (1900): 278.
2. John Dalberg-Acton, *Lectures on Modern History* (New York: Meridian, 1961 [1906]), 22.
3. Letter to Bettina von Arnim, February 6, 1828, Leopold von Ranke, *Das Briefwerk*, Walter Fuchs, ed. (Hamburg: Hoffman and Campe, 1949), 139; Letter to Heinrich Ritter, October 28, 1827, Ranke, *Sämmtliche Werke* (Leipzig, 1890), 53–54; p. 175. Letter to Ferdinand Ranke, November 11, 1836, Leopold von Ranke, *Neue Briefe*, Bernhard Hoeft and Hans Herzfeld, eds. (Hamburg: Hoffman und Campe, 1949), 230.
4. "Prefatory Note," *English Historical Review 1* (1886): 5.
5. *English Historical Review*, Reviews of S. Gardiner, *History of the Commonwealth and Protectorate 1649–1660* and Georg Busolt, *Handbuch der griechischen Geschichte 13* (1898): 125, 167. See also Lord Acton's praise for Ranke's writing "without adornment." *Lectures on Modern History* (New York: Meridian, 1961), 39.
6. "Gardiner's Personal Government of Charles I," *Saturday Review* (December 22, 1877): 774.
7. Quoted in Peter Novick, *That Noble Dream: The "Objectivity Question" and the American Historical Profession* (Cambridge: Cambridge University Press, 1988), 193.
8. *Atheneum* (1863): 392–393; (1869): 629.
9. Acton, *Lectures*, 29.
10. John J. Ign. von Doellinger, *Fables Respecting the Popes of the Middle Ages*, Alfred Plummer, trans. (London: Rivingtons, 1871), 9.
11. Acton, *Lectures*, 34–35.
12. Lucian, *How to Write History*, K. Kilburn, trans. (Cambridge: Harvard University Press, 1959) quoted in Donald R. Kelley, *Versions of History* (New Haven: Yale University Press, 1991), 65. For one small example of this phenomenon see C. H. S. Fifoot, *Frederic William Maitland: A Life* (Cambridge: Harvard University Press), 95.
13. Doellinger, *Popes*, 48.
14. Hope Mirrlees, *Outline of Jane Ellen Harrison's Life*, unpublished manuscript, Newnham College Archives, Cambridge University.
15. Information provided by Sir John Plumb, March 1985, Cambridge, England. Plumb asserts that Evelyn Waugh liked to use Power and particularly featured her in *Vile Bodies*. I have not been able to find a character like Power in that work; perhaps Plumb meant another of Waugh's works.
16. Copy of draft resolution of St. Hugh's administrative council found in Evelyn Mary Jamison papers, Warburg Institute, London.

17. Conversations with Westfield College archivist and historian, Janet Sondheimer, July 30, 1985. See also the Skeel collection in the Westfield College archives.

18. See the Vernon Lee collection at Somerville College, Oxford, for details of this situation and for indications that Vernon Lee had an inkling about preparations by hostesses for her visits.

19. Quoted in Peter Gunn, *Vernon Lee: Violet Paget, 1856–1935* (London: Oxford University Press, 1964), 105, 139.

20. Caroline Jebb, *Life and Letters of Sir Richard Claverhouse Jebb* (Cambridge: Cambridge University Press, 1907), 163–165, (Letter of Jebb to "C. L. S." [Caroline Jebb], July 20, 1873). The author thanks Kali Israel of Rutgers University for this citation from her forthcoming study of Lady Emilia Dilke.

21. Virginia Woolf, *The Death of the Moth* (New York: Harcourt Brace, 1942), 237.

22. Eileen Power, *Medieval People* (London: Methuen, 1924), 67.

23. Ibid.

24. Helen M. Cam, ed., *Selected Historical Essays of F. W. Maitland* (Cambridge: Cambridge University Press, 1957), 277.

25. Caroline Ware speaking informally at the first Evalyn A. Clark Conference, October 12, 1985, Vassar College. J. B. Ross also provided a similar picture of Salmon's classes in interviews, May 1985, Washington, DC.

26. Beatrice Berle, *A Life in Two Worlds* (New York: Walker, 1983), 49.

27. See Lucy Maynard Salmon Collection, Box 3, Vassar College Archives for details of the attacks on Salmon, particularly by James Baldwin, early in the 20th century.

28. Louise Fargo Brown, *Apostle of Democracy. The Life of Lucy Maynard Salmon* (New York: Harper and Row, 1943), 134.

29. Ibid., 83.

30. Lucy Maynard Salmon, "The Family Cookbook," *Vassar College Quarterly 11* (March 1926), 101–111.

31. Gaston Bachelard, *The Poetics of Space* (Boston: Beacon, 1969).

32. Salmon, "The Family Cookbook," 105.

33. Mary Beard, *On Understanding Women* (New York: Longmans, Green, 1931), 11–12.

34. Martha Bensley Bruere and Mary Ritter Beard, eds., *Laughing Their Way. Women's Humor in America* (New York: Macmillan, 1934), vi.

5

Making Geography Objectively: Ocularity, Representation, and *The Nature of Geography*

JOHN PAUL JONES III

You know everything *that has been observed for centuries, with your particular sagacity you arrange everything together, from much-used material you gain ever new and grand views, and you reproduce the whole in the most desirable clarity.*

—ALEXANDER VON HUMBOLDT[*]

"Geography," a prominent commentator once remarked, is the "Mother of Sciences."[1] While the irony of so describing a male-dominated discipline was lost on him, the performative function of the originary rhetoric was not: he went on to a claim a permanent position for the field based on the logic of genesis. Such efforts to center geography within the field of sciences characterize many of the programmatic statements that have reflected on the discipline's nature. Arguably, these maneuvers have enabled geography to make much "progress," both by justifying its

[*]To Carl Ritter, on the occasion of receiving his second volume on Asia; quoted in Hartshorne, *The Nature of Geography*, 56, emphasis in original.

67

presence within the academy and by delineating its boundaries vis-à-vis other disciplines.

Against the trunk-and-branch structure of lineate development that grounds evolutionary approaches to disciplinary history stands critical genealogy, a form of historiography critical of any claims of genesis. In this approach, disciplines are not positioned naturally like fauna in Linneaus' schematic, but are socially constructed endeavors formed by contextually contingent intersections of power and knowledge. Yet however fashionable the contextual approach may be in comparison to its naturalized alternative, it nonetheless remains the responsibility of those who would reject foundationalist histories to uncover the complex fields within which specific disciplines are produced.[2]

In this chapter, I am concerned with one such historically significant matrix of power/knowledge; that of objectivity. To focus on objectivity's role in constructing geography's identity is obviously to reject taken-for-granted histories that view the discipline as determined by a parade of pioneering figures struggling with disciplinary boundaries, the field's proper objects and methods, and its stances regarding numerous dualistic formulations (e.g., science vs. art). This is not to say, however, that these are not the stuff of geography's history. Instead, my aim is to show that resolution of these issues sometimes depended upon usually unexamined stances toward objectivity. More a silent partner in disciplinary pirouettes than the focus of explicit consideration, objectivity, like any ideology, was dependent upon its widespread acceptance as necessity by those who both made and charted geography's History.

More recently, the force of objectivity has changed considerably with the rise of hermeneutics and the collapse of consensual disciplinary politics during the 1960s and 1970s.[3] Commentators from diverse theoretical persuasions have become highly suspicious of objectivity, especially when defined as the careful practice of neutrality. Those who have acknowledged the impossibility of rigid adherence to the canons of objective social investigation have been persuaded to make known their situated affiliations by specifying—to the extent they are able—the effects these have on research processes and outcomes. One could even go so far as to argue that engagements with postmodernity, at least inasmuch as this admittedly polymorphous term is characterized by a mistrust of the universal subject, are little more than the aftermath of objectivity's collapse.

Still, objectivity is an elusive attribute.[4] In both historical and contemporary terms it does not sit as a fixed and unitary opposition to subjectivity, that is, it is not confined simply to an absence of bias toward contending parties. Objectivity is instead buttressed by the larger discourses of science, through which it continues to hold sway, resisting elimination in the face of what for some are the perceived consequences of its abandonment: irrationality, nihilism, relativism, and anarchy.

That objectivity's power in discipline making is partly the result of its polyvalent character is one of the central themes of this chapter. But my aim more directly is to uncover which aspects of objectivity have proven most important in the construction of geography. Before beginning, however, I want to delineate three limitations of my account. First, objectivity and geographic knowledge are best conceived as mutually determined: Not only has geography been disciplined by objectivity, so too has objectivity been constructed by the acquisition of "geographic" information.[5] The latter relation, however, is not examined here. Second, I must caution against the temptation to search for parallels with other disciplines. After all, it is not simply notions like objectivity that construct disciplines; they are equally vulnerable to other unevenly developed matrices of power, such as myriad institutional and individual forces both inside and outside the academy.

A third limitation of the discussion is imposed by my approach, a "close reading" of objectivity's invocation in Richard Hartshorne's *The Nature of Geography* (hereafter *Nature*).[6] His book is a propitious choice for my task, for not only does *Nature* reflect dominant understandings of objectivity in the mid-20th century, it also served to institutionalize them through what has quite probably been the most significant work in American geography.[7]

Throughout its nearly 500 pages, Hartshorne painstakingly examines the European origins of modern Western geography, paying particular attention both to the programmatic statements that have defined its objects, concepts, and methodologies, and to the discipline's position within the human and physical sciences. His account is more than review, however, for *Nature* also offers a thoroughgoing critique that purifies the discipline of much historical residue.[8] Although its importance waned in the 1960s under the onslaught of spatial science and behavioralism, and even more so after the rise of humanism and Marxism in the 1970s, *Nature* built an unparalleled consensus that defined geography as the study of areal differentiation. Required reading for two generations of scholars following its publication in 1939, *Nature* laid the foundation on which many subsequent theoretical developments were constructed.[9] Although Hartshorne's opus was not universally accepted as the canonical text,[10] it seems safe to predict that we are unlikely to witness ever again the degree of theoretical consensus produced by *Nature*. It was, quite simply, a founding text for American geographers who had long depended upon Europeans—especially the Germans and, to a lesser extent, the French—

for their "philosophy."[11] And its publication came at a heady historical juncture: Just as American geography was being wrested from the grasp of the "Old World," so too was the country asserting its primacy on the international stage following World War II.

In what follows I first sketch in broad terms the different coordinates of thought that undergird objectivity. I then turn to two aspects of this assemblage that significantly influence Hartshorne's work: geography's dependence upon visual apprehension in determining its objects of inquiry (and with this, its disciplinary boundaries), and the importance of distanced narration in discussing them. I end this section by discussing two competing ontologies of space: one that underpins Hartshorne's objectivity and one that asserts that subjectivity is the operative principle of everyday experience and that geography should therefore reveal the subjectively determined encounters between person and world. Against this *either* objective *or* subjective position, I conclude the chapter by offering some thoughts on a postdualisitc ontology of space based on the work of Henri Lefebvre.

OBJECTIVITY AS EXCESS

Objectivity, as Samuel Weber notes,[12] resists definition. It suffuses, spilling out beyond its apparent dualistic confines to become more than the "other" to subjectivity, bias, and willfulness. In so doing, it provides numerous opportunities for marshalling its persuasive power. For objectivity invokes, with profound moralizing overtones, a wide field of assumptions that enable context-transcendent truth claims. Among these assumptions are the determinacy of reality, the necessity for investigative rigor, the strict separation of subject and object, the transparency of meaning, and the teleology of scientific and social progress. It is these tenets to which we owe objectivity's excess over and above subjectivity, and that provide objectivity with the power to construct disciplines. My intent in this section is to describe briefly the scaffold that undergirds objectivity, in order to set the context for an analysis of some of its effects on Hartshorne's *edifice*: the discipline of geography.

Any number of metaphors might be usefully deployed to depict objectivity. That of a scaffold, however, seems particularly apt. It critically signals that objectivity is itself perched on a construction, a particular historically constituted approach toward viewing and representing the world. No less a social product than beliefs in divine intervention, the equally naturalized form of storytelling it supplanted, objectivity owes its reputation for insuring clarity and truth to its position atop late 18th- and early 19th-century Enlightenment epistemologies that privileged science over traditional beliefs, determinacy over indeterminacy, rationality over irrationality, and transparency over obscurity. Objectivity was thus not stabilized by a fixed and unitary dual—that is, subjectivity—but was braced by a complex of interconnected supports. As Peter Novick suggests in his widely celebrated account of the reception of objectivity in the discipline of history:

> The assumptions on which it *rests* include a commitment to the reality of the past, and to truth as correspondence to that reality; a sharp separation between knower and known, between fact and value, and, above all, between history and fiction. Historical facts are seen as prior to and independent of interpretation: the value of an interpretation is judged by how well it accounts for the facts; if contradicted by the facts, it must be abandoned. Truth is one, not perspectival. Whatever patterns exist in history are "found," not "made." Though successive generations of historians might, as their perspectives shifted, attribute different significance to events in the past, the meaning of those events was unchanging.[13]

Novick's summary shows objectivity to be a complex construction, one buttressed by the rejection of metaphysics in favor of direct experience with reality; a belief that reality is independent of the observer; the assumption that facts exist pretheoretically and are prior to the researcher's values; a conviction that the truth value of knowledge claims may only be judged vis-à-vis these facts; an acceptance of the division between factual and fictional representation; and, finally, the certainty that scientific progress is guaranteed by the continual reassessment of earlier knowledge claims.

It is in this sense that subjectivity, the putative other of objectivity, was not simply opposed to its dual, but to all that makes objectivity both possible and desirable. The stakes for objectivity are thus not only the distortions that arise when one fails to purify one's work from particularizing influences such as class or gender, but also, the conduct of science itself. For without objectivity, interpretation mediates facts rather than re-presents them, truth claims become suspect, and the telos of progressive knowledge collapses. Herein lies the basis of objectivity's power.

To be suspicious of objectivity, however, is to suggest that it is not a disinterested tool for the legitimation of the scientific enterprise. A critical skepticism is justified on the grounds that, even were its standards faithfully implemented, objectivity would assign to science an apparently eternal set of tasks. For one, it relied on the understanding that, in order

to continue the advancement of knowledge, science must progressively
sharpen its measurement tools so as to edge ever closer to direct apprehension and representation of reality. Accompanying this was the understanding that science must also continually reassess facts in order to insure
that their earlier formulation was not contaminated by the social position
of the observer. Both understandings are capable of legitimating disciplinary growth, as Hartshorne himself well recognized:

> When a single student studies a particular scientific problem, no matter
> how critically he examines his own work, there remains the possibility
> of error, whether through carelessness or through subjective influences
> affecting his observations and reasonings. . . . In order to make possible
> a higher degree of accuracy and certainty, therefore, it is a recognized
> principle of all science that studies should be carried on, organized, and
> presented in such a manner as to provide an accumulation of evidence
> of different students on the same problem.[14]

With such large stakes, it might come as some surprise to note that
we find in objectivity versus subjectivity a fundamental paradox of
dualistic oppositions that seemingly define themselves only through the
other: namely, the impossibility of maintaining an equality of force
between oppositions while also preserving the less powerful other. Why,
we might ask, did subjectivity not collapse in the wake of these stakes? In
other words, what accounts for the enduring creative tension between
objectivity and its other? At first glance, it seems that the power of
objectivity was ensured by the force of scientific rationality, while subjectivity's resistance was aided by the difficulty of conducting social investigation while hoisting oneself out of history, culture, and politics. Yet this
alone cannot account for subjectivity's resistance. For if objectivity could
be specified as merely a set of rules to which one adheres, then subjectivity
might have been readily overrun by its more powerful other. Such an easy
resolution could, however, pose dangers to those who used objectivity to
legitimate their work as scientists. By my estimation, what sustained the
opposition was not only objectivity's conflation with science, which
rendered its practice difficult, but also the assessment that those who
practiced social investigation outside of the academies and professional
societies did so subjectively. In this sense, objectivity as the other to
subjectivity makes the work of scientists not only difficult, but also
important. Objectivity thus displays itself as an instrument of disciplinary
power, with the capacity to separate science and art, knowledge and
politics, and the trained and untrained. In short, the representation of
truth is—as the emergence of professional societies demonstrates—not to

be confined to the ranks of amateurs. Novick thusly describes a widely held view of the historical profession:

> The objective historian's role is that of a neutral, or disinterested, judge; it must never degenerate into that of advocate or, even worse, propagandist. The historian's conclusions are expected to display the standard judicial qualities of balance and evenhandedness. As with the judiciary, these qualities are guarded by the insulation of the historical profession from social pressure or political influence, and by the individual historian avoiding partisanship or bias—not having any investment in arriving at one conclusion or another. Objectivity is held to be at grave risk when history is written for utilitarian purposes. One corollary of all this is that historians, as historians, must purge themselves of external loyalties: the historian's primary allegiance is to "the objective historical truth," and to professional colleagues who share a commitment to cooperative, cumulative efforts to advance toward that goal.[15]

This broad sketch serves to demonstrate that objectivity is far too complex and important to be posed as the mere other to subjectivity. Yet this still leaves open the discipline-specific question posed here, namely, what aspects of objectivity were influential in Hartshorne's own geography making?

OBJECTIVITY IN HARTSHORNE'S *NATURE*

Hartshorne assiduously submits a great number of concepts to detailed scrutiny, but objectivity is, unfortunately, not among them. This is not too surprising, for in Hartshorne's day objectivity's value for directing the progress of knowledge was largely unquestioned. So much so, in fact, that while the concept itself goes unexamined, Hartshorne is not opposed to invoking its presence throughout *Nature*. This is particularly the case when he offers his definition of science: "organized, objective, knowledge."[16] Beyond this rhetorical coupling with science lie two more nuanced invocations of objectivity that dominate discussions in *Nature*. The first of these concerns geography's "reality designation," that is, how its facts will be secured. Hartshorne reviews the discipline's historical dependency upon direct, visual "observation" of reality, and against the reigning belief that geography must limit itself to an ocular-defined "material" reality in order to be objective, he offers the dissenting view that visual perception neither guarantees nor is the precondition for objectivity. Thus in this instance, he deploys objectivity to widen the discipline's scope by arguing that geography should study more than what presents itself as visual evidence.

If objectivity in the first case enlarges the disciplinary project, in the second case it is used to delimit it. Objectivity is here deployed to separate geography from aesthetics in order to legitimate it as a scientific field. For Hartshorne, only "objective" representation qualifies to be called "science." As such, all geographic narration must be cleansed of any language that would reveal the subjectivity of the narrator. Thus objectivity, to Hartshorne, is dependent neither on specific objects of analysis nor on the methodologies brought to "witness" them. It is, instead, insured through the distanced re-presentation of reality. His objectivity thus bespeaks a particular way of representing the world, one whose value-neutral character is assured by uncompromisingly purging geographic description of the personal opinions of the author. In the following subsections I place these two aspects of objectivity within the larger context of geography and discuss their importance to key issues Hartshorne confronts.

Uncoupling Geography from Ocularity

I begin with the not uncommon claim that modernity privileged ocularity over other forms of sensory apprehension.[17] The predominance of vision—that "master sense of the modern era"[18]—has been linked to the rise of printing, the invention of the telescope and microscope, and the development of perspective in Renaissance painting. But perhaps it is the epistemological shifts brought about by the Cartesian distinction between mind and matter that provide ocularity with a ready connection to objectivity. Modernity's ocularity underwrote the canonical preconditions for science in that the objective optical order was the source of all the markers—determinacy, clarity, insight, and transparency—upon which the designation "reality" depended. Accordingly, the eye came to symbolize the emotional detachment necessary for hoisting the disembodied (but mostly male) observer out of the reciprocal subject–object milieu and into a terrain of decidability and independence that privileged a universalist subjectivity in which the world was "there" for all to see.[19] The objectivist gaze presupposed an abstract, isotropic, and rectilinear Cartesian perspectivalism, the functioning of which rested on the assumption of subject–object and mind–body separation. As Martin Jay summarizes it:

> Cartesian perspectivalism was thus in league with a scientific world-
> view that no longer hermeneutically read the world as a divine text

but saw it as situated in a mathematically regular spatiotemporal order filled with natural objects that could only be observed from without by the dispassionate eye of the neutral researcher.[20]

If a great many fields felt the weight of ocularcentrism, there were few domains of knowledge better positioned to implement its strictures than geography.[21] For one thing, incursions into "foreign" territories by European powers depended upon realist cartographic representation. Here, the blank spaces of maps were filled with iconographies instrumental to the state: topographic features, water and mineral resources, and the location of "native" peoples—all of which had been faithfully witnessed and recorded following the careful inductive procedures of Alexander von Humboldt, who set the standard for the collection and depiction of geographic data in the 19th century. The certainty of the trustworthy spectator was thus doubly important for geography—through the assuredness offered by a faith in mimetic representation in cartography on the one hand, and an adherence to Baconian induction that guided the collection and classification of phenomena on the other hand. Under such pressures, ocularcentrism assumed a preeminent position within geographic methodology well into the 20th century.

Importantly, the basis for Hartshorne's rejection of ocularcentrism as a precondition for objectivity was not a distrust of the epistemological canons upon which it rested. Rather, his critique develops along instrumental lines. Quite simply, an observation-dependent definition of objectivity threatened to limit the scope and potential of the discipline. In Hartshorne's eyes, spatial difference was more than merely the variation of visually manifest material phenomena that could be accurately described, measured, and mapped. Some aspects of variability simply could not be confined to the visual (e.g., cultural beliefs).[22] Put another way, in terms starkly indicating the hegemonic potential of geography as the study of areal differentiation, the discipline's objects of inquiry included anything that varied from one place to another. These need not be confined to "material" phenomena, since "immaterial" phenomena not only varied, but also contributed to the varying character of places.

Hartshorne thus identifies an alignment between the material and the immaterial on the one hand, and the visual and the nonvisual on the other. He traces the source of these pairings, at least as they relate to geography, to 19th-century German geography, and in particular to its two most prominent figures, von Humboldt and Carl Ritter. To both, geography must be an empirical science rooted in observation:

> In contrast with the blind dependence upon authority, characteristic
> of earlier periods, and the *a priori* construction of systems of supposed
> facts about the earth that characterized much of the work of the
> eighteenth century, many students toward the end of the this period
> emphasized the importance of determining first the actual facts.[23]

For von Humboldt, this required attention to the "scene itself," a strict
empiricism that avoided natural philosophy: "We need only fear and avoid
with difficulty: false facts."[24] Ritter, though devotedly religious and prone
to writing of "divine secrets," had proclaimed "we must ask the earth itself
for its laws."[25] In spite of their philosophical differences, both were
concerned that geography offer "objective descriptions of observations
of nature."[26]

By the latter half of the 19th century, the next generation of scientists
had purged geography of the organicism and theology that lingered in
the works of von Humboldt and Ritter, respectively:

> The new viewpoint in science . . . [was marked] by an increasing emphasis
> on the development of "scientific laws," and by a conscious isolation of
> science—and specifically of geography—from any particular *Weltan-
> schauung*.[27]

In an effort to make their endeavors as scientific as possible, many scholars
of this period argued that humans should be excluded as disciplinary
objects in geography. For example, Georg Gerland charged geography
with the study of the forces and changes in earth materials. His science
of geophysics had no room for humans, though, as Hartshorne notes, his
inclusion of animals and plants in geography created a potentially misleading hierarchy of causality.[28] Siegfried Passarge went even further,
excluding the study of animals from the field.[29]

Other geographers of the second half of the 19th century were
content to include humans, but only inasmuch as their activities could be
visually apprehended. Hartshorne presents an array of commentators
who tethered the objectively defined necessity for *direct apprehension* of
reality to material phenomena that could be *seen*. Leo Waibel and
Albrecht Penck, for example, both argued that geography should be
confined to that which exists within our "field of vision."[30] For Stanislaw
Pawlowsky, the discipline studies "all those objects and phenomena that
fill a certain space."[31] Hartshorne credits Finnish geographer Johannes
Granö for his specific attention to other sensory data (e.g., smells and
sounds), but even for Granö the senses provided the criteria for dividing
disciplines: Material objects alone have spatial extent and are therefore
significant to geography.[32] As Hartshorne tells it:

Although [Granö] recognizes that the material and immaterial phenomena of an area form a unity (*Einheit*) he insists that geography must consider directly only the material facts and leave the immaterial to sociology. By limiting ourselves in this way "we can comprehend and describe our objects naturally in the way that a normal (*gesund*) person sees them."[33]

By Hartshorne's reckoning, European dependence upon ocularity was transported to American geography via the landscape school of Carl Sauer. In a 1925 essay entitled, "The Morphology of Landscape," Sauer proposed that the cultural landscape be geography's "naively given section of reality."[34] In adopting this view of the division of the sciences, Sauer sought to assert geography as the discipline with territorial rights to the study of material landscapes. As Hartshorne characterizes it, Sauer's landscape school conflates observation with science:

The remaining efforts to reform geography that need to be considered appear to be much more definitely motivated by a desire to make it what apparently it has not been, a proper science. In the first place, since science must deal with observable phenomena, geography, in order to be a science, must deal with observable phenomena, and these it finds in the visible "landscape"—or, if it is claimed that some things are observable but not visible, geography must limit itself to material objects. These, in contrast with immaterial phenomena, we may observe and measure with some degree of accuracy and certainty.[35]

But for Hartshorne, "observable features" are no criteria for disciplinary boundaries. He questions the historical context that would give rise to such an equation:

The reader can hardly fail to have observed that underlying all the arguments of those who wish to consider only material objects—objects directly observable by the senses—is the spirit of physical science. Material things—and particularly visible objects—are the sort of phenomena that students trained in physical sciences know how to deal with. Geographers with that background—which includes most geographers today—would naturally prefer to have to study only such definitely tangible *things*.[36]

Sauer, who was a close associate of Berkeley anthropologists Alfred L. Kroeber and Robert H. Lowie, was of course aware that culture could be described in material as well as immaterial terms. Yet by ceding culture *qua* immaterial to anthropology, culture's material manifestation as "landscape" offered a young geography its own object of analysis. But, for

Hartshorne, to rely on materiality was to impose an arbitrary lens on the constitution of areas:

> If geography could confine itself to non-human aspects of the earth, it would perhaps be free of any difficulty of studying immaterial phenomena. Once geographers are agreed—as in general they always have been—that they will study human or cultural geography, they are committed to the study of things cultural as well as natural. Culture is basically immaterial and manifests itself both in immaterial and in material results, both of which are subject to scientific observation. If culture can be geographically significant in its material manifestations, it would be most extraordinary that it should not be geographically significant in its more fundamental, immaterial, aspects.[37]

For geography to cast such a wide net and still remain objective, it was necessary for Hartshorne to disentangle ocularity per se from objectivity. He does so by relying on objectivity's multiple meaning, employing one pillar of objectivity—that of distanced narration—against another, the certainty of visual observation:

> Even the sober scientist may on occasion see things that are not objective—as in the case of a mirage. In any case, even if we may assume that most of the things we see are objective, we do not see them objectively; indeed one of the most fundamental axioms of any science is that "things are not what they seem."[38]

The American geographer Vernor Finch had paired both these forms, arguing that, "How an area *is*, involves subjective ideas. You *see* only things which are *objective*."[39] For Hartshorne, by contrast, materiality was no guarantor of objectivity:

> Actually just the reverse is the case. Any given section of the shell of the earth's surface, containing material and immaterial facts, is a piece of objective reality. The immaterial phenomena are no less objective than the material objects. It is simply a problem of method to find the objective means for observing them.[40]

Hartshorne thus makes clear that the division between the material and the immaterial is an ontological distinction, and not one that disavows the epistemology upon which objectivity rested:

> The essential conclusion is that under the broad view of science as the pursuit of knowledge of reality by objective means, science, in general,

is not required to limit itself to any particular category of phenomena. The business of the scientist is to pursue knowledge wherever objective means of study permit, regardless of whether they be direct or indirect; if immaterial phenomena can be determined by indirect, but objective, means of measurement, they are phenomena for some scientists to study.[41]

These comments, while showing that objectivity possessed for Hartshorne the power of negation, still leaves open the question of its definition, and with this, its positive construction. It is to this issue that I now turn.

Objectivity as Scientific Presentation

As mentioned above, Hartshorne repeatedly pairs the appellation "science" with "objectivity." Though the latter is not defined in *Nature*, the strategic combination provides clues to Hartshorne's understanding of it. By way of entry, we might first ask what is at stake in defining geography as a scientific field.

The question of geography's scientific status has a long history, but within the German tradition that most concerns Hartshorne, the issue is explicitly addressed by Kant (1724–1804), who placed the field within the descriptive branches of knowledge.[42] Various successors to that tradition, most significantly von Humboldt (1769–1859) and Friedrich Ratzel (1844–1904), argued against the reigning body of largely descriptive empirical work undertaken by geographers in favor of a solid explanatory, that is, causal, basis for the field. These efforts notwithstanding, the tensions between the scientific claims and the actual work of geographers were by no means resolved by the late 19th and early 20th centuries.[43] As the English geographer Halford Mackinder, a leading environmental determinist and political geographer, wrote in 1887:

> At the moment we are suffering under the effects of an irrational political geography, one, that is, whose main function is not to trace causal relations, and which must therefore remain a body of isolated data to be committed to memory. Such a geography can never be a discipline, can never, therefore, be honoured by the teacher.[44]

Mackinder's fears emigrated to America when, at the turn of the century, geographers were faced with the problem of disciplinary legitimation within the growing network of academic institutions. As a fairly young discipline that emerged from under the shadows of geology as late as 1904,[45] geography at first did not enjoy a secure position within the academy. Numerous accounts of the prospects for the field during this period bear witness to an inferiority complex relative to geology and history, with which geography shared significant institutional and intellectual relations, as well as to the more developed social disciplines like sociology, political science, and economics.[46] In defending their position within the academy, most writers argued that geography had either a distinctive object of inquiry or a unique methodology. In either case, the question "Is geography a science?" assumed major proportions, not the least because many geologists viewed with skepticism those who, though trained in the physical sciences, later turned their attention to questions of culture.

While Hartshorne is sympathetic to the idea that causality is the highest stage of science, he refuses to make it a precondition for scientific practice. Indeed, he is quick to remark that there is an objective danger in defining science in terms of causal relations:

> As Schülter, Michotte, and Sauer have all stated, a definition of a field of science in terms of causal relationships *instructs* its student to seek and find such relationships, robs him of his impartiality, and easily leads to dogma.[47]

Having severed the connection between science and causality, it is left to objectivity to bear the weight of the former's definition. Hartshorne first links geography and science (*qua* objectivity) by arguing on behalf of independent scholarship; that is, the progress of scientific knowledge is altogether linked to its autonomous conduct. For him, it is the State that has jeopardized the discipline's scientific status and progress:

> The great majority of the writers of geographical works of the seventeenth and eighteenth centuries, however, did not attempt to translate the purpose of geography in terms of scientific interest. Rather, they were concerned with its practical utility. Over and over again they emphasized the value of the study of geography as a means for other purposes—for an understanding of history and as a practical aid to government. . . . It could make little headway, however, so long as geography was considered to be merely the handmaid of history and government.[48]

Hartshorne, writing mostly in Vienna at the end of the 1930s, could hardly have been ignorant of the contemporary resonance of this comment. Yet he resolutely avoids any comparison, turning his attention to a different threat to the discipline's scientific status: the work of preprofessionals. As

Novick has shown,[49] objectivity has proven to be a powerful weapon of authority, one that can be marshalled against those who write as "amateurs" outside of the legitimacy of the academy. Like the historians in Novick's account, Hartshorne questions the "dependability" of such writers:

> Certainly it is true that, just as history is studied and written by many who are not by training historians, there are many non-geographers willing and able to supply knowledge of areas. . . . But [such] study likewise illustrates the vast amount of work necessary simply to test the dependability of material gathered by untrained travelers, naturalists, agricultural students, literary writers or statesmen, and, particularly to organize it effectively into regional study.[50]

As indicated earlier, the credibility of the "untrained" was suspect because of the perceived difficulty such "prescientific" investigators had in purging subjectivity from their accounts. They simply could not be trusted to practice their craft under the academy's standards of objectivity and according to the methodologies developed to insure successful adherence to them. In making this point, Hartshorne again links geography with history, thus legitimating the former by the proven institutional success of the latter:[51]

> However effective may be the descriptions of artistic writers in presenting the character of an area, these descriptions cannot be expected to satisfy scientific standards of knowledge. One does not expect the writings of a Walter Scott or a Francis Parkman to supplant methodological historical narratives. Similarly, only trained geographers can provide objective, quantitatively measured, scientifically interpretative, and dependable presentation of an area. If, at the same time, this requires a high degree of skill in the use of maps, diagrams, and the written word, geographical literature is not lacking in skillful presentations. That is a question of style, and style in the presentation of knowledge does not remove it from the sphere of science. But if geography is to remain always objective . . . the describer is not to express his feelings, but to impart how he has comprehended the things objectively.[52]

In this view, the academy takes on the image of a mystic club whose secret rules of conduct are made secure by the time and effort one spends in seeking entry:

> We are concerned here, not with all knowledge, but with that sort of knowledge—by whatever name one chooses to call it—that is distinguished from either common sense knowledge or from artistic percep-

tion "by the rigor with which it subordinates all other considerations to the pursuit of the ideals of certainty, exactness, universality, and system."[53]

What lurks in opposition to objectivity here is not only the specter of preprofessional accounts, but also that of aesthetic representation, of contaminating the sterile accounts of the scientist with the emotive expressions reserved for the artist. In this view, the boundary between science and art is homologous to that of objectivity and subjectivity. Since objectivity, for its part, defined science, it clearly had the power to enforce the former division; moreover, for Hartshorne this is a boundary for which there is no legitimate trespass:

> Geography attempts to acquire knowledge of the world in which we live, both facts and relationships, which shall be as objective and accurate as possible. . . . If one compares these ideals, as the fundamental requirements for that form of knowledge, which hereafter for convenience we will call "science," with the ideals of artistic perception (in whatever form one finds them stated by students of art), it is clear that there can be no logical combination of the two and transition from one to the other.[54]

The incommensurability of the oppositions is forcefully demonstrated in the following passage, in which Hartshorne attempts to align geography with the first in the pairs of oppositions, science/art, distance/participation, and rationality/emotion:

> The subjective impression which the artistic worker (including both painters and literary writers) receives from a landscape or region, and which he desires to convey to others, is something very different from the objective description which the geographer must attempt to provide. So far as pure description is concerned, the method of the geographer is photographic in character, with the distinctive personal reactions of the observer reduced to a minimum.[55]

Thus objective geography, like the camera, "does not lie." Of course, the metaphor unwittingly defuses his ocularity argument, but concerning the character of objectivity he is nonetheless clear: Scientific representation is mere mimesis, that is, presentation without representation. While the artist "desires to convey," scientific description—to which all professional geographers must aspire—has to be purged of any language that bespeaks aesthetic or personal intentions. Thus described, *objectivity betrays itself to be nothing more than the adherence to modes of representation that successfully implement the contingently agreed upon standards of conventional scientific writing.* In other words, for Hartshorne, objectivity is a "performance" that properly enacted, can be called "science."

A Recap and an Ontological Excursion

I began my account of objectivity by invoking the analogy of the scaffold, the matrix of scientific discourses on which objectivity is perched. By my estimation, objectivity's discursive construction both provided the basis for Hartshorne's unquestioning acceptance of its value, and endowed the concept with a measure of power that, as he deployed it, had the capacity for defining geography's objects and its methodologies for representing them. In his case, objectivity as distanced narration enabled him to not only broaden the scope of geography by arguing for the possibility of objective representation of the immaterial world, it also supplied the basis for demarcating the field against its artistic and pre-professional competitors. His deployments thus demonstrated a twofold power: one that disciplined geography internally, in terms of its objects and forms of representation, and one that authorized it externally, by defining its border vis-à-vis those who geo-graph (i.e., write the world) outside of the confines of the discipline's established institutional arrangements (departments within the academy and professional organizations outside of it).

Given that any epistemology is inevitably linked to an ontology, it seems that we might usefully attempt a critique of Hartshorne's objectivity by examining his spatial ontology. As the above review of *Nature* has indicated, space has historically been conceptualized materially. As a concrete materiality, space included both the physical environment (i.e., "nature"), as well as human transformations of it that produce cultural landscapes, regions, places, built environments, etc. The description and explanation of variation—whether physical or human—across these settings has traditionally served as geography's *raison d'être* and marked its distinctiveness within the larger body of the sciences.

As the study of areal differentiation, geography assumed an ontological separation of space per se from the processes that give rise to variations across it. The consequences of such thinking have been twofold: first, the relegation of geography to the study of the *outcomes* of processes rather than the study of the processes themselves[56]; and second, a consequent failure to theorize spatiality as part of these processes.[57] In this view, Hartshorne's contribution can be seen as an attempt to widen the scope of what is considered to be an outcome of social processes (i.e., the "immaterial"), but his ontology nevertheless remains loyal to the divisions indicated earlier.

In opposition to the objectivist ontology sketched out above, during the 1960s and 1970s geography witnessed a profound critique that emphasized the subjectivity inherent in all of everyday life. Under the labels "humanistic," "phenomenological," "existential," and so on, geographers urged their colleagues to reject sterile, objectivist conceptions of space in favor of explorations of subjectively defined and experienced places.[58] In this sense, subjectivity as epistemology presupposed a different spatial ontology, one that saw the world not as a container of objects that varied across space, but as sites invested with meaning, emotive content, and human intentionality. In their attempts to uncover the richly varied meanings of place, these scholars rejected explanation in favor of understanding and stressed the importance of experiential and participatory methods over quantitative ones.

However successful this perspective has been in its critique of the objectivist ontology, it nonetheless retained as its basis the oppositional pairing of objectivity versus subjectivity. As a result, for many of this persuasion, both perspectives remained relevant. As Tuan writes, "Place is not only a fact to be explained in the broader frame of space, but it is also a reality to be clarified and understood from the perspectives of people who have given it meaning.[59] If, as Entrikin notes in affirming this position,[60] geography has both objective and subjective dimensions, then we are, as a consequence, left with a choice between one or another of two epistemological/ontological alternatives: Either we accept the canons of objectivity and its mechanized ontology, or we reject this approach in favor of one that describes the subjective worlds of everyday lived experience. But what, we might ask, emerges if we refuse to fall prey to these dualistic presuppositions? Or in other words, is it possible to posit an ontology of space whose epistemology is outside of objectivity *versus* subjectivity and that therefore avoids their ultimate destinations—omniscience and relativism, respectively? In the concluding section I hope to signpost a path toward just such a perspective.

CONCLUSION: THE SPACES BEYOND OBJECTIVITY AND SUBJECTIVITY

Let me begin by raising the two critiques of objectivity that have been widely disseminated over the past 30 years.[61] In the most general terms, the critiques take two forms: one that questions the presumed independence of subjects and objects necessary to secure pretheoretical facts (i.e., the double hermeneutic critique), and one that questions the possibility of true and unmediated descriptions of social reality (i.e., the "crisis of representation" critique). Rather than review the implications of these debates for geography, I chose instead to reverse the equation by focusing attention on a dialectical theory of space and evaluating objectivity's prospects in light of it. In this sense, what follows is an attempt to further dislodge objectivity from its position atop "science" by urging a reconsideration of space—certainly one of the most trenchantly objective objects of inquiry claimed by any discipline. My account reviews the concept of "social space" developed in the work of the French Marxist philosopher, Henri Lefebvre, and engages his thinking with the two critiques of objectivity.

For Lefebvre and his contemporary interpreters,[62] Space is both produced by and reproductive of social relations. This characterization suggests, at first glance, a straightforward dialectical relation between social structures, on the one hand, and spatial structures, on the other. A stripped down version of the "sociospatial dialectic" would thus argue that geographies are produced by social relations (e.g., of production, gender, race, etc.), while at the same time space mediates, reproduces, and transforms these relations by providing the possibilities for and constraints upon the social practices that reproduce society.[63] Space, as a result, is not a mere reflection of social relations, but an inseparable part of social reproduction. As Lefebvre argued, this requires that we shift our objects of analysis from *"things in space* to the actual *production of space.*"[64]

Lefebvre's version of geography, however, is more than the recognition of a *mutual determination* between the social and the spatial, for such a conceptualization might only reinscribe the separation between both moments. He goes further by developing "social space," a concept by which he sublates the social and the spatial such that neither can be conceptualized as existing—materially or immaterially—independent of the other. On the one hand, social space both embeds and signifies social relations; on the other hand, it is only through space that social relations are experienced and exert power. The social and the spatial are thus brought together as one moment in a dialectical relation of simultaneity: Space *is* the social order, produced by social processes that are themselves always spatial. As a consequence, space is never neutral, but always "political and ideological. It is a product literally filled with ideologies."[65] The social relations of production, gender, race, and sexuality are inscribed in, given meaning through, and activated, reproduced, and transformed by the social spaces in which they are embedded. As Lefebvre repeatedly emphasized, the social relations of space are never monolithic, nor are they "mirrored" in space such that they can be "read off" as essentialist significations of themselves. Social spaces are both complex and contradictory; they not only reveal but also veil the social powers that give rise to and work through them. Thus, like Barthes "text," social space is a plurality which lacks determinate meanings and fixed boundaries.[66] And like the historian's archive, which does not simply "exist" and therefore "express" history,[67] space is the product of social powers that determine what shall be revealed, in this case, as geography. *Space, then, is not the thing itself–a fixed and transparent materiality that re-presents social relations–but rather contingently defined representations of those relations, ones that not only reveal social powers, but through contradiction, juxtaposition, and withdrawal, also conceal them.*

Having summarized Lefebvre's argument, I can now sketch some of its implications. Pertinent to the first critique of objectivity raised at the beginning of this section, Lefebvre's ontology makes it possible to under-mine the separation of subjects and objects that has long sustained objectivity, for both must be taken as irreducibly social *and* spatial. Just as social relations are always present in space as an "object," so too are spatial relations always implicated in the social construction and position of the "subject."[68] These relations of subject and object cannot be detached from one another in the process of social investigation. Rather, both are bound together by and transformed through the contingent subject/object contexts within which understanding takes place. The familiar double hermeneutic is thus expanded to include not only a critique of subject/object separation that has its roots in social reciproc-ity; it is, through social space, also a spatial hermeneutic. Collapsed as a result are those models of knowledge–like Hartshorne's–that rely on divisions between subject and object, knowledge and opinion, and truth and error. These chasms mark not the secure route to ever better geographies, but rather their own social necessity–that is, the scientific origins of the desire to claim, know, and stabilize space through the objectivist epistemology.

If we assume that contingency defines not only sociospatial subjects and objects, but also their interaction in specific research contexts, what then do we make of the process of interpretation? By my estimation, this uneliminable contingency does not require that we succumb to relativism, reject the possibility of knowledge, and accept anarchy and nihilism and their paradox of "rules without rules." I would suggest instead the adoption of an epistemology of engagement that is ever vigilant in regard to the contingencies of interpretation. This shifts the focus from an oppositional model whose two choices are *either* the stabilization of space and our accounts of it via "objective" strategies *or* the denial of any of claims of knowing beyond whatever grounding is possible in "subjectiv-ity," to one that is attentive to the social spaces of subjects, objects, and the context of interpretation. Such an approach has affinities with Derrida's radical hermeneutics. As Bauman summarizes his argument,

> The central message of Derrida is that interpretation is but an extension of the text, that it "grows into" the text from which it wants to set itself apart, and thus the text expands while being interpreted which precludes the possibility of the text ever being exhausted in interpretation. Derrida's philosophy of deconstruction asserts the inescapability of multiple meaning and the endlessness of the interpretive process—not because of the impotence of the cognizing mind, but as the result of the awesome potency of cognitive capacity to regenerate the very text it aims to tame, arrest and ossify; to expand *the world* it strives to confine and enclose.[69]

Thus Derrida's charge suggests not the futility of interpretation, but the necessity of making all investigation part of an endless dialogue, an interplay whose purpose is found in its own undecidability and inconclusiveness.

Lefebvre's ontology carries forward to the second critique of objectivity, that is, to the domain of representation. If space distills and embeds social powers while also signifying and veiling them, then geography requires a language for this process. For Lefebvre, "representation" served this purpose:

> To make things even more complicated, social space also contains specific representations of this double or triple interaction between the social relations of production and reproduction. Symbolic representation serves to maintain these social relations in a state of coexistence and cohesion. It displays them while displacing them—and thus concealing them in symbolic fashion—with the help of, and onto the backdrop of, nature.[70]

I take this to imply that *space is not a presentation that can be re-presented, but is always already a representation to be represented.* Space thus effects a "double movement." The first is a difference that follows from its status as representation, that is, as an object of inquiry that is always displaced from and displacing its "origins" and hence forever unrecoverable as one-in-the-same of itself. The second movement is a difference that ensues from the process of representation itself, that is, from the problems inherent in any writing about, or mapping of, space.[71] To place this double movement in concrete terms one need only consider the representation of social "reality" in cartography. Clearly maps are vehicles of communication, that is, "texts," which do not simply reproduce space but are instead socially constructed representations of it. In the same way, space is a representation of social relations, and maps (and any other geographic description) a double movement from which verisimilitude can never be recovered. Such then are the differences that space both makes and is; they cannot be overcome by faithful subscription to forms of representation that claim either to be more objective by virtue of an absent narrator, or more truthful by the revelation of the narrator's subjective presence.

By my estimation, the tasks that ensue from the above discussion are twofold: first, to augment and extend the double hermeneutic and contemporary theories of representation via the concept of social space, and second, to further elaborate Lefebvre's ontology in order to overcome still dominant conceptions of objectivist space. What is clear about the latter task in particular is that the study of space can no more be confined to traditional disciplinary boundaries than the study of social relations.[72] The end of objectivist spatiality does not, however, signal the demise of geography, but rather a wider and more complex realization of it. Unlike its predecessor, such a geography cannot be legitimated through originary claims, nor disciplined through the epistemologies that framed earlier definitions of the field. Instead, the ontology of social space requires that we reject self-serving constructions of disciplinary boundaries in favor of a new, interdisciplinary science of space. That this space could never be studied as mere "object"—let alone objectively—surely helps to write the obituary of that ideology.

ACKNOWLEDGMENTS

I would like to thank Anne Buttimer, Stuart Daultry, Mary Gilmartin, Wolfgang Natter, and Ted Schatzki for discussions and comments.

NOTES

1. Harlan H. Barrows, "Geography as Human Ecology," *Annals, Association of American Geographers 13* (1923): 1–14; p. 1.
2. A recent example of this approach, and one that deserves wide readership, is David Livingstone's *The Geographical Tradition* (Oxford: Basil Blackwell, 1994).
3. For an account of the political escarpments of this period in geography, see Richard Peet, "The Development of Radical Geography in the United States," in *Radical Geography*, Richard Peet, ed. (Chicago: Maaroufa Press, 1977), 6–30.

4. Dorothy Ross, *The Origins of American Social Science* (Cambridge: Cambridge University Press, 1990), 117.

5. Derek Gregory's *Geographical Imaginations* (Oxford: Basil Blackwell, 1994), 16–33, examines the claim that the development of logical empiricism depended upon the rise of exploration, mapping, and classification in the 18th and 19th centuries.

6. Richard Hartshorne, *The Nature of Geography: A Critical Survey of Current Thought in Light of the Past* (Lancaster, PA: Association of American Geographers, 1939).

7. Witness the contemporary interest evidenced in James N. Entrikin and Stanley D. Brunn, eds., *Reflections on Richard Hartshorne's The Nature of Geography* (Washington, DC: Association of American Geographers, 1989).

8. I have in mind his discussions of organicism and environmental determinism.

9. I am referring to the Hartshorne–Schaefer "debates" of the 1950s, which revolved around such oppositions as idiographic–nomothetic, qualitative–quantitative, pattern–process, and inductive–deductive; see Fred Schaefer, "Exceptionalism in Geography: A Methodological Examination," *Annals, Association of American Geographers 43* (1953): 226–249; and Richard Hartshorne, "Exceptionalism in Geography Re-Examined," *Annals, Association of American Geographers 45* (1955): 205–244. The exchange influenced theory in geography well through the 1970s and, interestingly, continues to haunt contemporary arguments; see, for example, Neil Smith, "Dangers of the Empirical Turn: Some Comments on the CURS Initiative," *Antipode* 19 (1987): 59–68.

10. The Berkeley School of Carl Sauer—itself a focus of Hartshorne's critique in *Nature*—was the primary competitor in the United States. See Carl O. Sauer, *Land and Life* (Berkeley: University of California Press, 1963), especially "The Morphology of Landscape," 315–350. (Original work published 1925)

11. I am grateful to Anne Buttimer for pointing out this aspect of its American reception.

12. See Weber (Chapter 3, this volume).

13. Peter Novick, *That Noble Dream: The "Objectivity" Question and the American Historical Profession* (Cambridge: Cambridge University Press, 1988), 1–2, emphasis added.

14. Hartshorne, *Nature*, 376–377.

15. Novick, *That Noble Dream*, 2.

16. Hartshorne, *Nature*, 134.

17. See, for example, Lucien Febvre, *The Problem of Unbelief in the Sixteenth Century*, Beatrice Gottlieb, trans. (Cambridge, MA: Harvard University Press, 1982); Richard Rorty, *Philosophy and the Mirror of Nature* (Princeton: Princeton University Press, 1979); and Martin Jay, *Force Fields* (London: Routledge, 1993).

18. Jay, "Scopic Regimes of Modernity," in *Force Fields*, 114–133; p. 114.

19. That this was a decidedly male gaze has attracted comment from scholars in many fields. For a discussion in geography, see Gillian Rose, *Feminism and Geography* (London: Polity Press, 1993), especially Chapter 5, "Looking at Landscape: The Uneasy Pleasures of Power," 86–112.

20. Jay, "Scopic Regimes," 118. What is so remarkable about this comment is the fact that though directed at painting, it aptly describes modern geography.

21. The relationship between ocularcentricism and geography is explored at various junctures in Gregory, *Geographical Imaginations*.

22. That Hartshorne, who wrote *Nature* principally in Vienna during the years 1938–1939, could include such "immaterial" phenomena in geography while holding firm to a concept of objectivity, distinguishes him from some German geographers of the same period. Nazi sympathizers not only castigated "materialism," they also rejected as misguided both objectivity and a refusal to serve the state. For a discussion, see T. H. Elkins, "Human and Regional Geography in the German-Speaking Lands in the First Forty Years of the Twentieth Century," in Entrikin and Brunn, eds. *Reflections on Richard Hartshorne's The Nature of Geography*, 17–34.

23. Hartshorne, *Nature*, 48.

24. Alexander von Humboldt, *Vorlesungen über physikalische Geographie nebst Prolegomenen über Stellung der Gestirne, Berlin im Winter, 1827–1828*, Miron Goldstein, ed. (Berlin, 1934); quoted in Hartshorne, *Nature*, 67.

25. Carl Ritter, *Die Erdkunde*, Vol. I (Berlin, 1822–1859); quoted in Hartshorne, *Nature*, 55.

26. Hartshorne, *Nature*, 66.

27. Ibid., 87.

28. Ibid., 106–115.

29. Ibid., 152–153.

30. Ibid., 152.

31. Stanislaw Pawlowsky, "Inwieweit kann in der Anthropogeographie von einer Landschaft die Rede sein," *Comptes rendus d. Congr. Intern. d. Géogr., Amsterdam, 1938*, Tome 2, Sec. 3a; 202–208; quoted in Hartshorne, *Nature*, 153.

32. Hartshorne, *Nature*, 199.

33. Ibid., 195.

34. Sauer, "The Morphology of Landscape," in *Land and Life*, 316.

35. Hartshorne, *Nature*, 28.

36. Ibid., 228, emphasis in original.

37. Ibid., 201.

38. Ibid., 196.

39. Vernor C. Finch, "Written Structures for Presenting the Geography of Regions," *Annals, Association of American Geographers* 24 (1934): 93–107; quoted in Hartshorne, *Nature*, 195, emphasis in original.

40. Hartshorne, *Nature*, 195. Although he uses "observing" in this context it is clear from other statements that the term is meant to signal the collection of data rather than a necessary linkage to visual criteria.

41. Ibid., 196.

42. See Anne Buttimer, *Geography and the Human Spirit* (Baltimore: Johns Hopkins University Press, 1993), especially 106–118.

43. Attempts to secure such a foundation for geography—to wrest it from the "dining clubs" that celebrated traveler's accounts—are explored in David Livingstone's *The Geographical Tradition*, 139–215.

44. Halford Mackinder, "On the Scope and Methods of Geography," *Proceedings of the Royal Geographical Society 9* (1887): 141–160; p. 143.

45. This marker, though arguably arbitrary, is the year witnessing the founding of the Association of American Geographers.

46. In addition to the essay of Barrows, "Geography as Human Ecology," see William M. Davis, "An Inductive Study of the Content of Geography," *Bulletin of the American Geographical Society of New York 38* (1906): 67–84, and Nevin M. Fenneman, "The Circumference of Geography," *Annals, Association of American Geographers 9* (1919): 3–11.

47. Hartshorne, *Nature*, 126, emphasis in original.

48. Ibid., 36–37.

49. See Novick, *That Noble Dream*, 47–60.

50. Hartshorne, *Nature*, 132.

51. See the discussion in Novick, *That Noble Dream*, 47–60.

52. Hartshorne, *Nature*, 133.

53. Ibid., 374. He is quoting Morris Cohen, *Reason and Nature: An Essay on the Meaning of the Scientific Method* (New York: 1931).

54. Ibid., 375.

55. Ibid., 133.

56. As John Fraser Hart notes in a passage acknowledging Hartshorne, "Geographers are interested primarily in the results of processes, rather than in the processes themselves." In "The Highest Form of the Geographer's Art," *Annals, Association of American Geographers 72* (1982): 1–29; p. 14.

57. The larger implications of this failure, itself based on the idea that space is little more the "stage" on which social life unfolds, is examined in Ed Soja's *Postmodern Geographies* (London: Verso, 1989), especially pp. 10–75.

58. See, for example, J. Nicholas Entrikin, "Contemporary Humanism in Geography," *Annals, Association of American Geographers 66* (1976): 615–632; and David Ley and Marwyn S. Samuels, eds., *Humanistic Geography: Prospects and Problems* (Chicago: Maaroufa Press, 1978).

59. Yi-Fu Tuan, "Space and Place: Humanistic Perspectives," *Progress in Human Geography 6* (1974): 213–252, quoted in J. Nicholas Entrikin, "Introduction: The Nature of Geography in Perspective," in Entrikin and Brunn, eds., *Reflections on Richard Hartshorne's The Nature of Geography*, 2.

60. The oppositional options are highlighted in Entrikin and Brunn, ibid.

61. See the editors' introduction (Chapter 1, this volume).

62. Henri Lefebvre, *The Production of Space*, David Nicholson-Smith, trans., (Oxford: Basil Blackwell, 1991); also see Soja, *Postmodern Geographies*.

63. See Edward Soja, "The Socio-Spatial Dialectic," *Annals, Association of American Geographers 70* (1980): 207–225.

64. Lefebvre, *Production*, 37, emphasis in original.

65. Lefebvre, quoted in Soja, *Postmodern Geographies*, 80. Thusly characterized, space has parallels to Marx's analysis of the commodity: Both present themselves as "natural" and "uncontested" materialities, while veiling at the same time the social processes and contradictions that are embedded within them.

66. Roland Barthes, *S/Z*, Richard Miller, trans. (Oxford: Basil Blackwell, 1990). Also see Wolfgang Natter and John Paul Jones III, "Signposts Toward a Poststructuralist Geography," in *Postmodern Contentions: Epochs, Politics, and Space*, John Paul Jones III, Wolfgang Natter, and Ted Schatzki, eds. (New York: Guilford Press, 1993), 165–203.

67. See Smith (Chapter 4, this volume).

68. In this view, the various standpoint epistemologies concerned with subject positions are extended to include not only social positionality, but spatial positionality as well.

69. Zygmunt Bauman, *Intimations of Postmodernity* (London: Routledge, 1992), 131, emphasis added.

70. Lefebvre, *Production*, 32.

71. For a discussion see Natter and Jones, "Signposts," 191–195.

72. This is a point Lefebvre forcefully makes in *The Production of Space*, 89–90.

6

The American Historian of France and the "Other"

JEREMY D. POPKIN

At times, a historian who reads the accounts by some of our anthropologist colleagues of their experience of intercultural encounter can be overwhelmed by envy; our professional lives seem so drab by comparison.[1] When I first arrived on the foreign shore where I intended to carry out my historical research, the natives handed me forms to fill out, photographed me, assigned me a number, relieved me of a small amount of money, and provided me with written instructions in my own language for the use of their national library. Hardly an experience to match those of ethnographers struggling to set up their tents among the !Kung or the Jivaro—although I suspect that more than one ethnographer has had moments in the field when the prospect of doing research in Paris seemed awfully attractive.

There are a number of reasons why the theme of intercultural encounter does not occupy the same place in historical literature that it does in anthropology, starting with the history profession's perverse pride in being "the most reactionary members of the academy," "the last to know about current fashions" in methodological debate.[2] One is that the subjects of the historian's inquiry, unlike the flesh-and-blood people scrutinized by the ethnographer, are generally dead, so that we can play what Voltaire called our "pack of tricks" on them without having to look them in the eye. Furthermore, to the extent that historians do come into contact with living members of the culture whose past they are studying, their most extensive encounters are often with professionals engaging in activities similar to their own—that is, other scholars. Whereas the encounters described by ethnographers sharpen the field researcher's sense of doing something that makes no sense in the eyes of the "others," the historian's interactions are likely to reinforce the sense of participating in a common endeavor with "native" historians from the country under study.

Paradoxically, the most problematic recent encounters between academic historians in this country and the "others" they study have occurred among specialists in what we u-nself-consciously label "American history." Within this field, there has been in recent years intense debate about the proper approach to the history of minority groups and women, and on those frontiers, the question of the historian's encounter with otherness has frequently been heated.[3] An important characteristic of these debates that differentiates them from the issues facing anthropologists, however, is that members of the groups concerned have striven for and, to some extent, obtained professional positions within the discipline in this country. While there has been much rhetoric about white males imposing their representations of history on African Americans and women, the situation is obviously different from that in anthropology, where the subjects of research have no access to professional academic positions.

Whereas debate has raged about the teaching of the history of women and ethnic minorities within the United States, the fact that a substantial proportion of American academic historians devote their professional lives to the study of foreign cultures has generated relatively little discussion. When one does give it some thought, however, this situation seems to call for some exploration. In a global perspective, it is anomalous. Statistics are hard to come by, but the community of American academic historians is certainly more wide-ranging in its interests than our colleagues in foreign countries. Although no foreign university system of any size limits its historians exclusively to the study of its own national past, the normal pattern is one in which such history predominates. The great size and wealth of the American university system, compared even to those of the other "first world" nations, means that the number of American historians teaching and publishing about the history of some foreign countries exceeds the number of "native" historians working on the subject. Furthermore, there is a definite asymmetry in the flow of historical information: Very little foreign scholarship about

U.S. history gets produced and even less of it ever comes to the attention of historians in this country.[4]

The reasons for this country's relatively important investment in the understanding of the past of other cultures are many. A knowledge of the history of other countries is often justified as useful for pragmatic reasons: The societies that historians study (as opposed to many of those that interest ethnographers) are often those that have important strategic and economic ties with the United States, and an understanding of the way in which their values and institutions have been shaped over time, it is argued, is useful in making intelligent decisions in foreign policy and business. The fact that, in this country, historians are hardly ever consulted about such matters does nothing to diminish the profession's faith in this argument, which is widely respected within the academy but virtually ignored outside of it. The study of foreign cultures' history is also justified as a means of obtaining greater understanding of our own society. From the outset, European history in particular has always been treated partly as "prenatal American history," in Leonard Krieger's phrase, indispensable in understanding the origins of our own institutions. At the same time, however, as Krieger pointed out, foreign history defines American uniqueness by virtue of contrast. Thus, in the 19th century, an emphasis on the absence of democracy and the persistence of religious conflict in many European countries served to point up the special qualities of American civilization.[5]

A less often avowed motive, but one that certainly plays an important role in maintaining interest in "other" history, is that it performs certain psychological functions for the researcher. The specialist in a foreign culture acquires, to a greater or lesser extent, what the English historian of France Richard Cobb calls a "second identity," and the pursuit of such an alternative identity suggests, Cobb writes, that "the need for *la seconde patrie* was already there. . . ."[6] Consciously or unconsciously, one seeks something in this second culture that one misses in one's own. David Pinkney, the American historian of France who has written the most on the questions raised by our study of that country's past, recalls that, when he first visited France in the 1930s, "I was fascinated by the living presence of history that I had, until then, seen only in the reflection of other men's words . . . the long course of European history, the immense complexity of its many interweaving national elements, and the strangeness of much of it to an American raised and educated in the Middle West."[7]

In the half-century since Pinkney first saw Europe, much has happened to make United States history seem a more central part of world history, but when it is seen in the perspective of the history of civilizations such as China's or Europe's, that history can still look both short and monotonous. While ethnography usually involves the study of societies that at least appear simpler and closer to nature than our own, the study of foreign history most often brings Americans into contact with societies usually considered more complex, more "cultured." One American historian of France speaks of his long-standing "abject adoration" for a country whose traditions struck him as more sophisticated than his own.[8] Acquaintance with the history of such a culture confers a certain prestige back home in American academic society. Students and colleagues express envy and admiration when they hear that I am going to do research in France; they are less likely to do so in the case of my fellow department members whose work takes them to West Branch, Iowa, or Little Rock, Arkansas.

The American historians who specialize in French history are not entirely typical of the larger community of American historians of other cultures, but our situation serves to illustrate many of the issues raised by the interaction between American and "native" scholars. Two factors make the situation of the American historian of France atypical: first, the relatively privileged status of French history in the American historical profession, where it occupies a place out of all proportion to France's importance in American life, and second, the lofty status of our professional peers in France itself. Measured by the proportion of doctoral theses and of papers on the subject at the annual conferences of the American Historical Association, French history constitutes the third most important field in the discipline, behind U.S. history and British history and well ahead of the history of other nations whose impact on American life in the past century has unquestionably been larger, such as Germany, Russia, or Japan.[9] The reasons for this heavy investment in French history are difficult to pin down, but they certainly include the belief that French is an easier language to learn than most other foreign tongues, the romantic appeal of French and particularly Parisian life, and the centralization of French library and archive resources.[10]

Americans are also attracted to French history because of French historians' reputation as methodological leaders in the field. This reputation owes little to any interaction between French historians and the famous names of French structuralist and poststructuralist thought: While Michel Foucault's analysis of power relations in everyday life has had a definite impact on the writing of history in France, the other major figures in this group, such as Roland Barthes and Jacques Derrida, have made hardly any impression. French innovativeness is associated with the "*Annales* school" of historiography established in the interwar period by Marc Bloch and Lucien Febvre and continued by Fernand Braudel, Emmanuel Le Roy Ladurie, and a host of others whose influence has radiated far beyond France and indeed far beyond the confines of the historical discipline. Whether the *"Annales* school" still represents a coherent historiographical tendency or not is currently a subject of much debate, here and in France, but its influence, even if it is becoming increasingly diffuse, remains significant.[11] Aside from the formidable reputation of this group of scholars, the study of French history in France rests on a solid institutional foundation of universities and research institutes, scholarly journals, and a publishing industry about which French academics complain endlessly but that nevertheless puts out what seems to an American observer a considerable number of original scholarly books. Whatever the justification for American historians' interest in the French past, it cannot be maintained that we are fulfilling a function that the French are incapable of performing for themselves.

Although American interest in French history goes back to the origins of our republic—among the oldest books printed in the state of Kentucky and preserved in our university library is a translation of a history of the French revolutionary emigrés—American historians were largely content to transmit knowledge of the French past articulated by French and, occasionally, English scholars until the 1920s. In contrast to the situation in ethnography, the American academic community thus started out in the condition of an underdeveloped country, importing sophisticated products from abroad. At the end of the 19th century, American scholars rated French history as a secondary aspect of European history. German methods of historical scholarship dominated the field, and Albert Bushnell Hart of Harvard University could "set down 'the fundamental principles of American history,' maintaining . . . that 'our institutions are Teutonic in origin: they have come to us through English institutions.'"[12]

French history was, of course, a component of the history of European civilization, a historical outline of which became an increasingly common part of American college curricula in the years just before the First World War. As commentators on the American understanding of European history have pointed out, "the Western Civ course was a characteristically American invention," offering a vision of European history at odds with the prevailing representations of that history taught in Europe itself.[13] At a time when history in the European countries, France included, was being taught in an increasingly nationalistic mold, the American approach to the subject emphasized a "Western tradition" supposedly common to the advanced countries of the world.

By making the connection between the destinies of Europe and America unmistakably clear, the First World War provided a great stimulus to the study of European history in American universities, and, by pitting the United States against the Germans, the war opened the way to a more sympathetic understanding of the French past. During the war, the federal government called on historians to develop "War Issues" courses that would help students bound for the army understand the reasons for this country's involvement in the conflict. Institutionalized after the war, these courses in the history of modern European civilization created a steady demand for qualified teachers. The establishment in 1929 of the *Journal of Modern History*, the first academic publication devoted exclusively to European history, marked a major stage in the development of a community of specialized scholars.[14] Within this group of experts on the European past, there emerged for the first time specialists on French history prepared to make the effort to cross the Atlantic and carry out the archival research that had become the *sine qua non* for recognition as a leader within the American historical profession. Scholars such as Crane Brinton, Louis Gottschalk, Leo Gershoy, and R. R. Palmer began to make scholarly contributions that even attracted some recognition in France.[15]

The Second World War provided an even greater stimulus to American interest in European history than the first conflict. A generation of young historians found themselves recruited to the Office of Strategic Services (OSS), the State Department, and other branches of the government and posted overseas to provide expertise about the foreign countries they had undertaken to study; other future French historians made the acquaintance of the country by helping to liberate it. Some, like H. Stuart Hughes, a Harvard graduate student, found themselves in positions where they could try to exert some direct influence on both American and French national policy. Stationed in Algiers to follow the activities of the Free French provisional government there in 1943–1944, Hughes labored to move the U.S. government to a more sympathetic attitude toward De Gaulle while at the same time promoting a "reinvigorated and impregnable Popular Front" uniting left-leaning democratic forces in France itself.[16] For the group as a whole, "the imperatives of war taught . . . the reciprocity of historical and political analysis, the complementarity of the social sciences, the urgency of scholarship."[17]

The wartime experience also produced a distinct change in American scholars' view of their position vis-à-vis the societies they studied and the professional historians from those countries. The change had been most marked in German history, where even before the war, the rise of the Nazi regime and the consequent ideological distortion of the history produced in Germany itself encouraged historians working in the United States, many of them admittedly refugees, to consider themselves "the guardians of German history," able to approach the subject with an objectivity impossible for the native historical community.[18] In France, the war and the Vichy regime had a less drastic impact on the history profession, and there were not as many academic exiles, so that there was less sense that the mainstream of French historical scholarship had been transplanted to the United States. American historians of France nevertheless emerged from the conflict with the sense that they, as outsiders, had something important to teach the French nation about its own history.

Speaking for the contributors to a collective volume on *Modern France: Problems of the Third and Fourth Republics*, which included essays by most of the young scholars who were to shape American study of French history in the 1950s, Edward Meade Earle wrote,

> The authors are critical, as an affectionate friend would be critical. . . . They are sympathetic, since they are Americans who care enough about France to devote the major part of their professional activities to French studies. They are objective, as a physician would be objective, not merely for the sake of objectivity but for the larger purpose as well of understanding the situation and seeking its improvement.

In this vein, one contributor went so far as to declare that "with the exception of a few years under the government of Louis Napoleon, the entire period since Waterloo has seen the progressive failure of the French to adjust their development to the process in the other advanced countries of Europe."[19] This critical spirit was not simply an expression of *hubris* born of the contrast between the French catastrophe of 1940 and American military success: In many cases, the critiques in the Earle volume drew their inspiration from French journalists, social scientists, historians and political figures whose unsparing castigations of their own society from the 1930s onward prefigured the diagnoses offered by the Americans.[20] In fact, the tone of exasperation in many of these essays stemmed from disappointment at the fact that the French, gifted with so many intelligent domestic critics of their own shortcomings, nevertheless seemed to lack the will to implement changes that would be beneficial to their own society and to the western world as a whole.

At its worst, postwar American scholarship thus produced criticism of the French that verged on diatribe. At its best, it produced an explicit recognition of the otherness of French historical traditions. The economic historian David Landes underlined the necessity of understanding the cultural factors that kept French businessmen from behaving like the abstract models of entrepreneurs in American economics textbooks. To the French, he wrote,

> The business is not an end in itself, nor is its purpose to be found in any such independent ideal as production or service. It exists by and

for the family, and the honor, the reputation, the wealth of the one are the honor, wealth, and reputation of the other.[21]

Laurence Wylie's *Village in the Vaucluse,* based on field research carried out in 1950–1951 in a small French town and first published in 1956, achieved a deserved status as a classic both in ethnographic literature and in French history. Like Landes, Wylie succeeded in seeing the French he studied as human beings with values different from but not necessarily worse than ours. Noting the warmth of French family life and the absence of crime and alcoholism, he concluded that even if "there is a bit of madness in the relationship of the [villagers] with the rest of the world . . . when we look at life there and life elsewhere, it is not always clear on which side the madness lies."[22]

Wylie's book, much appreciated by historians and frequently assigned as course reading, nevertheless had only limited use to them as a research model. Wylie's subjects were living, he had interacted with them personally, and he had made little use of the sort of written documentation on which historical research is usually based. For most historians, the encounter with the French past continued to be a more impersonal one, conducted in libraries and archives. The postwar expansion of American universities, the unprecedented American involvement in world affairs that marked the Cold War era, and the creation of fellowship programs that facilitated travel and research abroad provided the opportunity for growth in the numbers of American historians specializing in France, as well as those studying almost every other foreign country. French historians followed the general tendency of all academic specialists: They tended to reproduce themselves. A growing number of American history departments began to offer not only undergraduate courses in French history but graduate seminars as well. In 1955, there were enough French history specialists to create their own professional association, the Society for French Historical Studies, and in 1958 it began to publish its own journal, the first learned periodical devoted exclusively to the subject outside of the Hexagon.[23]

Among the offerings in the first issue of the new journal was an article by David Pinkney, a member of the wartime generation (Ph.D. 1941, OSS 1941–1943, State Department 1946) and a specialist in 19th-century French history, entitled "The Dilemma of the American Historian of Modern France." Far from offering the upbeat forecast about the future of American historical studies of France that might have been expected during this era of expansion, Pinkney warned primarily of pitfalls. "Our contribution is startlingly small," he announced. The American specialist in French history, Pinkney warned, faced a double marginalization. The "natives," France's own historians, were in a position to produce much better history than Americans could ever hope to: The American scholar "simply does not have sufficient time to do the documentary research in French archives that is the first essential to original scholarly production." At the same time, because of this distance from the archives and the consequent relative superficiality of the research that they could perform, American specialists on France could not hope to produce work as interesting as the best scholarship on American history. The mission of the American historian of France was thus to accept a modest role, synthesizing and vulgarizing the results of the genuinely original research done by French scholars for the benefit of an American audience.[24]

This "Pinkney thesis" on the situation of the American historian of France is best remembered among Pinkney's colleagues as an unfortunate venture into prophecy: Writing just before the Sputnik-inspired boom in funding for academic research and the inception of cheap air travel to Europe, Pinkney forecast that Americans' opportunities to work in France were bound to diminish. The reality proved to be just the opposite: The years after 1958 saw a dramatic growth in both the quantity and sophistication of American work in French history, part of a substantial overall increase in American attention to the history of the rest of the world and part, as well, of the tremendous expansion of the American academic enterprise.

Pinkney was challenged periodically to reevaluate his position, thus making him virtually the only American historian of France to reflect on the issue at any length. As the years went by, he could not deny the obvious fact that Americans were producing more, not less, French history, but in articles published in 1975 and 1981, he continued to assert, on the basis of a statistical study of scholarly book reviews, that they still had not overcome French scholars' resistance to accepting the validity of their scholarship, and thus that there was still something problematic about the American scholar's relationship to the French past.[25] By 1991, however, when Pinkney returned to the subject for the fourth time, his article bore the title, "Time to Bury the Pinkney Thesis?" He had continued to follow the statistics on French book reviews, citations of American works, and translations, and he concluded that the old barriers had fallen. "We are clearly experiencing a growing integration of the French and American historical communities," he wrote, and, extrapolating from a few years in which the number of young French historians had declined, he now predicted that "France's history may be written increasingly in the next two decades by foreigners, and Americans, one may reasonably assume, will be prominent among them."[26]

One could certainly question the triumphalist tone of Pinkney's final evaluation (he died in 1993) in one respect: The enlarged volume of American scholarship in France, far from reflecting an ever-growing number of American historians working in the field, is the delayed result of the Ph.D. boom in the 1960s and early 1970s. The production of history Ph.D.'s has fallen sharply since then, and this, together with the gradual shift in interest from European to non-Western fields and, within Europe, to such areas of burning interest as the former Soviet Union, augurs an eventual diminution in the volume of American historical scholarship devoted to France. But he is certainly correct that French professional scholars now pay more attention to what American historians write about their country, and that more American books about French history get translated and thus reach a French audience extending even beyond the academy.

Before we conclude that American historians have shed their status as outsiders, however, we need to look at the way in which this transformation took place. In the immediate postwar period, as we have seen, American scholars of France, while continuing to concede to their French equivalents an advantage in technical qualifications, wrote unabashedly from the perspective of a general culture that they assumed to have overcome certain problems that French society had failed to resolve satisfactorily. Among the worst of those problems, as far as Americans were concerned, was the excessive level of ideological conflict in French life, which, they observed, had as one of its consequences a marked tendency among French academic historians either to avoid research topics touching on subjects directly implicated in those conflicts, or to take up those topics with the explicitly stated purpose of furthering an ideological goal. Thus French historians—especially the methodological innovators of the *Annales* school, whose energy was concentrated on the study of the medieval and early modern periods—refused to venture into the study of almost anything having to do with their nation's history since 1789, while topics with an obvious ideological charge, such as the French Revolution, became the exclusive property of historians identified with the French Communist Party.

Under these circumstances, American historians of France were able to profit from the fact that they were independent of the structures of French academic and political life. As Peter Novick has demonstrated in his important analysis of the presuppositions of American historians, the 1950s was the high tide of the discipline's faith in the possibility of an objective portrait of the past.[27] The spectacle of the French tiptoeing around so many obviously important historical subjects added to the American conviction that, in spite of the technical disadvantages of distance from the archives and lack of audience, the outsider was better placed to write an objective history. Even Pinkney, despite his pessimism about the possibilities for American historical research in France, had allotted to the American scholar one "great advantage . . . over his French counterparts, detachment and impartiality. . . . He can see French history in a dispassionate way that no Frenchman can."[28] The breakthrough that allowed American historians to produce a body of original historical literature that ultimately compelled acceptance even from French scholars resulted from the systematic exploitation of this magic shield of distance in such works as Eugen Weber's study of the protofascist *Action française* movement, Joel Colton's sympathetic biography of the Popular Front leader Léon Blum, Harvey Goldberg's life of the turn-of-the-century socialist Jean Jaurès, and the volume that stands as the classic example of the genre, Robert Paxton's *Vichy France*.[29]

Paxton's book had special impact because he dealt with one of the most sensitive subjects in modern French experience, the wartime regime of Pétain. *Vichy France* was by no means the first book on the subject, but, because the author was not French, his carefully documented assertions about the extent of French collaboration could not easily be dismissed as part of the partisan debate about the war years that had long divided the French public. While it is generally accepted that Paxton demolished once and for all the claim that wartime collaboration was imposed by the Germans on a reluctant French government, however, it is not so clear that the virtue of his book derived from its author's detachment. Paxton made little effort to disguise his deep feelings about his subject. Vichy's officials, he concluded, were men of a type who lost sight of ultimate values. "So blinded, they perform jobs that may be admirable in themselves but are tinctured with evil by the overall effects of the system." Not that Paxton intended to preach only to the French: His concluding lines suggested, first, that in such a crisis, even Americans "are far more likely to act . . . like the Vichy majority," and then that "it may be the German occupiers rather than the Vichy majority whom Americans, as residents of the most powerful state on earth, should scrutinize most unblinkingly."[30] There were, naturally, French critics to suggest that Paxton's conclusions were vitiated because he was an outsider, either incapable of fully fathoming the French experience or prejudiced against his subjects.[31] On the whole, however, Paxton's conclusions, somewhat nuanced but not fundamentally altered, have become the common wisdom of French and American scholarly writing on the subject: the success of the book is the clearest example of the successful integration of an outsider's point of view into French consciousness of their own past.

Although Paxton's passing suggestion of an identification between

Germany and the United States marks his book as a product of the era of the Vietnam war, its outspoken criticism of both French conduct during World War II and of French treatment of that subject since the war still stamped his work as part of the American scholarly tradition dating back to the war years. The Vietnam generation lacked, of course, the conviction that American society represented a successful model that France was called upon to imitate. Furthermore, they could not help but be influenced by the fact that the contemporary France they encountered on their research trips was no longer the crisis-ridden society of the 1940s and 1950s but the increasingly stable and prosperous France of the "*trente glorieuses*," the "thirty good years" that had propelled the country into the ranks of the world's modern consumer societies, greatly reduced the gap between American and French living standards, and consequently diminished the sense of entering a different world that had previously struck American scholars arriving in the country.[32] The 1960s generation also experienced, at least vicariously, the upheaval of May 1968, which gave France the prestige of having produced a contestatory movement on a scale completely different from the antiwar movement on American campuses. For many American students, May 1968 and the revival of French Marxist thought that accompanied it gave new life to the notion of France as the vanguard of the revolution with something to teach the United States, rather than the other way around. Furthermore, it was just at this point that the impact of the *Annales* school historians really began to be felt in the American scholarly world.

As the younger historians who had been students in the 1960s entered the profession, the tone of American scholarship on France began to change. Research methodologies became more polished and "professional," with increasing use of social-science concepts (the sociologist–historian Charles Tilly had a great impact on many of these scholars) and Americans developed growing adeptness in the pursuit of sources in obscure French archives. Under the influence of the *Annales* school and of the general turn toward social history, there was a questioning of the national framework in which most previous American scholarship about France had been cast in favor of studies dealing with a specific community, a specific social class, or a specific occupational group, as in such monographs as Joan Scott's *Glassworkers of Carmaux* and Bonnie Smith's *Ladies of the Leisure Class*.[33] One effect of this tendency was to blur the issue of the American historian's "otherness" with respect to his or her subject. The American scholar no longer wrote as a member of one national culture commenting on another, but, most often, as a representative of the "modern world" commenting on the process of modernization, a general phenomenon held to have transcended national boundaries. Detailed scholarship in the French context was justified in terms of a putative contribution to a collective project of comparative research that has, however, rarely been pursued in practice. The sense that scholarship on France was likely to contribute to any specific clarification of large issues in American life, so strong in much of the work produced in the 1950s and early 1960s, was greatly diminished, except in certain subfields, notably women's history and Jewish history. American scholars working in these fields exhibited a sense of purpose sometimes missing from their more generalist colleagues' monographs, and based on their conviction that their subjects were in fact not "others" but part of the same community as the historian describing them.

The sense of fragmentation and disorientation resulting from these trends was not peculiar to the subfield of French history: By the 1980s, it was widely held to characterize the discipline as a whole, as Peter Novick has shown in *That Noble Dream*. William McNeill, an older scholar, worried that "The study of European history in this country [has] tended to cut itself off from the mainspring of human curiosity that ultimately, in any society, must undergird whatever historical investigation occurs," and warned that, as a consequence, "the recent efflorescence of professionalized European scholarship [is] more precarious than most of us wish to believe."[34] Unable or unwilling to articulate the meaning of the American experience, American scholars lacked a vantage point from which to make a distinctive contribution to French or European history. Paradoxically, this has no doubt contributed to the broader acceptance of American scholarship in France itself: In many subfields, it has become increasingly difficult to distinguish American from French perspectives.

While the problem of French "otherness" has thus come to preoccupy American scholars much less than in the past, trends in France appear to be pointing the other way. This is not due to any chauvinistic effort to recapture "French history for the French," although the French would doubtless be unhappy if as David Pinkney predicted their history did come to be studied more extensively in our country than their own. It is more a consequence of such developments as the reassertion by French historians of the importance of politics and of the national state, on the one hand, and, on the other, an examination of the relationship between the historian and his or her subject that tends to celebrate the historian's embeddedness in the national culture.[35] The renewed emphasis on national politics, a subject neglected in the 1960s and 1970s, tends to emphasize the specificity of the French experience and thus to sharpen the contrast between the French tradition and our own; in particular, the current French tendency to evaluate their most durable postrevolutionary regime, the Third Republic of 1875–1940, in more positive terms than heretofore amounts to a belated reaction against the critical view articulated so forcefully by Stanley Hoffmann and other American scholars in the 1950s.

The vogue in France for *ego-histoire*, the critical study of the historian's relation to his or her subject, can only serve to remind American historians of their place as outsiders. Pierre Nora, the impresario of the movement, has put it in the context of postmodernist critiques of objectivity and has called on historians not to see themselves simply as "the voice of the past. . . . an erudite transparency, a means of transmission . . . in the end, an absence obsessed with objectivity." The scholar of the past must now become

> a new personnage, ready to confess, unlike his predecessors, the close, intimate, personal connection he has with his subject. Even more, to proclaim it, to analyze it, to make it not the obstacle, but the means of his understanding. For this subject owes everything to his subjectivity, his creation and his re-creation.[36]

In the abstract, this position does not exclude the American scholar, but it does bring the difference of backgrounds into sharp focus. In practice, reading the elegant essays in which leading French scholars tease out the many ways in which their personal experience has enriched their scholarly work, the American historian is likely to experience moments of despair: Who among us can hope to understand French history like Raoul Girardet, who begins his piece by writing, "My childhood was the time when the monuments to the fallen were still new?"[37] And a few French historians have taken positions that do frankly amount to an assertion that history is local knowledge, inherently more accessible to the insider than to the outsider. For example, in the introduction to the book to which he devoted the last years of his life, *The Identity of France*, Fernand Braudel, the longtime head of the *Annales* school, asserts that "the historian, in reality, is never fully at home except with the history of his own country, where he understands almost instinctively the side alleys, the winding trails, the things that are unique, the weaknesses. No matter how erudite he may be, he will never have such assets when he resides somewhere else."[38] Braudel's assertion surprised both his French and American colleagues, coming as it did from a scholar whose own previous works had always looked far beyond France's own frontiers. He has been severely criticized by other French historians for positing the existence of a fixed national identity and ignoring the clear evidence of continued contact and exchange with other cultures.[39] There has been less discussion of the implications of Braudel's apparent ambition to revive the romantic–na-

tionalist historiographical tradition of Jules Michelet. Perhaps most professional historians have chosen to interpret it as an offhand remark by
an aging scholar whose entire *oeuvre* seemed to point in other directions.

The renewed saliency of the issue of national identity in French
historiography offers both a challenge and an opportunity to the American community of historians of France, and, more broadly, to an entire
profession that has invested heavily in the study of foreign cultures
without always fully comprehending the implications of such an enterprise. The challenge consists in the need to articulate a justification for
our need to understand the French past, particularly in a context where
conventional definitions of the national interest hardly dictate a major
effort in that direction. The opportunity consists in the chance to
revitalize our own work by becoming more conscious of our position as
interpreters between cultures. Rather than falling back on the old claim
that, as outsiders, we naturally bring greater objectivity to the study of
the French past than the French themselves can, we should accept the fact
that the American scholar of France is also an engaged scholar. As the
English scholar Richard Cobb has written, "a sense of involvement is not
only inevitable but even necessary, for the historian is not a cold clinician."[40]

The risk is that such self-awareness might lead to a certain solipsism,
reinforcing the tendency of American scholars to accept a self-definition
as professionals isolated from any larger culture and limited to writing
for each other. The hope should be, rather, that American scholars could
fulfill the program set out a generation ago by Leonard Krieger, the most
acute analyst of the situation of the American scholar of Europe. Krieger
saw the American scholarly community as having a unique opportunity
to put the foreign past in a broad context because "epistemological
necessity" required us to do so: "The events can be understood only when
the categories linking the American subject with the European object are
articulated."[41] Paradoxically, then, the future vitality of American scholarship on French history may depend not on the merging of two academic
communities into one, but on a renewed and more sophisticated sense
of our differences.

NOTES

1. See, for example, the discussion of ethnographers' accounts of their arrivals
in Mary Louise Pratt, "Fieldwork in Common Places," in *Writing Culture:
The Poetics and Politics of Ethnography*, James Clifford and George E. Marcus,
eds. (Berkeley: University of California Press, 1986), 27–50.

2. Dan T. Carter, "The Academy's Crisis of Belief," *Chronicle of Higher Education* (November 18, 1992): A36; Gordon S. Wood, "Novel History," *New York Review of Books* (June 27, 1991): 12–16.

3. See, for example, the discussion by August Meier and Elliott Rudwick, in "The Dilemmas of Scholarship in Afro-American History," *Black History and the Historical Profession* (Urbana, IL: University of Illinois Press, 1986), 277–308; and, more generally, Peter Novick, *That Noble Dream: The "Objectivity Question" and the American Historical Profession* (New York: Cambridge University Press, 1988), especially Chapter 14, "Every Group its own Historian," 469–521.

4. See the plaintive articles of the leading French specialists in North American history, André Kaspi, Pierre Mélandri, Jean Heffer, and Claude Fohlen, in the special number of the *Revue d'histoire moderne et contemporaine* devoted to the subject, vol. 37 (1990), no. 2.

5. Leonard Krieger, "European History in America," in *History*, John Higham, ed. (Englewood Cliffs, NJ: Prentice Hall, 1965), 233–313; 243. Krieger's essay is still the most thoughtful and probing examination of the cultural reasons for American interest in the foreign past.

6. Richard Cobb, *A Second Identity: Essays on France and French History* (London: Oxford University Press, 1969), 1.

7. David H. Pinkney, "American Historians on the European Past," *American Historical Review 86* (1981): 1–20; p. 1.

8. H. Stuart Hughes, *Gentleman Rebel: The Memoirs of H. Stuart Hughes* (New York: Ticknor and Fields, 1990), 222.

9. Thomas Schaeper, "French History as Written on Both Sides of the Atlantic: A Comparative Analysis," *French Historical Studies 17* (1991): 233–248; pp. 235–236.

10. For a longer discussion of these issues, see Jeremy D. Popkin, "'Made in U.S.A.': Les historiens français d'outre-Atlantique et leur histoire," *Revue d'histoire moderne et contemporaine 40* (1993): 303–320.

11. For a critical assessment of the current state of the *Annales* tradition, see François Dosse, *L'Histoire en miettes* (Paris: Editions La Découverte, 1987); for a defense of the tradition's vitality by one of the younger members of the group, see Roger Chartier, "Le monde comme représentation," *Annales E.S.C.* 44 (1989): 1505–1520.

12. Fritz Stern, "Germany History in America, 1884–1984," *Central European History 19* (1986): 131–163; p. 139.

13. Gilbert Allardyce, "The Rise and Fall of the Western Civilization Course," *American Historical Review 87* (1982): 695–725; p. 699.

14. Allardyce, "Rise and Fall," 706–709.

15. R. R. Palmer, "A Century of French History in America," *French Historical Studies 14* (1985): 160–175; p. 170.

16. Hughes, *Rebel*, 148, 156.

17. Stern, "German History," 157; Krieger, "European History," 291.

18. Stern, "German History," 132.

19. Edward Mead Earle, ed., *Modern France: Problems of the Third and Fourth Republics* (Princeton, NJ: Princeton University Press, 1951), v–vii; p. vi; John

B. Wolf, "The Elan Vital of France: A Problem in Historical Perspective," in Ibid., 19-31; p. 21.

20. On French social and political criticism in the 1930s, see J.-L. Loubet del Bayle, *Les Non-Conformistes des années 30* (Paris: Seuil, 1969).

21. David Landes, "French Business and the Businessman: A Social and Cultural Analysis," in *Modern France*, E. Earle, ed., 334-353; p. 336.

22. Laurence Wylie, *Village in the Vaucluse*, 3rd ed. (Cambridge, MA: Harvard University Press, 1974), 336, 339.

23. Evelyn Acomb, "Letter on the Founding of the Society for French Historical Studies," *French Historical Studies 16* (1990): 702-706.

24. David H. Pinkney, "The Dilemma of the American Historian of Modern France," *French Historical Studies 1* (1958): 11-25.

25. David H. Pinkney, "The Dilemma of the American Historian of Modern France Reconsidered," *French Historical Studies 9* (1975): 170-181; and "American Historians of the European Past," *American Historical Review 86* (1981): 1-20.

26. David H. Pinkney, "Time to Bury the Pinkney Thesis?," *French Historical Studies 17* (1991): 219-223; pp. 222-223.

27. Novick, *Noble Dream*, Part III, "Objectivity Reconstructed," 281-414.

28. Pinkney, "Dilemma," 21.

29. Eugen Weber, *Action française* (Stanford, CA: Stanford University Press, 1962); Joel Colton, *Léon Blum: Humanist in Politics* (New York: Alfred A. Knopf, 1966); Harvey Goldberg, *The Life of Jean Jaurès* (Madison, WI: University of Wisconsin Press, 1962); Robert Paxton, *Vichy France: Old Guard and New Order* (New York: W. W. Norton, 1975). (Original work published 1972)

30. Paxton, *Vichy France*, 382-383.

31. See the discussion in Henry Rousso, *Le syndrome de Vichy de 1944 à nos jours*, 2nd ed. (Paris: Seuil, 1990), 287.

32. The phrase was coined by the French economist and sociologist Jean Fourastié. See his *Les trente glorieuses* (Paris: Hachette, 1979).

33. Joan W. Scott, *The Glassworkers of Carmaux* (Cambridge, MA: Harvard University Press, 1974); Bonnie G. Smith, *Ladies of the Leisure Class* (Princeton, NJ: Princeton University Press, 1981).

34. William McNeill, "Modern European History," in *The Past Before Us: Contemporary Historical Writing in the United States*, Michael Kammen, ed. (Ithaca, NY: Cornell University Press, 1980), 95-112; pp. 108-109.

35. For the resurgence of political history, see the collaborative volume edited by René Rémond, *Pour une histoire politique* (Paris: Seuil, 1988); the movement toward *ego-histoire* is exemplified in *Essais d'ego-histoire*, Pierre Nora, ed. (Paris: Gallimard, 1987).

36. Pierre Nora, "Entre mémoire et histoire: La problématique des lieux," in *Les Lieux de Mémoire*, 4 vols., Pierre Nora, ed. (Paris: Gallimard, 1984), Vol. 1, xxxiii.

37. Raoul Girardet, "L'Ombre de la guerre," in *Ego-histoire*, Pierre Nora, ed., 139.

38. Fernand Braudel, *L'Identité de la France: Espace et Histoire* (Paris: Arthaud–

Flammarion, 1986), 9. Braudel's assumption that there is a stable French cultural identity has come under fire from other French historians, notably Gérard Noiriel in *Le Creuset français* (Paris: Seuil, 1988), esp. 50–67.

39. See, for example, the chapter "Questions à Fernand Braudel," by the French immigration historian Gérard Noiriel, in his *Le Creuset français* (Paris: Seuil, 1988), 50–67. For a wider discussion of the resurgence of questions of national identity in French historiography, see Jeremy D. Popkin, "French Historians and French Identity since 1970" (paper delivered at the Conference on European Identities, Indiana University, February 1994).

40. Cobb, *Second Identity*, 46.

41. Krieger, in *History*, Higham, ed., 312.

III

Reconceptualizing Objectivity

7

Significant Others: Objectivity and Ethnocentrism

DAVID COUZENS HOY

The title of this book is *Objectivity and Its Other*. In this chapter I am raising the question of whether one such "other" is ethnocentrism. Of course, this relation of otherness is a conceptual one, but there is also a more concrete sense of otherness at stake, namely, the sense in which we talk about understanding other people and other cultures. Right from the start, however, I want to make clear that pitting objectivity against ethnocentrism as the "other" is itself problematic. The "otherness" involved in their relation could be of several varieties. *Opposition* is the first relation of otherness that comes to mind, but a central issue is whether these two concepts really are opposites. Instead of seeing them as opposites, one might urge that they are "other" to each other simply in being *unrelated*. Bringing them into conjunction would thus be like comparing apples and oranges. The view that I argue for in this chapter is that the relation of otherness here is a complex one: These two notions are indeed other to each other, but like many such pairings, each one needs the other term for its own identity. So they may be neither unrelated terms that are indifferent to each other, nor opposites that exclude each

113

other. Since these concepts contrast with each other significantly, I call them "significant others." The relation is significant because although the terms are not formally wedded to each other in a mutually defining bond or a higher synthesis (as in a dialectical coupling), they often show up together. However, like other postmodern couples their proponents also seem to make a point of their disconnection, or at least prefer to leave the degree of their connection uncertain.

The relation of objectivity and ethnocentrism appears to be one of simple otherness, such that the concepts appear antithetical. Attaining objectivity seems to imply overcoming ethnocentrism. Objectivity thus appears to be unequivocally good and ethnocentrism to be unequivocally bad. However, Nietzsche warned us a long time ago that cultural phenomena generally have both advantages and disadvantages, so this simple antipathy may not be all there is to the relationship. Let me turn to a prominent recent critic of Nietzsche, Allan Bloom, to test Nietzsche's hypothesis against what Bloom has to say about ethnocentricity and objectivity. Bloom's attack on ethnocentricity and his defense of objectivity comes in a more general criticism of what he calls openness. He grants that there is a good sense of openness, where one is open to the "quest for knowledge and certitude," that is, to objectivity.[1] But he deplores the new openness that is, he thinks, open to difference simply for the sake of difference. He sees this radical openness as rejecting any attempt to overcome difference for fear of committing the sin of ethnocentrism.

What upsets Bloom in the new form of openness is its suggestion of relativism. The lesson that I have learned from Bloom's critique, despite my disagreement with it, is that there are two different directions from which to criticize ethnocentrism. One is the more traditional or *modernist* direction (which I believe Bloom represents, however uncomfortable he is with some of its tendencies) whereby ethnocentrism is overcome by means of a move to universal knowledge and transcultural values, that is, to objectivity. Recently, however, there is also the *postmodern* direction, whereby ethnocentrism has to be overcome because there are no transcultural values and because no culture is to be condemned or condoned wholesale. So the problem of ethnocentrism looks different when it is paired with one "significant other" instead of another. When the significant other of ethnocentrism is objectivity, ethnocentrism appears defective because it seems relativistic. When its significant other is relativism, it appears objectivistic (or universalistic or essentialist). Ethnocentrism thus seems to be a conceptual form of bigamy.

This bigamy can easily lead to the logical fallacy of equivocation in argumentation, and indeed I think that Bloom's critique of relativism has the paradoxical result of appearing not objective, as he intends, but ethnocentric. Consider Bloom's opposition to the recent introduction in American colleges of required courses on non-Western cultures, these courses being in his opinion a central strategy for promoting relativistic openness. Bloom believes that these courses are most often taught with the demagogic intention of forcing students "to recognize that there are other ways of thinking and that Western ways are not better."[2] Bloom opposes the relativism that he finds in the assumption that "all cultures are equal" and defends the need to find standards by which to judge both ourselves and others. In "Western Civ" he tries to imagine an attempt to come to grips with modern Japan without such standards.

> Japanese society is often compared to a family. . . . But the family is exclusive. For in it there is an iron wall separating insiders from outsiders, and its members feel contrary sentiments toward the two. So it is in Japanese society, which is intransigently homogeneous, barring the diversity which is the great pride of the United States today. To put it brutally, the Japanese seem to be racists. They consider themselves superior; they firmly resist immigration; they exclude even Koreans who have lived for generations among them. They have difficulty restraining cabinet officers from explaining that America's failing economy is due to blacks.[3]

Now I would have thought that what we should have learned from openness (in either sense) is to avoid the blanket stereotyping in this overzealous "objectivity." While there might be Japanese who could be described this way, I would think that there were many who did not fit this description; or at least I would need some evidence other than the anecdotal reference to a reprehensible cabinet officer. Bloom also makes an invidious comparison between Japan and the United States, as if there were not large segments of American society that would be guilty of these same charges.

But Bloom's message is part of an even more striking claim that Western culture is unlike non-Western cultures in at least one major respect. All these other cultures, says Bloom, are highly ethnocentric. Each believes that it is the best. This situation presents a double paradox. On the one hand, the teachers of openness, who are opponents of ethnocentrism, seem to be forced to recognize and legitimate the ethnocentrism of other cultures. On the other hand, these advocates of relativism seem forced to respect this ethnocentrism of the others in the name of objectivity:

> Only in the Western nations, i.e., those influenced by Greek philosophy, is there some willingness to doubt the identification of the good

with one's own way. One should conclude from the study of non-Western cultures that not only to prefer one's own way but to believe it best, superior to all others, is primary and even natural—exactly the opposite of what is intended by requiring students to study these cultures. What we are really doing is applying a Western prejudice—which we covertly take to indicate the superiority of our culture—and deforming the evidence of those other cultures to attest to its validity. The scientific study of other cultures is almost exclusively a Western phenomenon, and in its origin was obviously connected with the search for new and better ways, or at least for validation of the hope that our own culture really is the better way, a validation for which there is no felt need in other cultures. If we are to learn from those cultures, we must wonder whether such scientific study is a good idea. Consistency would seem to require professors of openness to respect the ethnocentrism or closedness they find everywhere else. However, in attacking ethnocentrism, what they actually do is to assert unawares the superiority of their scientific understanding and the inferiority of the other cultures which do not recognize it at the same time that they reject all such claims to superiority. They both affirm and deny the goodness of their science.[4]

Part of Bloom's critique, it should be noted, is of social scientific objectivity itself. On his view, cultural relativism is the latest attitude that science has adopted to study the human situation, and this leads to the "suicide of science,"[5] since science thereby seems to be giving up its original goal of rising above cultural contexts to what is accessible to anyone anywhere through the universal human faculty of reason.

Bloom's argument in *The Closing of the American Mind* that science and the enlightenment's faith in reason undermines itself is thus reminiscent of what the Frankfurt School critical theorists Max Horkheimer and Theodor Adorno called the "dialectic of enlightenment." His conclusions, however, go in a markedly different direction from theirs, since his goal is to restore the enlightenment faith in reason. Most striking is Bloom's conclusion that in contrast to all other cultures, which are ethnocentric, Western culture is the only one that is not ethnocentric. He believes that Western culture has overcome ethnocentrism and has come to value universal objectivity. What seems paradoxical (if not simply false) about Bloom's sweeping assertion here is that the claim that only Western culture is objective and nonethnocentric sounds highly ethnocentric. Moreover, because he adduces no evidence for his claims, it sounds biased and unobjective.

Of course, he does qualify his position in the later essay on "Western Civ" by stressing that he is not debating the value of Western versus non-Western culture, but more strictly "the possibility of philosophy."[6] He wants us to recognize that philosophy is not like religion, which is cultural and which even defines cultures. Instead, philosophy is more like natural science, which is transcultural (if not in historical origin, at least in the sense that now no one would propose separate courses in Western and non-Western physics). Bloom defends "the possibility of philosophy" by arguing that it is at least possible that there are cultural products that transcend their temporal and social origins to become "contemporary at all times."[7] He believes that the texts of classical philosophy have achieved something approaching this transcendence, and he says that he is willing to consider admitting some non-Western texts into the canon as well. But I note that he is willing to include the non-Western texts not because of their non-Western origins, but because he thinks that they have transcended these origins.

Here Bloom's own insight into the dialectic of enlightenment should have warned him that the belief that one has attained such transcultural objectivity oneself may be an illusion veiling what from another perspective could be seen as cultural myopia. This assumption that one has risen to the transcultural standpoint may itself be blind to its own cultural biases, and thus risks constituting a form of ethnocentrism. This form of ethnocentrism would be more invidious than the explicit ethnocentrism of cultures that had the Nietzschean strength to believe in their own superiority. At least those cultures would know that they were ethnocentric, whereas Bloom's position threatens to slide back into an ethnocentrism that deceives itself and ends in the weak epistemological position of a false consciousness that decries ethnocentrism in others while failing to recognize it in itself.

The concepts of ethnocentrism and objectivity thus push the defender of objectivity toward paradox. Bloom's argument starts, after all, by defining ethnocentrism as the belief that one's own culture is the best. Then Bloom distinguishes Western culture from all others for not being ethnocentric. But since only Western culture is seen as not ethnocentric, Western culture is reaffirmed as the best culture. This reaffirmation is (by the original definition) ethnocentric. So Bloom's analysis remains trapped in the dialectic of enlightenment.

HERMENEUTICS

Let me now consider a way out of Bloom's dilemma, a way that still leaves a place for philosophy. "Objective" and "ethnocentric" are adjectives that apply to people, or more exactly, to understandings. The branch of

philosophy that investigates the theory of understanding is called hermeneutics. Hermeneutics has a long history, but in this century it has been
shaped by two German philosophers, Martin Heidegger and Hans-Georg
Gadamer, whose central thesis is that all understanding is interpretive. In
the rest of this chapter I discuss recent theorists who accept this thesis,
including its attendant difficulties, and whose work thus could be loosely
classified under the rubric of hermeneutics.

First, however, let me delineate how the same dilemma that I have
found in Bloom's discussion could also trouble the hermeneutic thesis
that all understanding is interpretive. While this thesis might seem
reasonably straightforward, it has had its opponents, and the issues have
been focused particularly on objectivity, relativism, and ethnocentrism.
Thus, the hermeneutical insistence on the interpretive character of
understanding has led some theorists to conclude (falsely, I believe) that
hermeneutics is opposed to the idea of objective understanding. For
instance, if to understand another culture objectively anthropologists
must free themselves of all their cultural assumptions, objective understanding would appear to be impossible given the hermeneutical insistence on the context-bound character of any understanding. This insistence would lead to the charge that hermeneutics holds that
understanding is always biased for its own culture—or, in short, is ethnocentric.

Curiously enough, this charge appears incompatible with another
charge that is often leveled against the hermeneutical insistence on the
interpretive character of understanding and its apparent denial of objectivity. This is the charge of value relativism. The position thereby attributed to hermeneutics is that values are relative to different cultures, so
hermeneutical interpreters should refrain from imposing their values on
others who seem to hold different values. The incompatibility arises from
the fact that if understanding is always ethnocentric, and always value-
laden, then it would seem impossible not to see the other culture except
through the veil of one's own values and thus, impossible not to condemn
deviation from those values. So if hermeneutics is committed to ethnocentrism, then it could *not* accept value relativism, in the sense I am using
here,[8] since hermeneutics denies that one can abstract entirely from one's
own values and come to evaluate the world as the "others" do (if the
"others" do evaluate the world completely differently, although hermeneutics also challenges the intelligibility of this assumption). But on the
other side, if hermeneutics is committed to value relativism, then it could
not accept ethnocentrism since it could not privilege its own values over
the contrasting ones of the other culture.

So *both* of these charges could not be true. In what follows I explain how the hermeneutic insistence on the interpretive character of under-standing is subject to *neither* of these lines of criticism, which I believe to be wrong not only in how they construe the tenets and arguments of hermeneutical philosophy, but also in that they presuppose a false picture of culture and of cultural understanding. The hermeneutic thesis that understanding is interpretive need not lead to the denial of objectivity, but only to the denial of an overly abstract picture of objectivity as a transcultural, atemporal ideal. Similarly, hermeneutics can continue to insist on the context-bound character of interpretive understanding without falling into a pernicious ethnocentrism, even if the hermeneutical insistence on the inevitability of context does make hermeneutics resis-tant to the modern enlightenment ideal of transcultural universality.

Since much more has been written about hermeneutics and the problems of objectivity than about hermeneutics and the problems of ethnocentrism, in this chapter I focus more on the debate within herme-neutics about ethnocentrism and multiculturalism.[9] Among recent theo-rists whom I would group within the hermeneutical camp because of their insistence on the interpretive character of understanding are the philoso-phers Richard Rorty and Charles Taylor, as well as the anthropologist Clifford Geertz. Jürgen Habermas must also feature in this debate, although in a more oppositional way. I also include the French poststruc-turalists Michel Foucault and Jacques Derrida, because although they have criticized some versions of hermeneutic theory, their lineage goes back to Heidegger's hermeneutical conception of understanding.

To formulate the issue as it arises from within hermeneutics, in the next section I work through the debate between Clifford Geertz and Richard Rorty. In that debate Rorty has been willing to accept the label of ethnocentrism for his own stance, which he calls postmodern bourgeois liberalism. Geertz also can be characterized as a postmodern liberal, but cannot accept an avowed ethnocentrism. They share a position that looks much like the relativistic openness that Bloom attacks, and Rorty and Geertz are both accused by critics of being relativists. Geertz has re-sponded that he is not a relativist, but an anti-antirelativist, where the double negation does not imply a positive. Rorty has also adopted the label of anti-anti-ethnocentrism, but he is more willing to drop the double negative and settle for the label of ethnocentrism. However, I would suggest that the best way to read Rorty's ethnocentrism is to see that his variant of ethnocentrism is not pernicious. I thus have to identify exactly what makes ethnocentrism seem pernicious (e.g., to Geertz), and then consider whether a more acceptable, postmodern version of ethnocen-trism is possible. I maintain that an avowed postmodern ethnocentrism is viable, and I contrast it below with a late-modernist, unavowed ethnocentrism that I find potentially lurking in the positions of Charles Taylor and Jürgen Habermas. Along the way I allude briefly to how I think that Michel Foucault's method of genealogy and Jacques Derrida's deconstructions can serve to prevent a postmodern ethnocentrism from becoming pernicious again.

The Geertz–Rorty Debate

Clifford Geertz may not think of himself as an advocate of hermeneutic philosophy, and indeed there may be no direct philosophical lineage from Heidegger and Gadamer to Geertz. His affiliations are more with "forms of life" (Wittgensteinian) philosophy, as well as with the related "natives' point of view" approach to anthropology. But he seems to me to accept the hermeneutic thesis that understanding is always interpretive when he asserts as his central thesis the corollary that "meaning is socially constructed."[10] His view thus contrasts with Bloom's emphasis on transcultural objectivity, and their opposition goes all the way down to how they perceive the problems. Bloom's remarks about other cultures suggest that he holds what Geertz thinks to be a mistaken picture of culture, especially today. Geertz thinks that cultures are mistakenly pictured as nearly windowless semantic monads. Even a modern structuralist anthropologist like Lévi-Strauss imagines the world as "integral societies in distant communication."[11] In contrast, Geertz concludes that times have changed and that this picture no longer applies (and maybe was always distorting anyway). There are no longer exotic cultures that have flourished in isolation from modern societies until their discovery by modern anthropologists. One result of living in a more crowded world is that it is harder to keep secrets, and unusual practices are becoming rare. As Geertz quips, "We may be faced with a world in which there simply aren't any more headhunters, matrilinealists, or people who predict the weather from the entrails of a pig. Difference will doubtless remain—the French will never eat salted butter. But the good old days of widow-burning and cannibalism are gone forever."[12]

In the place of this late-modernist picture of cultures as integral, autonomous, self-contained wholes, Geertz substitutes a postmodern picture. In the postmodern picture we live in a crowded world where difference is not exotic and far away, but right next door. Crowded conditions have not made diversity disappear, as there has not been a *convergence* of views, only a *mingling* of them. This mingling has not led to a melting pot, where there is a shared conception of what is good, just, beautiful, reasonable, or decent. The postmodern culture is not a self-contained whole, an autonomous integral "we" that confronts other such cultures as "theys." "Otherness" is again, in my terms, not simple opposition, but is better described as *significant* otherness. We are other to ourselves, not at one with ourselves. Foreignness, says Geertz, starts "not at the water's edge but at the skin's."[13] In the postmodern world we do not inhabit a serene, harmonious, self-contained web of meanings, but we live in a collage.[14] To live in a postmodern collage we must cultivate different virtues from those required by the modern picture. We will have to learn that diversity has its advantages and its disadvantages, and that it can be neither ignored nor embraced.

Let me now test Geertz's sentiments against the worries that certainly spring to mind. Is this postmodern picture a version of "anything goes" relativism? How does anyone retain any commitments without retreating to a beleaguered ethnocentrism that asserts "here I stand" or "*my* values, right or wrong"? Has objectivity gone out what Bloom would consider a too widely open window, along with rights and human nature? Behind these questions about objectivity, relativism, and ethnocentrism are some more general philosophical problems about the nature and limits of understanding. If there are diverse understandings of the world, does not each side really believe that others would come to accept its point of view under ideal conditions? Does understanding another standpoint require agreeing with it? Does not disagreement imply that some agreement must be possible or that some consensus must emerge from the tumult of dissent? Would not even the most thorough-going advocate of cultural pluralism have to accept the possibility of a *single* framework that allowed diverse practices and values to coexist? Would pluralism even be possible unless we were nonpluralistic about at least one point of agreement, namely, our agreement to disagree?

This barrage of questions requires some care to sort out, but let me first return to the lesson I would like to draw from Geertz. The questions will not be answerable, I think, if we are stuck with the windowless semantic monad picture of cultures, which I would like to characterize more generally as the *closed horizon* model of understanding. Nietzsche in an early essay, the second *Untimely Meditation* on "The Use and Abuse of History for Life," criticizes an objectivist model of modern historiography, but fails to generate a positive solution precisely because he takes over from the scientistic conception of historiography the closed horizon model. According to this model, which also applies to contemporaneous but separate cultures, the past and the present are each self-contained horizons. "Scientific" historiography is thus that which abstracts from the present standpoint, and recreates the past horizon, "the way it really was." The paradox in which Nietzsche traps this objectivist historiography results when this same objectivism leads to relativism and to nihilism. The suspension of present values for the sake of recreating past values leads to an inability to privilege any set of values over others, and thus to an inability to act. So on Nietzsche's account the rise of objectivist historiography leads to a weakening of the modern age, and to an inability to act in a historically new way instead of simply reacting haphazardly to constant change.

However, Nietzsche himself seems trapped in the paradox, since he cannot tell his own age how to overcome the problem, and he ends with the empty hope that a new generation will somehow be able to forget history. But forgetting about other ways of thinking and acting hardly seems like the best means of regaining the courage to act boldly. For one thing, voluntarily deciding to forget seems psychologically impossible. For another, this courage would be undermined by the worry that what one wanted to do had already been tried, perhaps unsuccessfully. These problems aside, the young Nietzsche seems unclear about what exactly the use of the knowledge of historical diversity is. Geertz makes clearer the "uses of diversity," and in this I think he is complemented by Hans-Georg Gadamer's critique of the closed horizon model and the substitution of a hermeneutical model for understanding the diversity of understandings.

Gadamer believes that Nietzsche's model of horizons as closed to one another is a vestige of Romanticism: "Just as the individual is never simply an individual because he [or she] is always in understanding with others, so too the closed horizon that is supposed to enclose a culture is an abstraction."[15] On Gadamer's view, while objectivist historiography is right that we should be careful not to assimilate too hastily the otherness of the past or the foreign culture to our own expectations, he also believes that we can never disregard our own commitments entirely. As Geertz also believes, the problem of ethnocentrism and relativism is badly posed by thinking either that we have to commit ourselves to our own commitments, as a self-conscious ethnocentrism would have it,[16] or that reading too much anthropology will result in becoming so open to the claims of other cultures that one will cease to have any views about what is decent or reasonable.[17] The antirelativists are too anxious because they overestimate our ability to transcend our parochialisms, and the self-conscious ethnocentrists surrender too easily to the comforts of provincialism.[18]

Gadamer, however, makes a move that Geertz would resist when he goes on to account for how we do expand our horizons. Gadamer would agree with Geertz that understanding otherness consists neither in an empathy based in some underlying human nature or shared psychology, nor in the direct application of our own standards to other persons. However, Gadamer does suggest that this expansion is a "fusion" of horizons, one that "always involves rising to a higher universality that overcomes not only our own particularity but also that of the other."[19]

This assertion may sound like a neo-Hegelian claim that understanding ascends dialectically a pyramid of different views until it finally attains the peak where it arrives at the one universal view, and at absolute knowledge. However, Gadamer's critique of Hegel shows that if hermeneutics resembles a Hegelian account that understanding can develop, the account suggests a Hegel without the absolute, since there is no ideal closure that is finally posited. From a Gadamerian perspective what is wrong with both ethnocentrism and the supposition of a transcultural, objective universality is the projection of an ideal closure, a peak to the pyramid, in the evolutionary history of the human species. For Gadamer, since interpretation is always motivated by the specific needs of concrete situations, and since these situations always change (sometimes precisely through the introduction of new interpretations), new interpretations will always be needed. The final closure supplied by the ideal of "the one right interpretation" misconstrues the phenomenon of understanding, which always remains (and this is his term) *open.*

Geertz would, I believe, accept this Gadamerian line, or at least this criticism of ethnocentrism and of universal, transcultural objectivity. Geertz identifies the two extremes that are to be avoided as ethnocentrism, on the one hand, and on the other hand what he calls UNESCO cosmopolitanism, an attitude aspiring to noncultural objectivity.[20] Both ethnocentrism and cosmopolitanism are blind and insensitive to diversity, although for different reasons. Cosmopolitanism assumes that universal reason can be attained, whereas ethnocentrism believes that it has been attained (at least by "us," and anyone who is not one of "us" will eventually come to our point of view). Both ethnocentrism and cosmopolitanism believe that their view is the best for everybody, and thus that the position is innocuous because it is one that anyone should adopt willingly. But Geertz believes that their indifference to difference is not as innocuous as it may seem, since it can lead to the repression of diversity, whether forcefully or simply through an inability to imagine diversity. Thus he believes that ethnocentrism represses difference by treating it as mere unlikeness, and UNESCO cosmopolitanism not only marginalizes but often denies the reality of difference altogether. In contrast, Geertz believes that cultural diversity presents us with viable alternatives to our own way of thinking and acting. He asserts that we might want, literally, to "change our minds."[21]

Now hermeneutics would not agree that we could really change our minds into different ones, at least in the sense of becoming totally other than we are. But one reason for this qualification is that the very idea of being "totally other" relies on the "closed horizon" model, and is to be rejected. For hermeneutics understanding is never explicitly totalizable, as this model implies. Instead, understanding presupposes a large background of beliefs, desires, and practices, such that we can never become completely aware of our entire background all at once. On the hermeneutical account, if relativism is pictured as the confrontation between two entirely different sets of beliefs, then relativism is not really possible, because we could never be faced with the choice of rejecting everything about ourselves and making ourselves totally other by explicitly choosing an entire set of new attitudes. However, we can expand our horizons by incorporating the effects of becoming aware of diversity, and for Geertz this effect on our own self-understanding is a primary positive *use* of diversity.

The disservice of ethnocentrism, for Geertz, is that in closing us off from the other, we close us off from ourselves. Ethnocentrism is pernicious because it represents an easy "surrender to the comforts of merely being ourselves, cultivating deafness and maximizing gratitude for not having been born a Vandal or an Ik."[22] Even relativism has the effect of making us more acceptable to ourselves, by suggesting that the other is *simply* other to us, and that it is "okay" for each of us to be as we are. On Geertz's view, the use of diversity is not that it is simply other, but it is, to use my phrase, "significantly other." The point of letting diversity be visible is not to make us *acceptable* to ourselves, but to make us *visible* to ourselves. A central feature that we will find, in this crowded world, is that we are ourselves diverse. We are our own other. We will find that the world is "full of irremovable strangenesses,"[23] and in a world without headhunters and widow burnings, the strangeness is more likely to be found at home than abroad. We will find that "we" are really not a single outlook on the world, but instead, an aggregate of "theys." An ethnography practiced on ourselves would show not only agreement, but disagreement. Finding the other already at home in ourselves is also not going to make us love the other, but at least we will know more about ourselves; we will find that we are not really what we think we are, and we may not like to be so divided against ourselves.

Geertz sums up the uses of diversity by saying that the point is not to love one another, or die, since in that case we are doomed. Instead, the point is to know one another, and live with difference. Of course, we may not come to desire to be like others, but Geertz suggests that "we must learn to grasp what we cannot embrace."[24] That is, we must at least try to understand the significance of the otherness, and how the foreign practices are acceptable to others even if we could not participate in them ourselves. Geertz's sentiment here is an admirable one, but there are at least two problems with it. One is whether understanding can remain as agnostic as Geertz implies. This objection is raised by Habermas to pluralism in general. The second problem is whether there are not some differences with which it would be impossible to live.

Let me discuss both problems in light of the example that Geertz raises as a counterexample to the complacency of ethnocentrism, a complacency that he fears will result from Rorty's explicit avowal of ethnocentrism. The case is one where an alcoholic Native American in the southwestern United States gets access to treatment on scarce artificial kidney machines, thereby excluding other patients who also needed dialysis. When he is told that the treatment will not work unless he stops drinking, he deliberately keeps on drinking and indeed dies in several years. The moral dilemma for the doctors arises from their being faced with someone who gets on the machine only so that he can drink a little longer before dying, thereby leading to earlier deaths for some other people who might have been socially more productive. What Geertz finds in this story is that neither the doctors nor the Native American gave up any of their commitments, but instead, they simply failed to understand each other, and "the whole thing took place in the dark."[25] Geertz himself believes that if the doctors had been better ethnographers, they would have appreciated that the drinking problem of the Native American may well have been a response to the ethnocentrism he had to face everyday in the mainstream of American society, an ethnocentrism that is indeed guilty of serious crimes toward Native tribes.

Rorty's response is to maintain that Geertz is obviously a better ethnographer than the doctors, but that the outcome of the case was the right one, so it cannot be faulted from the standpoint of either justice or morality. That is, it was right to leave the alcoholic on the machine once he was on it, since that was procedurally the just response. From the moral point of view, furthermore, there is no command that the doctors love or empathize with their patients, only that they do the best that can be done to cure them. Finally, our society is not to be condemned for the physicians' failure to understand the Native American's position. Our society provides the anthropologists, the "connoisseurs of diversity," for precisely that task. Rorty thus thinks that liberal society can be praised for having both functions: "specialists in particularity" to draw attention to those whom society has failed to notice, and "guardians of universality" to treat everyone alike.[26]

This defense of liberal society may seem to put Rorty in Bloom's camp, but I hasten to add that there is a crucial difference. Whereas Bloom is a modern liberal, attacking ethnocentrism and defending the drive toward transcultural objectivity, Rorty is a postmodern one, attacking transcultural objectivity and defending ethnocentrism. This is not to say, however, that Rorty and hermeneutics deny objectivity altogether, since objectivity is possible within the conventional constraints of "normal" or nonanomalous discourses; what hermeneutics denies is only a particular philosophical picture of how objectivity is possible. Whereas Bloom thought it necessary to defend transcultural objectivity by pointing to human nature as a rational foundation for universal rights, and is thus a *modern* philosopher in the tradition of the enlightenment, Rorty thinks that philosophy is unable to provide the strong legitimations that are required by the appeal to transcultural criteria of rationality. Postmodern liberals have learned from anthropologists, historians, and novelists to go case by case: "we postmodernist bourgeois liberals," he says, "no longer tag our central beliefs and desires as 'necessary' or 'natural' and our peripheral ones as 'contingent' or 'cultural.'"[27] I draw attention to the words *central* and *peripheral* here, as they suggest that no belief is absolutely founded or permanently fixed. In principle, any can be moved from the center to the periphery or from the periphery to the center. Furthermore, there *are* beliefs that are central, so there are commitments that we would be loath to give up even if we did not think we could give absolutely convincing arguments for them. So the position is not nihilistic or relativistic, since there are commitments that are felt strongly to be "central."

The difference between the modern and the postmodern thus turns not only on different substantive values but even more pointedly on the philosophical metaquestion of whether rationality is cultural or transcultural. Rorty is an anti-anti-ethnocentrist because he wants to drop a hard and fast distinction between cultural bias and rational judgment, and more generally a sharp distinction between the necessary and the contingent. Rorty's anti-anti-ethnocentrism is really an attack more on enlightenment rhetoric than on enlightenment values:

> [Anti-anti-ethnocentrism] urges liberals to take with full seriousness the fact that the ideals of procedural justice and human equality are parochial, recent, eccentric, cultural developments, and then to recognize that this does not mean they are any the less worth fighting for. It urges that ideals may be local and culture-bound, and nevertheless be the best hope of the species.[28]

But Rorty's position is really not the same as simple ethnocentrism because he does not want to overcome diversity, and he recognizes the significance of otherness. Thus, the postmodern, unlike the defender of modernity and enlightenment objectivity, does not recommend "a philosophical outlook, a conception of human nature or of the meaning of human life, to representatives of other cultures."[29]

Universality versus Plurality

If both Geertz and Rorty are postmodern liberals, there is still some tension between their perceptions of whether to be anti-ethnocentrist, as Geertz is, or anti-anti-ethnocentrist, as Rorty is. Geertz thinks that Rorty's explicit defense of liberalism can lead to a complacency that might lead to an insensitivity to cultural diversity. Rorty's assessment is that cultural diversity is not an endangered species, and that liberalism is not a windowless monad but on the contrary, the outlook that is currently the most sensitive to the significance of otherness. Within hermeneutical philosophy, however, the more obvious debate is not between these two so much as between them and others who think that their rejection of rational, universal objectivity has led to a vacuous pluralism. As I mentioned, two philosophers who work within a hermeneutic framework but who object to this pluralism are Jürgen Habermas and Charles Taylor. Two others who are advocates of pluralism are Jacques Derrida and Michel Foucault. While ethnocentrism and multiculturalism have not been at the center of these thinkers' reflections (except for Taylor), let me apply their more general arguments to this issue, and draw some conclusions favoring a hermeneutical pluralism.

Habermas can be placed within the framework of hermeneutics because he acknowledges as a direct influence on his own theory the primacy given to understanding by the hermeneutical tradition from Dilthey to Heidegger and Gadamer.[30] His own thesis is that "reaching understanding is the inherent telos of human speech."[31] This claim goes beyond Heidegger and Gadamer, however, insofar as reaching understanding (*Verständigung*) means for him reaching agreement, and he gives "agreement" a special analysis. "Agreement" is the English translation for the German word *Einigung*, which carries the sense of becoming one. There are, of course, rational and irrational ways of becoming one, and Habermas does not mean that understanding is reached when people are forced to agree, or are brought up in a general like-mindedness. The telos of human speech is achieved not in all uses of language, but only in the special case of rational, uncoerced discussion that leads to consensus. However admirable Habermas's ideal is, it becomes problematic when he asserts that this special case of rational agreement is the "original mode" of language use, such that all other uses of language are "derived from" or logically dependent on it.

In this mode "the speech act of one person succeeds only if the other accepts the offer contained in it by taking (however implicitly) a 'yes' or 'no' position on a validity claim that is in principle criticizable."[32] Habermas thus offers a strong analysis of what is involved in rational understanding insofar as he claims that understanding the other entails either accepting or denying the other's assertions. There is no middle ground, such as abstention or agnosticism. Furthermore, it would seem that as long as people kept saying "no," they would not really be understanding one another since they had not reached agreement. In contrast to Habermas's position, then, Gadamer holds the more moderate position that understanding does not entail believing or assenting to the other's claims: "Whoever understands," he says, "does not need to say 'yes' to that which is understood."[33]

On this issue Michel Foucault is, I believe, more on Gadamer's side than on Habermas's. Foucault makes the admittedly more ambiguous remark, when asked about the Habermasian thesis on consensus, that "the farthest I would go is to say that perhaps one must not be for consensuality, but one must be against nonconsensuality."[34] I take this assertion as indicating that when confronted by someone with different views, there is some need to overcome apparent disagreement by trying to see why there is divergence. But this movement toward understanding need not entail the formation of a single stance or an ideal consensus. Being "for consensuality" Foucault believes to be dangerous if it leads to an inability to understand and thus to tolerate divergence.

Because hermeneutical philosophy starts from the idea of understanding arising within a particular context, it is sometimes accused of seeing interpretation as a process of taking what at first seems strange or incomprehensible and turning it into something familiar. A central tenet of hermeneutics comes from Heidegger's phrasing of the hermeneutic circle: "Any interpretation which is to contribute understanding, must already have understood what is to be interpreted."[35] However, a crucial point that follows from Heidegger's analysis is that we are not always aware of how our own prejudgments are influencing our interpretations, so we must try to make our own self-understanding as problematic as that which we are interpreting. So hermeneutics is not the one-sided task of making the strange familiar. A good reading will often make what we at first take in a text as familiar seem strange. The confrontation with cultural diversity is one way in which to make us aware of our self-understanding, since it highlights and questions features that for the most part we take for granted and barely notice. Geertz thus praises ethnography for showing us that "the sovereignty of the familiar impoverishes everyone."[36] Gadamer thinks that the same result can come through the confrontation with the alienness of past texts, including those that have become the canonical classics and thus that might seem so familiar to us as to have become second nature. He thus explicitly distances himself from Schlegel's ironic "axiom of familiarity," which reads, "things must always have been just as they are for us, for things are naturally like this."[37] Gadamer criticizes historians who never let the texts of the past call their own knowledge into question. Gadamer does not say so, but he might be able to accept deconstruction as practiced by Derrida and others as an appropriate method for maximizing such strangeness. Alternatively, Foucault's archaeological and genealogical methods are intended to estrange us from the present by getting us to see what we take to be *necessary* features of the present as historically *contingent*.

Within the hermeneutical camp, then, there is disagreement on what is required to speak of successful understanding. Habermas's conception of the role of philosophy is that philosophy must explain how "the requirement of objectivity is to be satisfied," and the way to do this is to work out a theory of rationality and show it to be *"universally valid."*[38] Gadamer's failure to satisfy the "requirement of objectivity" can be seen, Habermas believes, in Gadamer's inability to account for the case of anthropology. For Habermas Gadamer is too confined to the model of textual interpretation, where there is a *prima facie* duty to assume that when there is divergence between the text and the interpreter, the text must be right or must at least be reconstructible to emerge as the correct account:

> In opposition to this [says Habermas] stands the anthropologist's experience that the interpreter by no means always assumes the position of a subordinate in relation to a tradition. To understand the Zande belief in witches satisfactorily, a modern interpreter would have to reconstruct the learning processes that separate us from them and that could explain wherein mythical and modern thought differ. Here the task of interpretation expands to what is actually the theoretical task of discovering patterns of development of rationality structures. Only a systematic history of rationality would keep us from falling into sheer relativism or naively positing our own standards as absolute.[39]

So if we are to avoid the alternatives of relativism or ethnocentrism, philosophy for Habermas must project a universally valid theory of rationality. Of course, Habermas's philosophy thus comes to a point that resembles ethnocentrism insofar as both posit "our own standards [of rationality and objectivity] as absolute." However, the difference is presumably that ethnocentrism does so naively, and Habermas does so legitimately by giving an empirically testable theory of stages of rational and moral development (which Habermas derives from Piaget and Kohlberg).

This appeal to an evolutionary theory of development gives pause to many who might otherwise agree with Habermas about the need for a universal theory of rationality to avoid both relativism and ethnocentrism. One might fear that ethnocentrism is already built into developmental theories like Kohlberg's. One could therefore try to work out the universal theory of rationality without the "systematic history of rationality." However, these moderns would still have to convince the postmoderns that the philosophical project of demonstrating a universal theory of transcultural rationality could succeed, or that it would do so without results that were only procedural and so thin as hardly to apply.

Since the postmoderns do not have a knockdown argument that such a universal theory could not be constructed, the issue is still an open one, and can be debated only as particular constructions of a theory of universal rationality come along. One candidate for a solution comes from Charles Taylor, in his essay "Understanding and Ethnocentricity."[40] On Taylor's view Gadamer's notion of a fusion of horizons is on the right track, so long as it avoids the one-sidedness of ethnocentrism. Taylor agrees with the hermeneutical view that understanding always starts from one's own context. Taylor has also been a critic of objectivistic social science that disregards other peoples' self-understandings in the explanation of their behavior. But Taylor disagrees with the view (associated with Peter Winch) that proper understanding must go entirely native and get completely inside the other point of view to the extent that criticism becomes impossible. For Taylor, as for Habermas, criticism must be possible, but Taylor adds that *self*-criticism must be possible as well. That is, our interaction with others might lead us to see our own standpoint as deficient in certain ways, and thus it might lead us to compensate by trying to alter our comportment. He would thus agree with Geertz that a principle use of diversity is to get us to see ourselves better, and to *make* ourselves better as well.

Taylor's response to the anthropological problem of understanding the tribal belief in magic is thus different from Habermas's. Habermas suggests that we will have to see these magical beliefs as an earlier stage of cognitive development than our own scientific one. Taylor suggests that although right now we may have to see our scientific beliefs as correct and their magical ones as incorrect, we might also come to understand exactly how our standpoint is different from theirs, and what the advantages and disadvantages of both are. Thus, he thinks that although we have made clear gains by separating the task of gaining knowledge about nature from the task of being in harmony with nature, tasks that were not differentiated in the tribal practice of magic, we might come to admire their greater harmony with nature and try to achieve it again for ourselves.

On Taylor's account, then, we try to understand the natives in their own terms, but we also have to understand them in our terms as well. But although we use our own terms, we are not condemned to ethnocentrism because our own language does not remain unchanged. What happens, he believes, is that a new language is created, a "language of perspicuous contrast," one that includes both "their" language as well as "our" old language and assesses each against the other.

This solution is tempting because it accommodates Geertz's sense that understanding diversity leads to altered self-understanding. At the same time it accommodates Habermas's insistence that the anthropologist be able to criticize the other culture. However, Taylor's model does not completely escape the worry of ethnocentrism, I believe, because finally it is still "we" who speak the new language of perspicuous contrast. While we can recognize its advantages over our old one, it does not thereby automatically seem more objective and less culture-bound. Taylor does not say so, but his model suggests that this formation of a language of perspicuous contrast is a step in the direction of a rationality that could become transculturally universal. To me it suggests a residual belief that the multiple prior languages will *converge* in a single language of perspicuous contrast.[41] A contrast could not be perspicuous, after all, unless it were seen from a "higher," "better" perspective, or a greater, "objective" distance. So Taylor's reliance on the traditional metaphorics of light, with terms like clear-sighted, clairvoyant, and perspicuous is what leads me to suspect that he thinks of these languages as converging, and thus of plurality and diversity being dialectically synthesized in a more encompassing, unified language with greater consensus. Of course, Taylor is writing from within the hermeneutical tradition, and does not advocate the neo-Hegelian goal of attaining final closure through absolute knowledge. Hermeneutics will thus not be able to buy wholeheartedly the metaphorics of light and truth, given the hermeneutical tenet that understanding can never make its background practices fully transparent. So if perspicuity is gained, it is always only partial, and can never validate the whole by making the whole completely transparent to itself.

Anyone working within the hermeneutic tradition, I must stress, will need to be suspicious of the enlightenment ideal of rational convergence, an ideal that suggests that plurality and diversity must finally be comprehended in a higher, single, unifying whole. To postmoderns this ideal is illusory, and I will try to give some reasons why it might plausibly appear so. Consider the case of anthropology again, but recognize that anthropologists are more often in the situation today of Geertz when he recently returned to Bali. He found on his return many years later that the once apparently pure culture had become a curious and perhaps incomprehensible mingling of traditional Balinese and modern "Western" practices. Included in his visit were encounters with other anthropologists. However, these anthropologists were not "Westerners," but members of the cultures studied and analyzed by earlier Western anthropologists. As one might expect, these anthropologists, who had grown up reading these earlier Western accounts, often had different understandings of their cultures than the Western anthropological ones.

This example suggests to me one practical difficulty with Taylor's model of the formation of a synthesizing language of perspicuous contrast. Who is to say that there is only *one* such language formed? Why is it not more likely that the "other" who is studied, who is after all not a mute object but a significant, signifying being, also forms a language of perspicuous contrast? I see no argument, furthermore, to suggest that these two languages of perspicuous contrast will necessarily converge. Each of the new languages will appear to itself as perspicuous, but one of them will still be "ours" and not "theirs."

Does this outcome imply that hermeneutical philosophy condemns us to ethnocentrism? To answer this question, and to come to my conclusion, I can now state more clearly what I think is pernicious about ethnocentrism. There are two claims that seem to imply ethnocentrism, but only one seems to me to be pernicious. The first is the hermeneutical claim that understanding always arises from within a particular context, culture, or tradition. Because self-understanding can never make the background practices completely translucent, it will always carry with it much of this context. The second claim is that understanding always entails agreement and convergence. I think that the first claim is right, but I find the second claim doubtful. Of course, even if one accepts the second claim, it would not necessarily be ethnocentrist if it were possible that the agreement might come about by "going native," with "us" giving up most of our beliefs and going over to "theirs." Given the first claim, however, which implies that we cannot alter most of what we take as true, the second claim really means that for the most part we expect "them" to converge on and agree with "us," and not the other way around.

So if these two claims are held in conjunction, ethnocentrism of a pernicious sort may well result. Now we can see, furthermore, what contributes the pernicious element. If I am right that the first claim is not by itself pernicious, then it is the second claim that is suspect. But the second claim became suspect only when the expectation became explicit that the convergence would have to be on "our" standpoint and not on that of the other. What seems pernicious is thus the thought that genuine understanding results only when there is *convergence* on our understanding. So what seems regrettably ethnocentric is not the hermeneutic view that understanding always arises from and is tied to a specific culture or tradition, but the additional, antihermeneutic requirement of convergence on the one objective standpoint, with the expectation of that standpoint being our own.

COROLLARIES

With this conclusion I hope to have clarified some of the current debate about ethnocentrism and multiculturalism. Let me now try to put this clarification to use by reflecting briefly on some corollaries. Specifically, I want to say more about two concepts that featured in my discussions: language and self-criticism.

One thing that my discussion of these various essays on ethnocentrism and objectivity may have shown is that the problem of pernicious ethnocentrism often arises inadvertently from the same concepts used with the intention of avoiding ethnocentrism. Thus, I suggested that the notion of horizon was misleading in Gadamer's argument, since it invariably suggests the closed horizon model that he explicitly wanted to avoid. Similarly, although Taylor thought that a model using the notion of language instead of the phenomenological notion of horizon would clarify the discussion, that notion of language is also misleading. When we start to use language as a count noun (for instance, in distinguishing "our" language from "theirs"), we seem to fall back into the model of languages as clearly demarcated entities. The notion of "a language" thus does not move the discussion beyond the problems raised by the notion of "a horizon." Furthermore, as Donald Davidson has argued, "there is no such thing as a language, not if a language is anything like what many philosophers and linguists have supposed."[42] So if Davidson is right, Taylor may be making a mistake in thinking that one can individuate languages in the way his argument presupposes. By a language Taylor means our expressions of our beliefs and desires, and what is at stake is divergence between our practices and those of other cultures. To think of all these as enclosed in something called "a language" adds only a metaphysical supposition that somehow all our practices must form a singular, cohesive unity. If Geertz is right, a closer ethnographical reading of ourselves should make us skeptical about such a degree of unity. Correlatively, we may have to avoid making a metaphysical supposition about the autonomy and unity of cultural contexts, given our crowded, postmodern world.

If we gave up the assumption of the necessary coherence and unity of our own ways of existing in the world, and allowed for the fractures, multiplicities, and tensions in our individual selves and in our social existence, perhaps we could be more understanding of these when we find them in other people's modes of existence as well. This thought leads me to question the importance placed by philosophers like Habermas on the ability to *criticize* other cultures. There is obviously tension between Geertz and Habermas on this point, since Geertz, and perhaps Gadamer, do not agree with this claim that cultures must be rationally assessed and criticized. These pluralists believe that there is no standpoint from which an entire culture can be criticized; at most some particular practices will be recognized as ones that we could not practice ourselves.

Now Habermas too admits that an entire society cannot be praised or condemned as a whole. Presumably criticism on his account could only be piece-meal. The pluralists might add that perhaps *all* that could really be expected is criticism of ourselves. The pluralists might even allow for appeals to objectivity in such self-criticism, since such appeals would no longer seem to serve as an ethnocentric billy club as they do when used in criticizing others. That is, we can understand how we might be moved to change some of our beliefs and practices if we came to understand ourselves better or more objectively (perhaps through seeing how others differed from us). But we would not know how to change our entire mode of life. So if criticism of other cultures means simply that we cannot condone some of their practices and cannot imagine ourselves going over to those practices, that is only a point about ourselves. It cannot be a blanket condemnation of another culture. The most that we could hope for through criticism of others would be that they would change some of their practices, especially those that were not tolerative of our practices and did not allow for our mutual coexistence.

Such criticism of self and others might thus appeal to the need for tolerance, but tolerance is possible without the universal consensus posited by highly abstract conceptions of rationality from Kant through Habermas. Tolerance may indeed be likely to follow more from mutually recognizing that we are never likely to share all of one another's beliefs than from forcing everyone to accept the same set. We recognize the significance of otherness, I believe, not by overcoming it in the higher synthesis of universal consensus, but in the pluralism of tolerant diversity.

NOTES

1. Allan Bloom, *The Closing of the American Mind* (New York: Simon & Schuster, 1987), 41. More recently, see his essay, "Western Civ," in *Giants and Dwarfs: Essays 1960-1990* (New York: Simon & Schuster, 1990), 13-31.

2. Bloom, *The Closing of the American Mind*, 36.

3. Bloom, *Giants and Dwarfs*, 22-23.

4. Bloom, *The Closing of the American Mind*, 36-37.

5. Ibid., 39.

6. Bloom, *Giants and Dwarfs*, 28.

7. Ibid., 27.

8. Different definitions of value relativism are possible, but I am using the term specifically for the view that each culture has its own set of values, and that each one is equally viable. What is relativistic in this view is the suggestion that there is no way to judge another culture negatively. Of course, relativism is always paradoxical, and here the problem is how a culture can continue to value as it does when it allows for the possibility of another culture valuing differently. The next section will show that before worrying about relativism, we should first ask whether the picture of cultures that seems to lead to these issues is correct. If the picture of cultures can be changed, the conceptual paradoxes about relativism may no longer be applicable.

9. For a survey of hermeneutical responses to the problems of objectivity see my article, "Hermeneutics," *Social Research*, XLVII (4)(1980): 649-671.

10. Clifford Geertz, "The Uses of Diversity" (The Tanner Lecture on Human Values, University of Michigan, November 8, 1985), *Michigan Quarterly Review* (Winter 1986): 105-123; p. 112.

11. Ibid., 114.

12. Ibid., 105.

13. Ibid., 112.

14. Ibid., 121.

15. Hans-Georg Gadamer, *Truth and Method*, 2nd rev. ed., Joel Weinsheimer and Donald G. Marshall, trans. (New York: Crossroad, 1989), 304.

16. Geertz, "The Uses of Diversity," 112.

17. Geertz, "Anti Anti-Relativism," *American Anthropologist*, 86 (June 1984): 263-278; p. 265.

18. Geertz, "The Uses of Diversity," 110.

19. Gadamer, *Truth and Method*, 305.

20. "Cosmopolitan" is to be taken, I believe (although Geertz does not specifically mention this reference), in Kant's sense of the ideal historical end state where perpetual peace is attained because people transcend their particular affiliations and identify with one another globally, with all being alike; Kant posited a league of nations, and Geertz's reference to UNESCO also suggests a strategy of the United Nations to bring about a world agreeing on fundamental questions about what is just, rational, decent, or beautiful. See Immanuel Kant, "Idea for a Universal History from a Cosmopolitan Point

of View," in *Kant on History*, Lewis White Beck, ed. (Indianapolis: Bobbs-Merrill, 1963): 11–26.

21. Geertz, "The Uses of Diversity," 114.

22. Ibid., 110.

23. Ibid., 120.

24. Ibid., 122.

25. Ibid., 117.

26. Richard Rorty, "On Ethnocentrism: A Reply to Clifford Geertz," *Michigan Quarterly Review* (Summer 1986): 525–534; p. 529.

27. Ibid., 531.

28. Ibid., 532.

29. Ibid., 533.

30. See Jürgen Habermas, *The Theory of Communicative Action: Vol. 1. Reason and the Rationalization of Society*, Thomas McCarthy, trans. (Boston: Beacon Press, 1984), 107.

31. Ibid., 287.

32. Ibid., 287.

33. Hans-Georg Gadamer, "Replik," in *Hermeneutik und Ideologiekritik* (Frankfurt: Suhrkamp, 1971), 283–317; p. 313.

34. Michel Foucault, "Politics and Ethics: An Interview," in *The Foucault Reader*, Paul Rabinow, ed. (New York: Pantheon, 1984), 373–380; p. 379.

35. Martin Heidegger, *Being and Time*, John Macquarrie and Edward Robinson, trans. (New York: Harper & Row, 1962), 194 (German page 152). For an account of Heidegger's hermeneutical theory of understanding see my essay, "Heidegger and the Hermeneutic Turn," in *The Cambridge Companion to Heidegger*, Charles B. Guignon, ed. (Cambridge: Cambridge University Press, 1993), 170–194.

36. Geertz, "The Uses of Diversity," 119.

37. Gadamer, *Truth and Method*, 361.

38. Habermas, *The Theory of Communicative Action*: Vol. 1, 137.

39. Ibid., 134–135.

40. Charles Taylor, "Understanding and Ethnocentricity," *Philosophy and the Human Sciences: Philosophical Papers 2* (Cambridge: Cambridge University Press, 1985), 116–133.

41. Professor Theodore R. Schatzki suggested to me that convergence can go in different directions, and thus there can be different convergences for different interactions. He thus reads Taylor as being closer to Gadamer on the movement of understanding over time, and as being more pluralistic than my own reading suggests. But my stronger reading at least shows some difficulties in Taylor's model that would need to be explained and that pose difficulties for his way of picturing cultural contrasts on pages 125–126 of "Understanding and Ethnocentricity."

42. Donald Davidson, "A Nice Derangement of Epitaphs," in *Truth and Interpretation: Perspectives on the Philosophy of Donald Davidson*, Ernest LePore, ed. (Oxford: Basil Blackwell, 1986), 433–446; p. 446.

8

Objectivity and Rationality

THEODORE R. SCHATZKI

For many thinkers, objectivity is a property of ideas, propositions, thought systems, and the like. An entity of one of these sorts is objective if it is an accurate, or intersubjectively acceptable, representation of the world. So conceived, objectivity is more or less identical with truth, and its other is falsity or opinion. Objectivity can also, however, be thought of as a property of individuals and groups. On this rendition, it is people and communities that are objective or nonobjective, and what they say and think that is true or false.[1] On this conception, moreover, humans are objective or not by virtue of their behavior: how they proceed, think, question, form beliefs, adopt ideas, and so forth. The other of objectivity becomes injudiciousness and willfulness. Furthermore, certain sometimes presumed relations among truth, objectivity, and their others cease to hold. No longer, for instance, does objectivity guarantee truth, and willfulness falsity. A person can act objectively and yet accept false ideas. Similarly, he or she might proceed in the most arbitrary fashion and still arrive at truth. If these possibilities seem obvious, remember that the conflation of truth and objectivity in many discussions has obscured them.

This chapter treats objectivity as a property of persons and their communities. Its first task is to analyze objectivity so understood as a cluster of intellectual virtues. The bulk of my discussion, however, concerns the relations of rationality to these virtues, with special attention to the realm of social investigation. Mine is not an Aristotelian concern with rationality as constitutive of virtue. Rather, I argue that there are other types of especially close ties between objectivity and rationality. Not only does being an objective social investigator require keen awareness of rationality, but objectivity and rationality coincide in the case of certain practices, paradigmatically those investigating social life.

OBJECTIVITY: AN INTELLECTUAL VIRTUE

Widespread convergence exists today concerning the nature of objectivity *qua* property of the cognizing individual or community. This convergence is partially veiled because participating writers often contribute to it under rubrics other than objectivity. To indicate the contours of the emergent consensus, I will review the well-known work of two scholars, one each from the continental and analytic traditions in contemporary philosophy.

Hans-Georg Gadamer provides the exemplary discussion in continental thought. His analysis of hermeneutic experience in *Truth and Method*[2] starts off from Heidegger's conception of understanding as a constitutive structure of human existence (as opposed to one cognitive operation among others). A key feature of understanding so construed is historicity. Gadamer concretizes Heidegger's notion of the "throwness" of human life into tradition with the idea that understanding is both constituted and made possible by preunderstandings that are acquired from the traditions in which a person is brought up. Prejudgements provide the context that not only makes it possible to have a view on/of something, but that also helps form the views thereby opened up. It is impossible, consequently, to have an understanding free from pre-understanding. The enlightenment ideal of freedom from prejudice is illusory as a result. Understanding is a development of tradition that occurs whenever a historically constituted individual interprets an object, text, person, or action, access to which is mediated by a past tradition of interpretation.

The historicity of understanding problematizes the "scientistic" conception of objectivity according to which (1) a person is objective when his or her knowledge-gathering apparatus functions correctly, and (2) this apparatus functions correctly when everything particular about the knower is bracketed and cognition merely mirrors the world. The historicist school in late 19th-century German historiography, for example, claimed both that correctly understanding a past era requires the historian to project himself back into that era, and that doing this requires that he bracket his attitudes, opinions, and personality, lest the mirror-like projective apprehension be contaminated by something of himself. For Gadamer, this ideal is not only mistaken, but self-defeating. To bracket oneself, to eliminate all prejudgments, is to annihilate understanding itself. If understanding a past era means projecting oneself into it, what must be projected is *oneself*.

What, then, becomes of objectivity? Is all understanding subjective or illusory? Such a conclusion might be warranted when objectivity is taken as a property of understanding. But when it is viewed as a property of the understander, certain ways of being and acting can qualify a person as objective. One cardinal mark of objectivity is striving to become conscious of the prejudgments forming one's understanding. Although accomplishing this is a difficult and never fully attainable task, there is a difference between those who try and those who do not, between those who are capable and inclined and those who are incapable or disinclined to acquire self-knowledge when the opportunity arises. The more a person strives to become aware of his or her preunderstandings, the more objective he or she is.

A related mark of objectivity is the willingness to revise or abandon prejudgments when they obstruct understanding. Gadamer distinguishes between legitimate and illegitimate prejudgments. Even without detailing his account, the appropriateness of the distinction is obvious. Some of our ideas about past eras and other peoples clearly conflict with what was or is going on in those eras or with those peoples. Dogged adherence to these ideas would obviously obstruct satisfactory understanding. The bald misunderstandings many people have had of one another throughout history clearly differ from the more successful efforts of myriad explorers, travelers, and anthropologists to appreciate the peoples they encounter away from home. This is so regardless of the difficulties bedeviling the analysis of satisfactory understanding and the abundant instances in which the distinction between adequate and inadequate preunderstandings is not clear-cut.

Widespread agreement exists today on these marks of objectivity. In contemporary anthropology, for instance, numerous writers call upon ethnographers to include detailed self-descriptions in their texts. This call mirrors pleas heard in other disciplines for authors to preface their works with clear declarations of perspective. Gadamer offers additional marks of objectivity, which apply in the first place to the human sciences alone and do not command universal assent even there. To be objective, he suggests, an interpreter must be (1) open to learn something from the object under interpretation and (2) able to question and to carry out a conversation with that object in doing so. These claims arise from his more specific analyses of what is involved in understanding. In brief: Understanding X is grasping X's meaning, where its meaning is what it has to say, the truth it expresses about some subject matter. To grasp the truth X expresses about something is to learn something. Hence, understanding X is a learning experience, in which one rises to a more insightful and comprehensive vantage point that corrects and relativizes one's previous understanding of some subject matter. The more receptive one is to learn something from the object of interpretation, the more objective one is. Gadamer goes on to analyze being open to learning experiences as a matter of being able to pose questions to and to carry on a conversation with the interpretand. Possessing and utilizing these capacities is thus a further mark of objectivity.

Obvious difficulties attend the application of the latter claims about questioning and conversation to objects such as actions, events, and even texts. Nonetheless, it seems to me that, apart from these more specific claims, Gadamer's perspective does capture what objectivity consists in when the goal is to understand other people, whether they be the compatriots encountered in daily life or the foreigners met in distant neighborhoods or lands. To be objective is to be aware of one's prejudgments about the people one seeks to comprehend; to be willing to correct or abandon these judgments when they obstruct understanding; to be open to learning something from hitherto unfamiliar or incomprehensible outlooks; and to engage in dialogue in a sincere and evenhanded manner with those one wishes to understand. Even when one aims merely to observe and measure, and not also to interact with the subjects studied (assuming this is possible), objectivity still requires the first two of these virtues.

Hence, in Gadamer's view objectivity is a set of virtues, or character traits. A parallel view is found in the work of Thomas Kuhn.[3] What makes the parallel possible is Kuhn's celebrated shift from a philosophy of science concerned with the logic of scientific investigation to one emphasizing science as a form of activity. In Kuhn's eyes, scientists are united into communities by "disciplinary matrixes," sets of shared beliefs, theories, judgments, skills, paradigms, values, and languages. Kuhn famously maintains, further, that the history of a scientific discipline exhibits a succession of dominant scientific systems, each defined by a different disciplinary matrix. The transition from one dominant system to the next is characterized as a "revolution," in which a more or less complete changeover occurs in the reigning beliefs, skills, paradigms, and so on.

It is not necessary to explore the complexities and nuances of Kuhn's picture to extract his view of objectivity. For many readers, Kuhn's picture is a relativistic one, in which "incommensurable" systems of thought and action succeed one another without it being possible to judge the superiority or inferiority of an ascendent system vis-à-vis its predecessors. Particularly galling to some commentators is Kuhn's use of such expressions as "conversion" and "gestalt switches" to describe the process/experience in which scientists' allegiances migrate from one system to the next. To many, this suggests that changes in scientists' beliefs, and successions in dominant systems, are irrational, uncontrollable processes in which anything goes. This is not, however, Kuhn's view. He claims, instead, that a scientist, in evaluating scientific ideas and hence the merits and demerits of different scientific systems, employs a host of standards such as scope, simplicity, fruitfulness, and accuracy of predictions. Where Kuhn does contravene the dominant "scientific method" account of science (for which scientific activity serves as the paradigm of rationality) is in holding (1) that a given scientist, using different standards, might evaluate one and the same system differently, and (2) that different scientists might reach different conclusions about one and the same theory when employing the same standard. There is ample room for evaluative disagreement among scientists, and not only among those adhering to different systems. So there is no sure-fire scientific method, only fallible human beings making risky judgments from a variety of points of view. To counter accusations of extreme relativity and even nihilism, Kuhn adds that natural languages, along with cultural ideas and practices, constitute metalanguages and metaperspectives that ensure that scientists can understand and rationally discuss one another's diverging ideas and evaluations—even though disagreements might remain ineliminable.[4]

In sum, Kuhn portrays science as a bundle of activities, which are embedded in wider forms of sociohistorical continuity, in which rational argumentation takes place by reference to disparate values and concepts, and in which people are able to grasp, discuss, and dispute one another's viewpoints without thereby being converted. On this picture, evaluating scientific ideas and systems requires the scientist to be open, dexterous, evenhanded, experimenting, and reflective. Accordingly, although Kuhn does not highlight objectivity, the following characterization of it emerges from his work: To be objective is, first, to be open to opposing viewpoints, arguments, and judgments; second, to be able and willing to consider, weigh, and balance them; and, third, to be prepared for conversion to a different viewpoint through a preponderance of considerations and evidence. The only dimension of Gadamer's account absent from this characterization is seeking knowledge of one's preunderstanding (the beliefs, worldviews, and criteria relied on but not explicit in one's work). The compatibility of this idea with the Kuhnian perspective is, however, obvious.

Again, I believe that a view such as this is acceptable to a broad range of thinkers today. This is especially true of those who, following Kuhn, stress the social dimension of scientific work. Helen Longino, to take one example, writes that a scientific community is objective if, among other things, it recognizes avenues of, has shared standards for, and is responsive to criticism.[5] The Gadamerian–Kuhnian flavor of this characterization is obvious.

I conclude that objectivity *qua* property of the cognizing subject is a relatively unproblematic notion. It involves self-knowledge, openness to change, and the capacity to learn. It is a property that can characterize the natural scientist, the social investigator, and the friend, though the more specific forms it takes in these and other cases vary. Its possession, moreover, does not imply the possession of truth. Objectivity is a way of being, truth a property of beliefs. In the remainder of this chapter I will discuss why objectivity has an intimate connection with rationality, especially in social inquiry.

INTELLIGIBILITY AND RATIONALITY

Discussions of rationality are clouded by the multiplicity of understandings people have of it and by the plurality of types of objects to which it is ascribed (e.g., actions, practices, institutions, persons, beliefs, and preferences). This is not surprising given the centrality of the concept/phenomenon in Western life and thought and the tendency for pivotal notions in all traditions to undergo varied interpretations. My analysis focuses on actions and practices alone. Moreover, it outlines a "broad" or "thick" conception of rational actions and practices, one that differentiates them from the closely related phenomenon of intelligible actions and practices.

An action or practice is intelligible if it makes sense *that* the actor or actors perform it. What someone does "makes sense" if (1) it arouses no perplexity or incomprehension when encountered or learned about, or (2) whatever perplexity and incomprehension it has previously occasioned has been eliminated. This characterization leaves open why actions fail to arouse perplexity and which interpretations dissolve incomprehension. Moreover, it prescinds, from requiring that those understandings that render actions and practices intelligible be true, undistorted, or nonillusionary. Not prerestricting the possible causes and content of intelligibility avoids begging crucial questions and introducing veiled norms. In particular, I see no reason to maintain that an action is intelligible only when one's understanding of it is in some sense "accurate." An action or practice is intelligible when its becoming the object of attention does not occasion hesitation or breakdown in ongoing activities.

An action or practice is rational, on the other hand, if it makes sense *to* perform it. Here the issue is not whether it makes sense that people do it, but whether, given the circumstances, doing it was a sensible course of action. I do not think, however, that the notion of its making sense to X can be further analyzed as the notion of X's making sense just was. What it is for it to make sense to perform a given action or practice varies among contexts and cannot be comprehensively spelled out in a formula. I do think that its making sense to perform an action quite often amounts to the action's being intelligent, appropriate, and responsible in the circumstances. On those occasions, an attribution of rationality implies the possession of these three attributes. Not every action, however, that possesses these attributes is one that it makes sense to perform; for reasons that will become clear shortly, voting behavior is a perspicuous example. But, although the concept/phenomenon of rationality does not coincide with that of intelligence, appropriateness, plus responsibility, the two sets greatly overlap. I will therefore sometimes write below as if an action is rational if and only if it possesses these three features.

When it makes sense to perform an action or practice, it follows that, had one been the actor oneself or one of the actors in question, then that action or practice would have been a way of proceeding recommended for oneself. Herein lies a key difference between intelligibility and rationality. Intelligibility requires only that one's understanding of something not occasion problems. Rationality demands endorsement of the action in the sense of acknowledging its propriety.[6] When evaluating intelligibility, a person sets aside his or her commitments to particular ideas, rules, customs, and ends and judges whether what people do either fits somewhere into or smoothly extends the known mosaic of human existences. (For theoretically minded observers, intelligibility might consist more particularly in subsuming what people do under a theory of human life.) When ascertaining rationality, on the other hand, a person cannot bracket his or her deep-seated commitments to particular ideas, rules, ends, and the like (cf. the voting behavior referred to in the previous paragraph). For it is possible to judge whether it made sense to perform a particular action only on the background of these commitments. If actors' commitments contravene one's own, what they do might be intelligible, given their commitments, but it cannot be rational.

Because judgments of sensibleness rest unavoidably on the judger's large-scale commitments, in particular on the ways of being that he or she desires or finds valuable,[7] rationality is relative to the judger. This is also true, of course, of intelligibility, although for different reasons. Intelligibility is relative to the judger because it is defined in relation to his or her understanding, and because whether and as what an action or practice proves intelligible depends on his or her knowledge of human beings and of the variability of human lives.

The distinction between intelligibility and rationality differs from that between thin and broad rationality as employed by Jon Elster and his followers.[8] For Elster, an action is thinly rational when it follows from the agent's (consistent) beliefs, commitments, desires, and so on, and broadly rational when the relevant beliefs, commitments, and desires are themselves rational. My notion of intelligibility obviously parallels his notion of thin rationality. My rationality, however, differs from his broad rationality because finding an action to be rational, unlike finding it to be broadly rational, does not require judging that the actor's background commitments, beliefs, and so on are rational, that is, sensible. It requires only that one share much of the actor's background, irrespective of whether one thinks that particular background "elements" are irrational or nonrational. Broad rationality is thus in one sense a more demanding notion than rationality as I construe it. This is because broad rationality is really a notion of a rational person, whereas intelligibility and rationality on my account (and thin rationality on Elster's) characterize actions and practices. To those who would suggest that there is no need for this second type of rational action, I reply that it offers a perspicuous analysis of the use, as applied to actions, of "rational," its cognates, *and its translations* in a broad variety of natural languages.

To summarize, both intelligibility and rationality can vary among individuals and groups, depending on the variability among them in sensitivity, power of empathy, knowledge, self-knowledge, commitments, intelligence, wisdom, and what is deemed valuable or desirable. Note, however, that variation in these matters is less than absolutist scaremongers sometimes suggest. Considerable commonality in the above characteristics factually exists among individuals and groups, even among those with different cultural backgrounds. As a result, people's judgments of intelligibility and rationality are widely similar. Differences obviously exist. But with the passage of time, human beings are increasingly finding one another intelligible, even while there is admittedly slower convergence in their appraisals of rationality.

MARKS OF RATIONALITY

I noted above that the objective person is conscious of his or her preunderstandings. Does objectivity also require that a person be aware of his or her grasp of rationality, of what he or she goes on in judging what it makes sense to do? Self-consciousness helps constitute objectivity because it fosters the identification and eradication of prejudgments that obstruct satisfactory understanding. An interpreter whose understanding and judgments of rationality affect his or her comprehension of people whose sense of rationality differs from his or her own, will most likely misunderstand or have difficulties making sense of them. Consequently, because judgments of rationality vary among individuals and peoples, it is incumbent upon an objective investigator to become aware of his or her own understanding of this matter. This conclusion is general in scope, but especially pertinent in social investigations whose object of study is people different from the investigator. I also maintained earlier that further character traits such as openness to learning and readiness to revise preunderstandings likewise help constitute objectivity, because unaddressed differences can inhibit satisfactory understanding. It follows, once again, that an individual who seeks objective understanding of others (paradigmatically the social investigator) must make explicit his or her understanding of rationality and the differences between that understanding and those of others.

Some writers, however, argue that rationality does not vary among peoples, indeed cannot. Given the ferocity of the disagreement on this issue, I need to make my relativism more precise and perspicuous and to combat several conceptions of the universal characteristics of rationality. I divide my discussion into two parts, one concerned with individual behavior and the other with social practices.

The Individual

An individual's actions are governed by a number of factors, including ideas and thoughts, moods and emotions, ends, projects, customs, rules (explicitly formulated directives and instructions), paradigms, and believed states of affairs. To say that sets of these factors govern the continuous being-directed-toward-and-performing of actions that pervades the stream of moment-to-moment existence is to say that such sets specify why, at a given moment in a particular situation, an actor performed a particular action. Note that an actor need not be aware of these factors in order for them to govern his or her action.

Any given action is governed by a set of such factors. For instance, it is because John seeks to please his mother and knows that she expects him to take out the trash, that he picks up the trash barrel and heads down the stairs. (For the purposes of this chapter, it is not necessary to take a stand on the causal nature or otherwise of this "because.") In each case, furthermore, we can ask whether the action is intelligible or rational. An action is intelligible when it coheres with the factors governing it, and rational when it can be endorsed given these factors. Practically all actions can be rendered intelligible. Even emotionally determined nonteleological behavior can be understood as following coherently from the emotions at work. Stubbornly unintelligible actions are performed mostly by people locked up in mental asylums. Even these actions, however, often prove intelligible when extensive effort is expended at comprehending them. Many actions, on the other hand, are not rational. One is often unable to endorse behavior as sensible, in particular as intelligent, proper, and responsible. This can work in many ways. One might not accept the believed state of affairs on which someone acted, one might think that pursuing a given end in a given situation was inane, one might not see the point of a given form of customary behavior, one might feel that a given rule does not apply in a given situation, and so on. Especially when emotions and moods are in play does it often not make sense to do what someone does. For instance, if John is scared of the demons living in the garage, he might leave the trash at the garage door. It does not make sense (to us adults) to do this, though of course it makes perfectly good sense *that* he acts so.

The very plurality of grounds on which actions can be judged not rational (or lower in rationality) indicates the likely variability in such judgments. Some writers have nonetheless insisted that certain marks automatically qualify an action as nonrational. The feature most prominent in 20th century thought has been noninstrumentality, the failure of an action to be a prudent, intelligent, or efficient means toward the end for which it is performed. Two other traditional marks of nonrationality are unquestioning adherence to tradition and susceptibility to emotion and passion.

In many, especially Western, traditions instrumentality, thoughtful grappling with tradition, and/or neutralization of emotions are signs of rational action. But other peoples (and perhaps Western women too) might deem otherwise. Traditional peoples often considered it intelligent, proper, and responsible to follow tradition unquestionably—for example, because this is how their ancestors did it. Western disapproval of this norm signals a different understanding of rationality, not greater rationality on our part. Similarly, for some peoples acting unemotionally would count as a perversity of human nature. Although I disagree, I see no reason to treat the dimming of emotions as more than a circumstantial mark of sensible ways of proceeding. Even lack of instrumentality is less than a universally wielded criterion of nonrationality. It is not hard to imagine cases in which instrumental action is an affront to good sense, the gods, the ancestors, or the holiness of nature. Indeed, such cases are not unknown in the West. Intelligent and efficient pursuit of personal ends, for instance, might not be at all what it makes sense to do in the presence of the archbishop, and not merely because unseeming behavior undermines their attainment.

It is worth pointing out that these claims do not succumb to the barrage of arguments Hilary Putnam once raised against the relativity of reason. For instance, I do not defend a "criterial" account of rationality according to which what is rational depends on the (institutionalized) norms of a given people.[9] Rationality is not relative to norms of any sort on my account, where norms are explicitly formulated directives or formulas. Judgments of rationality are instead the product of unformulable skills developed in the context of public practices of judging.[10] Many of Putnam's other past arguments do not directly contravene the position developed here, since they attack relativism about truth. It is worth mentioning, however, that the position survives the test of self-reflexivity. Against the Cultural Imperialist, who claims that a statement is true only if it satisfies the norms of modern European and North American culture, Putnam argues that this claim itself neither conforms to or contravenes such norms; no such norms decide the issue.[11] The claim, consequently, is false. I concur, and add that there are no modern European/North American norms according to which it is either rational or not rational to claim that the rationality of action can vary among cultures. After examining considerations and arguments pro and con, however, it can and does make sense to claim that this type of rationality varies. So the claim applies to itself. Notice that substituting "styles of reasoning" (*à la* Ian Hacking) for "norms" in Putnam's arguments undercuts the latter.

So the intelligibility and rationality of individual actions are relative to a cluster of features that can and do vary among individuals and peoples. Someone might respond that Western practices of judging what it makes sense to do are definitive of rationality. This move, though not incoherent, is nonetheless dangerous. It pries rationality away from the more general notion of its making sense to X. It also highlights a way of being that, at least until recently, was more strongly pursued in the West than in other locales. In itself innocent, this fact can become pernicious in conjunction with the Western valorization of rationality. Finally, this move ignores the fact that there is no unified "Western" understanding of rationality, that our own tradition is not a single voice, but rather a chorus of we's. It thus treats but one prominent strand in our own tradition as definitive of a singularly prized notion.

In any case, judgments of sense do vary among individuals and peoples. Moreover, while just about any action can with sufficient effort and insight, be rendered intelligible, especially when its sociocultural context is considered, this is far from the case vis-à-vis rationality. Hence, given this variability, the lack of guarantees of rationality, and the Western valorization of its specific understandings of what it makes sense to do, it is incumbent upon the objective interpreter of human affairs to become conscious of his or her judgments of rationality and the sorts of considerations on the basis and background of which he or she pronounces them.

Practices

Moving beyond the individual takes us to unclearly demarcated terrain. For some, it is the level of the collective or group, for others that of structures and systems. Discussions of rationality have scrutinized entities of both general sorts. Here, I want to examine a type of entity of the group/collective sort: practices. I do so, first, because I am generally suspicious of attributions of structure, function, and systemicity to social life, and second, because standard analyses of collective rationality construe collectivities too narrowly. Collective rationality is usually tied to collective decision-making involving a group of people who deliberately and knowingly reach decisions on matters affecting them. Although decision-making of this sort occurs extensively in social life, too many of the activities whose rationality has been impugned—for example, witchcraft—are neither the implementation nor the result of such processes. A more inclusive notion is needed for examining the rationality of a wider range of social entities.

By a "practice" I mean an interrelated, open-ended manifold of actions linked by actors' shared understandings. Although actions, in order to form a practice, need not possess any particular degree of interdependence, coordination, coherence, similarity, or agreement, those composing a practice will exhibit these features sufficiently to distinguish themselves from the sets of actions that form other practices. More importantly, the actors involved will share understandings about what they are doing and about the relations among their activities, for example, that and why particular actions are appropriate responses to others. Their agreement, however, need only be partial. Participants in a practice can have conflicting interpretations of it. Such conflict, however, occurs within a wider (although revisable) background of agreement concerning what the practice is and which actions generally belong to it.

Like actions, practices can be queried concerning intelligibility or rationality. Let me say a word about intelligibility before turning to rationality. Explaining why it makes sense that a group of people carries out a particular practice usually involves citing such general factors of their lives as widespread attitudes or goals, pervasive background practices in their society, general features of their environment, and propensities of human beings and groups generally. For instance, female infanticide in China might be understood by reference to attitudes toward women; Eskimo euthanasia by reference to an inhospitable natural environment; the maintenance of the U.S. military by reference to the human propensity to expand and defend territory and interests; and the pursuit of social science via modern society's need for self-knowledge and regulation, together with its esteem for systematic, methodic understanding. Other possible explanatory factors in this context include basic motivations toward the world, "limit" situations (e.g., birth, death, and sex), and universal cognitive interests.[12] Quite often, however, general factors of the above sorts are compatible with a range of practices, and/or which general features are relevant to a given practice is not obvious. The paradigm cases discussed in the literature—such as Azande witchcraft, Australian rain-making ceremonies, and the beliefs of Tully Valley Blacks—fall into this category. In such cases, there is no ready explanation of a practice's intelligibility.

It is with respect to livable practices that are difficult to understand that a host of ideas concerned with the limits of understanding find their greatest application. These ideas all suggest that understanding a strange but livable practice requires the interpreter to transcend him- or herself. Examples of such ideas are that cross-cultural understanding involves learning from (wisdom), and that it entails ceaseless striving toward greater universality through the synthesis and mutual adjustment of particular understandings.[13] In achieving such understanding, the strictest demands of objectivity are in order. Self-consciousness, openness to learning and revision, and the capacity to engage in dialogue in an evenhanded manner are character traits indispensable for the gradual appreciation of strongly particular practices.

Turning now to rationality, I stated above that there is no general mark of rational actions. Is there one of rational practices? I will approach this topic by examining several of the most prominent phenomena promoted in Western thought as criteria of rationality: instrumentality, consensus, reflexivity, and truth.

The most paramount of these putative criteria is instrumentality. A practice is rational if it achieves the end for which it is carried out, or more weakly, if it achieves something valued by its practitioners. This criterion applies to any practice that is carried out for an end. I call such practices "institutions." There are, I claim, two types of institutions.

The first are practices that people intentionally set up and implement for the purpose of realizing a particular end or valued phenomenon. The success of such an institution at realizing its guiding end usually qualifies it as intelligent and proper. (Failure, however, does not automatically certify it as not rational.) I say "usually" since, as widely noted, success achieved in unexpected ways might not reflect on either the rationality or nonrationality of the practice. Although the proportion of a people's practices that are institutions of this sort grows as people increasingly strive to plan and control their lives, vast numbers of practices are not institutions. This is just as true in modern Western society as in the most traditional and custom-bound times and places. Religion is a perspicuous example. Although the founders of religions may have had particular purposes for inaugurating them, subsequent expansion, development, and reinterpretation of religions' tenets and practices disassociates the latter from founding purposes. Religions today no longer have any clear end that they are intended to realize. They certainly have manifold effects, some of which are highly valued by practitioners. But it is the rare case in which they were initiated in order to achieve these effects.

The second type of institution embraces practices in which practitioners standardly pursue a particular end as part of carrying out the practice. Here, the pursuit of a particular end is immanent in the practice's "culture." At least most of its practitioners, consequently, pursue the goal and do so simply by virtue of their participation. This end differs from whatever ends (if any)the practice's founders might have intended be fulfilled, and it is probably not the only end individuals pursue in carrying out the practice. A good example of such a practice is social science. In being trained into, and as part of, this enterprise, social scientists pursue the end of better understandings of social life. They work, of course, for all sorts of other ends as well, such as power, prestige, control, and livelihood. At least most of them, however, share this particular end. Religion, to my mind, does not qualify as an institution of this second sort. There is no generally shared end that church members pursue as part of engaging in church activities.

Instrumentality can serve as a criterion of rationality only for institutions, since institutions alone among practices have ends. Of course, generations of social theorists have not only attributed ends to all sorts of practices, but also ascribed ones that differ from whatever ends either the practices were designed to serve or are actually pursued in common. Although I cannot discuss this topic here in depth, let me offer a few considerations against their efforts.

One consideration is the problem of identifying how many and which ends a given practice subserves. Functionalists tended to treat any "beneficial" effect resulting from a practice as an end of that practice. This penchant proliferated the number of ends that any practice pursues. Moreover, it runs counter to the notion of an end to maintain that any contingent beneficial effect of X counts as one of X's ends. Ends can only be that subset of a practice's effects that in some sense the practice "pursues," subserves, or by virtue of its design or structure is likely to produce. This requirement led to extended discussions of feedback loops, the idea being that an effect is an end if it so affects the practice producing it as to secure its own continued production.[14] Relatively few effects, however, satisfy this criterion. Furthermore, it proved difficult to differentiate "beneficial" effects from nonbeneficial ones. Benefit is something very much in the eye of the beholder, and attempts to define it in an allegedly neutral fashion in terms of contributions to system maintenance, equilibrium, or directional change soon confronted difficulties in applying the latter concepts to social life.[15] Defining ends in this manner also simply assumed without justification both that beneficial effects alone qualify as ends and that something's ends must be registered in its effects.

Another consideration is that practices need not have ends at all. This idea is familiar from the numerous analyses that, in opposition to the intellectualist construal of practices as goal-oriented activities, treat them instead as "expressions" of some attribute, orientation, or sentiment. For such theories, human beings not only pursue ends, but also act in ways that are essentially manifestations, embodiments, or articulations of human propensities, attitudes, orientations, and drives. One need not endorse the notion of an expression to agree that not all actions and practices are end-oriented. If, for instance, John, who is in a bad mood, berates his wife when she enters the kitchen, it might be that he does this not so as to achieve some end, but simply out of an irascible countenance toward the world. Someone could reply that because John might be unconsciously pursuing an end, it might remain appropriate to judge his behavior on the grounds of instrumentality. Although I do not deny this possibility, it would be dogmatic to insist that this is true of all nonovertly teleological behavior. In any case, neither this nor the related suggestion that groups unconsciously pursue ends can be further examined here.

A brilliant attempt to employ the instrumental versus expressive duality in interpreting practices is Charles Taylor's idea of a practice oriented toward a predifferentiated amalgam of instrumentality and expressivity.[16] On Taylor's analysis of the history of Western science, the distinction between the instrumental stance of attempting to control nature and the expressive attitude of being attuned with it did not exist in pre-Galilean science. Only after Galileo did the distinction manifest itself, and did so as a bifurcation of cultural practices. Prior to Galileo, science pursued an amalgamation of the not yet differentiated orientations. Taylor suggests that Azande witchcraft practices be analyzed similarly. In engaging in these practices, the Azande are out neither to control nature, as Sir James Frazer supposed, nor to become attuned with it, as analyses like those of Peter Winch and John Beattie would have it. Rather, they are out to attain both, or more exactly, to achieve some fusion of the alternatives not yet differentiated for them.

Taylor's analysis abets those who would crown instrumentality as a general mark of rationality, for it assures that some practices that seem to us uninstrumental and possibly "expressive" do nonetheless pursue control. It also, however, invokes a theory of history: that out of which something arises is a fusion of this phenomenon with other phenomena that similarly have yet to emerge as distinct. I believe we should think about history in line with a different theory that does not construe historical phenomena as present in amalgamated configurations prior to their emergence as distinct entities. On this theory, historical phenomena are something new. They arise, of course, out of previously existing phenomena, but do so by transcendence rather than by developmental differentiation. Pre-Galilean science is not an amalgamation of what follows it, but a prior, different thing from which there arises the differentiation, and hence the first existence (distinct or fused) of mastery-seeking scientific practices and attunement-expressing spiritual ones. This picture requires that the pre-Galilean stage be characterized in its own positive manner and not only as a synthesis, *pre ante*, of the two subsequent sets of practices. If we adopt this picture, orientation toward controlling nature may or may not be an aspect of the earlier stage. Whether it is, whether the earlier practice was end-oriented at all, and hence whether instrumentality is an appropriate mark of the rationality of pre-Galilean science or Azande witchcraft, are questions whose resolution requires specific analysis of these practices.

The fact that instrumentality marks the rationality of institutions alone severely restricts the scope of this criterion.[17] As I shall now show, however, instrumentality constitutes the context within which the next two putative criteria operate.

A second possible mark of a practice's rationality is consensus. Thinkers emphasizing that intellectual work is carried out by members of communities often view ideal consensuses or a community's capacity to engage in consensus-building activities as marks of objectivity, truth, or rationality. Their discussions usually focus on the formation of beliefs: a set of beliefs is deemed rational, roughly speaking, if it is formed consensually through dialogue. Lying behind this analysis are the ideas that rational beliefs are those that are well-grounded, and that well-grounded beliefs are those that survive group discussion. It is not much of a leap from here to the thought that groups and communities are rational if they are willing and able to engage in processes of dialogical, consensus-producing belief formation. I will discuss dialogue further below; let us first consider consensus alone.

How does the idea of consensus as a mark of rationality apply to practices? The most prominent approach is to say that a practice is rational if it permits and encourages the formation of consensuses. This idea is *prima facie* most plausible in the case of intellectual practices. By an "intellectual practice," I mean a practice in which practitioners methodically and systematically seek understanding of a particular domain of phenomena. Intellectual practices are thus a type of institution. Given the end of better understanding and the fallibility of individual investigators, the practice is more likely to succeed if its members work cooperatively; and a crucial feature of cooperative work is the attainment, maintenance, and evolution of consensuses. So the pursuit of consensus marks intellectual work as rational. Notice the role instrumentality plays in reaching this conclusion.

It is not obvious that this idea applies to practices other than intellectual ones. The rationality (or nonrationality) of practices such as going to church, going to school, political elections, and watching ballgames has nothing in particular to do with consensus or the capacity to reach them. A great deal of consensus is, of course, woven into these practices; but this situation reflects the fact that any practice contains considerable consensus, and thus tells us little about the putative rationality of particular activities. Neither the existence nor the pursuit of consensus qualifies any of the above activities as intelligent, proper, and responsible.

In fact, even in the case of intellectual practices it is not consensus per se but the interactive activities carried out in its pursuit that qualify a practice as rational. Intellectuals and academics in all fields disagree among themselves to remarkable degrees. Consequently, it cannot be consensus, but, if anything, the dialogues in which they participate, that marks their activities as rational. Most importantly, it is not the fact that these dialogues occasionally yield consensuses, but instead their pursuit alone that qualifies intellectual practices as rational. If consensuses were never reached, practitioners might eventually despair of them. But the point of intellectual activities is better understanding, and there is no guarantee that consensuses will always build around better understandings. In saying this I consciously contravene theorists who define "better" understanding in terms of ideal consensus—in the real world consensus does not always follow quality. In any event, the real world suffices to shift attention from consensus toward dialogue as a mark of rationality.

Dialogue, however, must be subsumed under a wider mark, namely, reflexivity. Reflexivity is the capacity to know and to work upon oneself.

It is the cluster of capacities for self-awareness, self-analysis, self-criticism, and self-development. These capacities are usually treated as properties of individual people. But practices, too, are reflexive when they allow for and encourage the development, dissemination, teaching, and exercise of these skills. Applied to practices, the notion is reminiscent of the idea of an open, as opposed to closed, society, which a number of writers have utilized to claim that modern Western practices are more rational than traditional ones.[18]

Reflexivity has three central components: self-knowledge, openness to self-criticism and change, and dialogue. These are the qualities I describe above as constitutive of objectivity. If they are also marks of rationality, then objectivity is a mark of rationality. I think that this indeed so, but primarily vis-à-vis intellectual practices alone.

I will defend this claim by reference to two prominent thinkers. In *Whose Justice? Which Rationality?* Alasdair MacIntyre utilizes a three-stage model of development to analyze the rationality of traditions.[19] In the first stage, beliefs, texts, and authorities are blindly accepted; in the second, inadequacies in these are identified; and in the third, reformulations, reevaluations, and new ideas respond to these inadequacies. In this third stage, the tradition institutionalizes methods and intellectual virtues, develops standard forms of argumentation, and formulates theories of its own activities of inquiry. It also often has to grapple with "epistemological crises," which can lead it to recognize that only a different tradition possesses the resources needed to resolve the seemingly insuperable difficulties it faces. A rational tradition is one capable of passing through these three stages, including the possible acknowledgement of the superiority of a different tradition. Clearly, rationality requires that the tradition permit the development and exercise of the capacities constituting objectivity.

Even this thumbnail sketch makes it clear that MacIntyre analyzes the rationality of intellectual practices. Only of practices that seek systematic understanding of a domain of phenomena can rationality require a possible evolution of this sort. In particular, although all sorts of practices can benefit from awareness of problems as well as their rectification, the epistemological apparatus developed in the third stage pertains to intellectual practices alone. We should not, however, too hastily prescribe even self-knowledge and self-criticism as a mark of the rationality of other sorts of practice. In extremely traditional societies, it might be deemed highly unintelligent and improper to question authority; and unless the activities involved undermine institutional ends, we are in no position to criticize them on grounds of lower rationality. On the other hand, practices aiming at egalitarian coexistence clearly do require the battery of capacities constituting objectivity. Only if people are self-aware, open to change, and capable of dialogue can egalitarian life be realized.

Another defense of objectivity as rationality is found in Jürgen Habermas's notion of communicative rationality.[20] On Habermas's analysis, a person is communicatively rational if he or she is willing and able to respond to criticism directed at any validity claim (truth, normative rightness, sincerity, effectiveness) raised by his or her speech acts and actions. A practice, correlatively, is rational if it requires and enables participants to respond to criticisms directed at their validity claims. Since Habermas believes, roughly speaking, that properly carried-out argumentation yields consensus, he expands this minimal specification as follows: A practice is rational if it is oriented toward the attainment and maintenance of consensus resting on the intersubjective recognition of criticizable validity claims.[21] Without proceeding into the intricacies of Habermas's position, let us ask whether this conception of rationality extends beyond intellectual practices.

That it applies to the latter should be clear. If the point of an activity is better understanding, and if individuals are more fallible than groups, then cooperative inquiry embracing disputation, criticism, and argumentation is a mark of the excellence of the activity. This conclusion extends beyond intellectual activities to all those truth- and/or mastery-seeking practices that would be enhanced by critical cooperation. Why, however, should this orientation be the mark of the rationality of culinary, sexual, recreational, political, and other social practices? I see no reason why it makes sense to carry out practices of any of these sorts only if they both allow for and exploit argumentative dialogue. Many practices of these types are and can be sensible, that is, intelligent, proper, responsible, and satisfying in their context, even though they eschew or restrict such interaction.

Replies to this claim usually invoke theses about practices in general. For instance, in a society where egalitarianism is deemed appropriate for all domains of life, its making sense to carry out a given practice might require that the practice accommodate and utilize evenhanded argumentative dialogue. Habermas and others might even say that doing this is necessary for the realization of justice. A different Habermasian response is that practices utilizing argumentative dialogue stand at the top of a learning curve, at whose lower reaches are arrayed the various practices eschewing such discourse. It is beyond my competence to comment on the veracity of claims of the latter sort; and it is beyond the scope of this chapter to debate whether a just society is one in which egalitarian decision-making operates in all areas of life. But it does seem to me indisputable that there are and have been myriad human practices that were perfectly appropriate, intelligent, and responsible, even though they did not exploit the capacities constituting objectivity. Contrary to Habermas's intuitions, it does not automatically qualify a practice as the sort it makes sense to engage in if participants in that practice give reasons for their actions and speech acts when questioned. Only of mastery-seeking or intellectual practices can objectivity be a mark of rationality.[22]

In the case of social investigation, moreover, there is an additional reason why objectivity, or reflexivity, is a mark of rationality. As discussed above, the point of being objective when studying others is both to identify and extirpate those preunderstandings that obstruct adequate understanding and to be able, perhaps through interaction with one's subjects, to learn of wider and more insightful understandings and perspectives from which to understand them. Objectivity, consequently, is crucially and essentially instrumental in realizing the end of social inquiry. So, apart from arguments applicable to intellectual practices generally, the end of social investigation establishes that it always makes sense for this institution to encourage objectivity/reflexivity.

One last putative mark of a practice's rationality is that its central ideas and beliefs be true. Space considerations preclude the close attention to the notion of truth required to do this idea justice. Consequently, I will argue simply that truth is an inadmissible criterion of rationality on a commonsensical correspondence theory of truth. I will show this by discussing the converse thesis, that falsity is a mark of deficient rationality.

If a practice lacks the resources required to discover the inaccuracy of its constitutive ideas, this inaccuracy cannot qualify it as lacking in rationality. Falsity can serve as a criterion of lower rationality only when an individual or practice possesses the capability, but fails to discover the falsity of central tenets. To take a stock example, Azande witchcraft is nonrational by virtue of the falsity of its beliefs only if the Azande have the capacity to discover this falsity and have simply not done so.

However, even when a practice possesses the capacity but fails to uncover falsehoods, it cannot automatically be considered deficient in rationality. For the falsehoods might be nestled in a network of convictions that safeguard them from exposure. This is a familiar point in the philosophy of science. An example from social science is provided by the much ballyhooed fact that Tully Valley Blacks were ignorant of the connection between human intercourse and pregnancy even though they understood the role copulation plays in animal procreation. Although I cannot know the specifics of the case, I assume that Tully Valley Blacks had a way of thinking about human sexuality that tied so strongly into their beliefs about other phenomena that they either did not notice the similarities between human and animal sexuality or had a way of understanding them that did not force them to draw the conclusions about human intercourse and pregnancy that we find obvious.[23] In either case, there is no reason to convict them of a lack of rationality. Only on an intellectualist interpretation that construes all their practices as attempts to control and explain can their beliefs here be taken as a sign of lesser rationality. Notice that failure to respect these conditions on falsity as a mark of lesser rationality leads to the conviction of non-Western and past Western intellectual traditions as lower in rationality.

Perhaps, however, the falsity of their beliefs is irrelevant to the Tully Valley inhabitants. Even when the above conditions are fulfilled, falsity can serve as a mark of lesser rationality only if the practitioners *care* about whether their leading ideas are true or false. Suppose inaccuracies and contradictions in their practices convince us that the Azande or the Tully Valley Blacks should have noted them and revised their activities accordingly. This holds, as Winch (following Evans-Prichard) emphasized,[24] only if these peoples care about the contradictions and inaccuracies involved. If they do not, they can be accused definitively of doing something that does not make sense only if these contradictions obstruct the attainment of the point or end of the practice—and as the discussion ignited by Winch's article demonstrates, there is less than unanimity on this point.

So, the use of falsity as a mark of lower rationality is subject to severe limitations. Unlike objectivity, it does not even automatically serve as a criterion vis-à-vis intellectual and mastery-seeking practices. The same conclusion results if truth is viewed not as correspondence, but as warranted assertability or some other type of coherence. I do not, however, develop here the different sort of argument that would show this.

CONCLUSION

What should we conclude from this long discussion of the marks of rationality? I demonstrated above that there are general criteria of rationality only vis-à-vis institutions, where instrumentality serves as a mark, and that subset of institutions comprising intellectual and mastery-seeking practices where objectivity counts as such. Social investigation is an institution of the latter sort; thus instrumentality and objectivity are marks of its rationality. Judging whether it makes sense to carry out practices other than institutions requires considering the particulars of the situation without the help of a general criterion. In making such judgments, the judger's powers of insight, empathy, sensitivity, knowledge, and so on come into play, and objectivity once again is required as a prime virtue. Such traits are less called upon when judging the rationality of institutions, in particular intellectual and mastery-seeking activities. Here, judging is a matter of applying a standard, although uncovering the features necessary to apply this standard (e.g., the practice's end[s]) likely demands some combination of the above traits.

The variability of judgments and senses of what it makes sense to do means that an objective person, especially a social investigator examining others, must be self-conscious about her own judgements and sense of this. She must seek to understand the considerations on the basis of which she judges as she does. Moreover, she must be prepared to learn new judgments and senses from her subjects and to pass judgment on them only after engaging them in dialogue. The variability of rationality thus demands that an objective investigator make rationality the object of the capacities constituting objectivity.

Finally, it should not be surprising that objectivity is the mark of rational social inquiry. As we saw, the goal of understanding others makes objectivity the sensible, that is, the rational way of proceeding for the social investigator. Indeed, one mark that an investigator acts rationally is his or her objectivity. But we have also seen, conversely, that in order to be objective an investigator must be conscious of his or her sense of rationality. Thus, what the objective social scientist is keenly aware of is something itself partly marked by his or her objectivity. Rationality and objectivity thus coincide for the social investigator. An objective investigator is one who acts rationally, and a rationally proceeding investigator is, *inter alia*, an objective one. This coincidence marks the life of the social scientist as strange and esoteric. For objectivity is not the normal way of the world. It is of little interest to most people, and attaining it requires continuous vigilance and effort. The objective investigator must keep in mind the differences between him- or herself and the people being investigated. The presence of objectivity often constitutes one of the biggest differences of all.

ACKNOWLEDGMENT

I would like to thank Piers Rawling for his illuminating and constructive criticisms of an earlier version of this chapter.

NOTES

1. Helen Longino draws a distinction between two senses of objectivity which parallels this distinction between truth and objectivity. See her *Science as Social Knowledge: Values and Objectivity in Scientific Inquiry* (Princeton, NJ: Princeton University Press, 1990), 62.
2. Hans-Georg Gadamer, *Truth and Method*, 2nd rev. ed., Joel Weinsheimer and Donald G. Marshall, trans. (New York: Crossroad, 1989).

3. The *locus classicus* is Thomas Kuhn, *The Structure of Scientific Revolutions* (Chicago: University of Chicago Press, 1962).

4. See the Postscript to the 2nd edition of *The Structure of Scientific Revolutions*.

5. Helen Longino, *Science as Social Knowledge: Values and Objectivity in Scientific Inquiry*, Chapter 4.

6. Allan Gibbard draws a similar distinction between its making sense that they X and its making sense to X. Although he does not develop this distinction in the direction I do, he agrees that (what I call) rationality, though not intelligibility, involves endorsement. See Allan Gibbard, "Rationality and Human Evolution, " in *Naturalism and Rationality*, Newton Garver and Peter H. Hare, eds. (Buffalo, NY: Prometheus Books, 1986), 217–233.

7. On this theme, see David B. Wong, "Three Kinds of Incommensurability," in *Relativism: Interpretation and Confrontation*, Michael Krausz, ed. (Notre Dame, IN: University of Notre Dame Press, 1989), 140–158, especially 153–154.

8. Jon Elster, *Sour Grapes: Studies in the Subversion of Rationality* (Cambridge: Cambridge University Press, 1983), 2–26.

9. See Hilary Putnam, *Reason, Truth, and History* (Cambridge: Cambridge University Press, 1981), 105–113.

10. For a similar response, see Richard Rorty, "Solidarity or Objectivity?," in *Relativism*, Michael Krausz, ed., 35–50; pp. 39–41.

11. Hilary Putnam, *Reason, Truth, and History*, 110–113; Hilary Putnam, "Why Reason Can't Be Naturalized," in *After Philosophy: End or Transformation?*, Kenneth Baynes, James Bohman, and Thomas McCarthy, eds. (Cambridge, MA: MIT Press, 1987), 222–244; pp. 233–234.

12. See, respectively, Stanley Jeyaraja Tambiah, *Magic, Science, Religion, and the Scope of Rationality* (Cambridge: Cambridge University Press, 1990), especially Chapter 6; Peter Winch, "Understanding a Primitive Society," in *Understanding and Social Inquiry*, Fred G. Dallmayr and Thomas C. McCarthy, eds. (Notre Dame, IN: University of Notre Dame Press, 1977), 159–188; and Jürgen Habermas, *Knowledge and Human Interests*, Jeremy J. Shapiro, trans. (Boston: Beacon Press, 1968), cf. the appendix.

13. On these ideas, see Hoy (Chapter 7, this volume). See also Peter Winch, "Understanding a Primitive Society, 183; Hans-Georg Gadamer, *Truth and Method*, Part II, Section II; Karl Mannheim, *Ideology and Utopia*, Louis Wirth and Edward Shils, trans. (New York: Harcourt, Brace, and World, 1936), especially Chapter 5; and James Boon, *Other Tribes. Other Scribes: Symbolic Anthropology and the Comparative Study of Cultures, Histories, Religions, and Texts* (Cambridge: Cambridge University Press, 1982), Chapter 1.

14. For discussion, see, for example, Jon Elster, *Explaining Technical Change* (Cambridge: Cambridge University Press, 1983), 55–65.

15. For discussion, see, for example, George Homans, "Bringing Men Back In," in *The Philosophy of Social Explanation*, Alan Ryan, ed. (Oxford: Oxford University Press, 1973), 50–64.

16. Charles Taylor, "Rationality," in *Rationality and Relativism*, Martin Hollis and Steven Lukes, eds. (Cambridge, MA: MIT Press, 1982), 87–105.

17. Another approach to instrumentality ties the instrumentality of a practice to the realization of its participants' interests. Since the notion of interests is tied to the notions of the human good and the good life, it leads to a discussion different from one concerned with ends. It is not possible to pursue this issue within the confines of the present chapter.

18. See, for example, Robin Horton, "African Traditional Thought and Western Science," *Africa 37*, nos. 1–2 (1967); 50–71, 155–187, and Ernest Gellner, "The Savage and the Modern Mind," in *Modes of Thought*, Robin Horton and Ruth Finnegan, eds. (London: Faber, 1973), 162–181.

19. Alasdair MacIntyre, *Whose Justice? Which Rationality?* (Notre Dame, IN: University of Notre Dame Press, 1988), Chapter 18, "The Rationality of Traditions."

20. See Jürgen Habermas, *The Theory of Communicative Action: Vol. I. Reason and the Rationality of Society*, Thomas McCarthy, trans. (Boston: Beacon Press, 1984), Chapter 1, sections 1, 2, 4.

21. Ibid., 17.

22. This should be enough to answer those who think that, in treating argumentative dialogue as a mark of rationality only when it helps achieve the point or end of a practice, I have misunderstood Habermas's intention to place communicative rationality alongside instrumental rationality as a distinct species. As just indicated, the presence of such dialogue, the fact that people are able and willing to defend their acts with reasons, does not *ipso facto* mark a practice as being of the sort it makes sense to carry out. I believe that, in order to make communicative rationality autonomous from instrumental rationality, Habermas must contend that calling X communicatively rational does not entail endorsing it.

23. Another standard move here is to interpret their claims either "symbolically" as not meaning literally what they say or "expressively" as nontruth functional expressions of attitudes toward life and nature. These strategies raise issues about belief and speech that cannot be discussed here. Examples of such interpretations can be found in Edwin Leach, "Virgin Birth," *Proceedings of the Royal Anthropological Institute for 1966* (London, 1967) and Ludwig Wittgenstein, "Lectures on Religious Belief," in *Lectures and Conversations on Aesthetics, Psychology, and Religious Belief*, Cyril Barrett, ed. (Oxford: Blackwell, 1966), 53–72; see also the discussion in Steven Lukes, "Relativism in its Place," in *Rationality and Relativism*, Martin Hollis and Steven Lukes eds., 275–292.

24. Peter Winch, "Understanding a Primitive Society," 170–171.

9

Beyond Objectivism and Relativism: Descriptive Epistemologies

ANDREW J. GRIMES
DEBORAH L. ROOD

Most organization studies researchers now agree that researchers' values affect research. This recognition has been one of the most important insights of the last several decades (Alvesson, 1987; Bendix, 1956; Burrell & Morgan, 1979; Gubrium & Silverman, 1989; Fischer, 1984; Krupp, 1961; Sjoberg & Nett, 1968; Steffy & Grimes, 1986). There continues, however, to be disagreement about how to respond to the impact of values on research.

The most common response advocates reducing the impact of values on research by adhering more closely to scientific values (Miner, 1990; Pfeffer, 1982). According to this response, scientific values protect research from the undue influence of other values. Scientific values consist of the scientific method and its basis in the objectivist epistemology[1] of positivism. Positivism seeks "to establish science as a form of true knowledge subject to validation that depends neither on metaphysical, ontological, nor other unfounded assumptions, nor on mere opinion of investigators" (Hall, 1990, p. 332).

A less common and more controversial response is epistemological relativism. This position is advanced by Gibson Burrell and Gareth Morgan (1979) in *Sociological Paradigms and Organizational Analysis*.[2] According to this relativism, scientific values are just values. They are unable to protect research from other values, and they do not deserve special privilege.

In organizational studies, the objectivism/relativism dichotomy is represented as an irreconcilable opposition (Miner, 1990; Pfeffer, 1982). If objectivism and relativism are viewed as oppositions, then abandoning objectivism leaves us no way to do research, no way to pursue knowledge, and no criteria for truth. This representation is part of "Cartesian anxiety" (Bernstein, 1983): Either we maintain objectivism or we lapse into relativism (Geertz, 1989).

In this chapter, we propose a third response. It is a response beyond the objectivism/relativism dichotomy, and is inspired by Bernstein (1983). To explain our response, we must first define several phrases. We use the phrase "local epistemologies" (Hall, 1990) to refer to ways of knowing shared by inquiring communities such as disciplines. Each local epistemology recognizes distinct ways of knowing and bases for knowledge. Local epistemologies tend to endorse only their ways of knowing. They do not reflect on the relationship between their ways of knowing and other aspects of the inquiry, such as the aims of their research, what and who they observe, how they make their observation, and how they validate knowledge (Steffy & Grimes, 1986). These normative epistemologies reduce a way of knowing to a prescribed set of strategies and rules for knowing. In this sense, they reduce epistemology to methodology (Bunge, 1983; Steffy & Grimes, 1986).

To reveal these hidden extramethodological aspects of normative local epistemologies such as aims, observed, observer, and knowledge validation, is to create a "descriptive epistemology." A descriptive epistemology describes the explicit methodology of a normative local epistemology. It recounts aims, observed, observer, the process of observation, and how knowledge is validated (Steffy & Grimes, 1986) as well as other information unique to it. This preparation requires a sort of reflection not usually endorsed in traditional objectivist research. Descriptive epistemology "expands" methodology to normative epistemology since it reflects on the context in which it is applied, so that aspects of inquiry not previously reflected upon may be identified.

How different must local epistemologies be to be considered distinct? Distinct local epistemologies disagree strongly about research issues, settings, objects, questions, tools and techniques, and/or assumptions. They also have few common bases for discussing their disagreements.

What is the difference between local epistemologies and substantive theories? For the objectivism of positivism, the difference is clear. Epistemology prescribes the correct strategies for research; theory describes the objects of research. However, beyond objectivism, this distinction breaks down. Here there are multiple normative local epistemologies, none of which is privileged. In this situation, epistemology is clearly implicated in knowledge and theory. "Correct" strategies of research are not independent of conceptions of the objects of research.

Normative and descriptive epistemologies do not have a one-to-one correspondence. The same normative epistemology may require several descriptive epistemologies if it is used by researchers with significantly different aims or values. The same descriptive epistemology may include several local normative epistemologies if it identifies common elements with which to compare or contrast them. These encompassing epistemologies are called "bridging epistemologies."

To get beyond relativism and the objectivism/relativism dichotomy, then, we recommend several devices for developing bridging epistemologies. Our purpose is not to integrate local epistemologies. Integration may be neither desirable[3] nor possible. Instead, the purpose is to present bridging devices that enable us to contrast and compare different epistemologies. More generally, our purpose is to show that sufficient respect for, description of, and reflection about the common aspects of different normative ways of knowing may take us beyond objectivism and relativism.

DESCRIPTIVE EPISTEMOLOGIES: BEYOND OBJECTIVISM AND RELATIVISM

In this chapter we describe five ways to generate bridging epistemologies. While there may be a number of ways to generate such epistemologies, we choose these because they have been useful to our own study of organization. These bridging devices are derived from theorists in the philosophy of social science, theorists actively engaged in investigating kinds of knowledge and strategies for arriving at them. They have "untied," or at least loosened, the privilege of any normative epistemology, and have recognized the need to transcend the objectivism/relativism dichotomy and the possibility of understanding disparate ways of knowing. After we describe our five devices to generate descriptive epistemologies, we present examples of their application from the literature on the anatomy of power.

Limiting Notions

According to Winch (1977), limiting notions are "certain fundamental notions" that are implicated in our common human experiences: birth, death, and sexual relations. Limiting notions are

> inescapably involved in the life of all known human societies in a way that gives us a clue where to look if we are puzzled about the point of an alien system of institutions. . . . The specific forms which these concepts take, the particular institutions in which they are expressed, vary very considerably from one society to another; but the central position within a society's institutions is and must be a constant factor. In trying to understand the life of an alien society, then, it will be of the utmost importance to be clear about the way in which these notions enter into it. (Winch, 1977, pp. 183–184)

Winch's limiting notions are objective in the sense that they are extreme experiences that must be dealt with in all human communities. Thus, they may form a commonality among humans regardless of how differently they are interpreted or handled.

While Winch's limiting notions are bridging devices between dissimilar cultures, we apply them here for disparate epistemologies of organization. In this context, limiting notions might include health, pain, stress, safety, and security; sexual identity and preference; physical and mental ability and disability; the impact of nature and the environment; time and space; tools and technologies; organization of work and the labor process.

To apply limiting notions to organizational epistemologies, one must describe how different epistemologies treat the same extreme of human experience, search for agreements and disagreements in these treatments, and investigate why they occur. For example, functionalist and nonfunctionalist epistemologies of worker commitment might be bridged by limiting notions of worker health and safety. These epistemologies assume different levels of worker commitment to organizational goals. Functionalist perspectives assume workers are committed; nonfunctionalist perspectives do not make this assumption. When prescribed work practices threaten worker health and safety, functionalist assumptions of harmony (Krupp, 1961) become suspect.

Since the concept of limiting notions recognizes commonality at the physical extremes of human experience, it is inconsistent with perspectives that view even such "physical extremes" as sex to be socially constructed (Butler, 1990; Laqueur, 1990). Our position is not that limiting notions necessarily exist, but that different epistemologies may treat them as doing so.

Oppositional Science

According to Longino (1990), oppositional science situates objectivist epistemology within a descriptive epistemology that recognizes the influence of cultural, social, and personal "contextual" values on scientific findings. Oppositional science is "always local and respectful of some of the standards of a specific scientific community. And it requires a mainstream or established tradition to which it is opposed and with which it is in some form of dialectical tension" (Longino, 1990, p. 214).

From a feminist perspective, Longino reinterprets the results of traditional (nonfeminist) biological gender research. Her reinterpretation indicates that traditional research results are significantly different for the two sets of values. Longino's oppositional science uses the same normative objectivist epistemology as traditional science, but transcends the objectivism/relativism dichotomy by generating a descriptive epistemology for each value perspective and bridging these by explicitly identifying difference in values and the relationship between values and research results. This bridge provides a way to compare and contrast the different perspectives.

In organization studies, feminism and antifeminism are contextual values, but there are others: applied versus theoretical, manager versus nonmanager, profit versus nonprofit, non-Marxist versus Marxist, ability versus disability, modernist versus postmodernist. Thus, non-Marxist researchers who are aligned with management and thus report the advantages of technological change and Marxists who stamp it as deskilling (Orlikowski, 1992) may be using the same objectivist epistemology. Oppositional science helps us understand these differences. Technological change may decrease the number of skilled, organized (well-paid) workers that managers require; in this sense, it promotes managerial interests. It may also reduce computational and physical job demands; in this sense, it ignores worker interests. Similarly, disabled researchers might employ theories or evidence at variance with those of mainstream research because their daily experiences alert them to conditions that the able-bodied do not see, hear, or feel (Hasenfeld & Chesler, 1989).

Oppositional science does not bridge *normative* epistemologies. Rather, it generates descriptive epistemologies for each value perspective and bridges these by explicitly identifying both differences in values and relationships between values and research results. In this way, the different values perspectives can be contrasted or compared. Longino's oppositional science relies upon the normative epistemology of positivism, but oppositional science is a device that could be used for other normative epistemologies as well.

Synthesis of Partial Truths

According to Mannheim (1936), the perspectives of sociohistorically embedded groups present partial truths about reality. Partial truths can be synthesized by analyzing the social and historical differences between groups. The synthesis overcomes the partiality of perspectives. It is just another sociohistorical perspective, but one that is more objective because it is more comprehensive:

> By juxtaposing the various points of view, each perspective may be recognized as such and thereby a new level of objectivity attained. . . . The false idea of a detached, impersonal point of view must be replaced by the ideal of an essentially human point of view which is within the limits of a human perspective, constantly trying to enlarge itself. (Mannheim, 1936, p. 296)

Mannheim's partial truths refer to forms of sociohistorical embeddedness (e.g., generational embeddedness). Sociohistorical embeddedness is relevant to organizational studies as well. First, it can synthesize conflicting perspectives of research subjects. In his study of a British rainwear manufacturer, for example, Young (1989) synthesizes the sociohistorical embeddedness of his research subjects. He describes the conflicting perspectives of two worker groups: single women working for their sole support and older married women who work to supplement their husbands' incomes. Young synthesizes these partial views by situating them in the context of organizational history and operations. He recognizes that the conflict, fostered by management, is the personnel strategy of weeding out uncommitted women in the younger group.

Second, it can synthesize conflicting normative epistemologies, at least those with different sociohistorical origins, such as, interpretivist and positivist epistemologies (Burrell & Morgan, 1979). Frequently, the later is aligned with management, the former with the managed (Bendix, 1956). In their research on emotional display, Sutton and Rafaeli (1988) synthesize interpretivist and positivist epistemologies. They first adopt a positivist epistemology to test the hypothesis that friendly cashiers increase store sales. This hypothesis is not supported, and they switch to an interpretivist epistemology to understand the perspectives of cashiers and customers. Finally, they combine results from both to conclude that the relationship between the emotional display of cashiers and sales is moderated by how busy the store is. Customers do not want cashiers to be friendly when the store is busy; they expect it when the store is not.

Switching Rules

Habermas's knowledge–interest scheme[4] (Habermas, 1971; Held, 1980) provides a set of epistemological rules for switching between kinds of science (empirical–analytic, hermeneutic, and emancipatory) based on kinds of knowledge–interest (technical, practical, and emancipatory). Thus, these switching rules are as follows: If you have a technical interest, use empirical–analytic science; if you have a practical interest, use hermeneutic science; and if you have an emancipatory interest, use emancipatory science. Since interest determines the science chosen, the "switch" in this scheme is knowledge–interest. The switch has three possible positions: technical, practical, and emancipatory. Habermas makes use of these rules when he chooses emancipatory science (critical theory) because his interest is ultimately emancipatory.

Habermas's switching rules are applicable to organization analysis (see Steffy & Grimes, 1986), but there are other switches as well: trust versus mistrust of knowledge (Rao & Pasmore, 1989); aim of research (Sjoberg & Nett, 1968); structure versus process (Giddens, 1976; Reed, 1985; Willmott, 1990). Additionally, new switching rules can be generated. To generate rules for switching between normative epistemologies, one must first generate descriptive epistemologies for each normative epistemology and compare them. One must then find the switch. The switch is the difference between epistemologies that allows us to prescribe choices among them.

Conversation

Bernstein's (1983) notion of conversation provides us with another device for bridging epistemologies. Conversation is a metaphor for the continuing written and oral give-and-take between people, theories, perspectives, and paradigms, and within and across different epistemologies. Epistemologies may be bridged by considering them parties in a conversation. Parties engage one another and respond to one another. During the process, parties present their positions and react to the positions of others. Disagreements are elaborated and agreements may be reached. Additionally, new standards for comparison may arise out of the process.

In *Beyond Method*, Morgan (1983) engages in conversation to bridge different epistemologies in organization studies. His book is an insightful report of a conference to "advance the cause of a reflective social science" (p. 7). In the book, 15 organization researchers detail in separate chapters their research assumptions, interests, and strategies. Morgan reports the results of his (misguided, as it turns out) attempt to create a conversation among these heterodox organization researchers.

Morgan assumed that the conference would unfold within his pre-planned framework based on four sociological paradigms (functionalist, interpretivist, radical humanist, and radical structuralist) presented in Burrell and Morgan (1979). However, true to the nature of conversation, the conference participants would not be constrained by either Morgan's framework or his vision of the conference. Morgan captures the spirit of this conversation:

> One of the fine flexible things about conversation is that it can begin anywhere and explore many different themes according to the way it becomes structured by those involved. A conversation usually only needs a starting point . . . ; those whose interest is engaged can usually be relied on to do the rest . . . , [to] use the course of conversation to confront and reflect on the views they hold and to act on any significant conclusions that emerge. (p. 376)

In a series of provocative introductory and concluding chapters that compares, contrasts, and bridges many of the researchers positions Morgan creates the conversation between them. According to Morgan, these research strategies cannot be evaluated in any absolute sense: "All social phenomena may have many potential ways of revealing themselves and the way they are realized in practice depends on the mode of engagement adopted by the researcher" (p. 389). Different research strategies and different local epistemologies simply do different things. In his conversational bridging of research strategies, Morgan concludes that it is the usefulness of research strategies that provides criteria for their evaluation: Whose view of reality do they express? Whose interest do they serve?

Bernstein (1983) and Morgan (1983) are both aware that power influences conversation. For them, if power interferes in the conversation, if the powerful speak louder and more often, knowledge is distorted as a result. Thus, knowledge is only knowledge to the extent that it is free of distortion caused by power.

We need to temper the notion that knowledge is analytically separable from power with a reminder from Foucault[5] (1979, 1980a, 1980b). For Foucault, knowledge presupposes and is inseparable from the power relationships under which it is created: Anything described as knowledge already contains and requires certain power relationships. But this does not mean that knowledge is distorted by power. Since knowledge recursively creates and is created by power, whether knowledge is "distorted" becomes a different issue.

Foucault's conception of knowledge tells us that the descriptive epistemologies identified in the process of conversation emerge within power relations and counsels that we be aware of those relations in utilizing and considering these epistemologies. In a conversation between different local epistemologies, the standards of comparison that come out of the conversation reflect the power relationships in which they are embedded. But this does not mean that they are "distorted."

POWER: AN EXAMPLE

In this section we present, as an example of theory and research beyond objectivism and relativism, John Gaventa's (1980) empirical examination of power, which is informed by Steven Lukes's (1974) "radical" theory of power. We select this example for two reasons. First, Lukes's theory embraces both objectivism, and, by Lukes's own account, relativism. However, Gaventa applies Lukes's theory in a way that gets beyond the objectivism/relativism dichotomy (Clegg, 1989a). To do so, Gaventa uses techniques similar to our bridging devices.

Second, while power is an important topic to most students of organization, Lukes's model and Gaventa's study tend to be ignored in mainstream North American organization studies (see Mumby, 1988, for an exception). Lukes's elegant three dimensional power model (which explains much of what we experience as power in organizations), together with Gaventa's careful empirical study, can add greatly to our understanding of organizational power.

Lukes's Radical View of Power

Lukes's (1974) first dimension of power is derived from Dahl's pluralist, behavioral model. In this dimension, power is exercised when person A causes person B to do what B would not do otherwise. The empirical identification of power in this dimension requires behavioral evidence: observable conflicts of interest between A and B about decision-making issues, observable participation assumed to reflect preferences and interests of A and B, and observable decisions or actions through which A gets B to do what B would not have done otherwise.

Lukes's (1974) second dimension of power is derived from a model by Bachrach and Baratz. In this dimension, power may be exercised by A to prevent B from acting or when B acts in anticipation of an action by A. Power now includes the ways B's decisions and actions are prevented by procedures and structures promulgated by A. The empirical identification of this dimension of power requires evidence other than behavior: observable or covert conflicts of interest between A and B about issues or potential issues; observable participation by A or B and/or grievances by B, assumed to represent preferences and interests of A and B; and observed decisions and events or inferred "nondecisions" and "nonevents" by which A keeps B from doing what B would have done otherwise.

In Lukes's third dimension of power, "A exercises power over B when A affects B in a manner contrary to B's interest" (1974, p. 27). This dimension of power occurs in asymmetrical relationships when As or their processes and mechanisms exercise power over Bs by influencing them to prefer outcomes more instrumental to the As than to themselves. In this dimension, the empirical identification of power requires evidence that would not be acceptable to a mainstream behaviorist perspective: latent conflicts of interest between A and B over a political agenda; inferred lack of participation or grievances assumed to represent the preferences but not the interests of B's; inferred "nondecisions" of B by which A keeps B from acting; and determination of B's "objective" interests by investigating the counterfactual—what B would have done in the absence of influence by A.[6]

For Lukes, each of the three dimensions of power is based on a "normatively specific conception of interest" (1974, p. 26). The first dimension rests on a liberal, the second on a reformist, and the third on a radical conception of interest. How does one choose among dimensions? Choices are determined by interests, interests represent values, and values are not objective. Thus, choice among dimensions is relative. Paradoxically, if one chooses the third dimension, one can then determine B's interest objectively—by solving the counterfactual (what B would do if not subject to A's power).

Lukes sharply distinguishes between the relativism of values and the objectivity of facts (Lukes, 1977). He assigns model choice to the realm of values and objective interests to the realm of facts. With this stance, Lukes stands squarely in the objectivism/relativism camp.[7]

Lukes and Epistemologies

Lukes's three dimensions use very different definitions of power: actions by A and changes in actions by B in the first dimension; B's inability to act because of rules, procedures, and traditions established by A in the second; and B's choices not to act because of agreements with or false presumptions about A in the third. At least two of Lukes's dimensions relate to distinct local epistemologies: the first and the third. The first, with its evidence of A's overt action and B's overt reaction, represents an objectivist epistemology of behavioral science. The third, with its evidence of a theorized counterfactual, is associated with the epistemology of critical theory (Geuss, 1981).

Gaventa and Descriptive Epistemologies

In a historical, economic, and interpretative case study of an Appalachian valley company town, Gaventa (1980) applies Lukes's three-dimensional theory of power to explain the quiescence of coal miners and citizens. Gaventa adopts the theory because he has an emancipatory interest. This interest is evident in two ways. First, rather than assume it is either natural (Geuss, 1981) or reflects agreement with union officials, coal company owners, and political leaders (the As), Gaventa attempts to explain the quiescence of the citizens and coal miners (the Bs). This motivates him to examine the causes and mechanisms of powerlessness, a concept consistent with both the second and third dimensions of power.

Second, Gaventa uses a colonial metaphor[8] to study powerlessness in the company town: The town, owned by an absentee British corporate landlord, is, in effect, a colonial territory administered by a hidden foreign political and economic power. This metaphor leads Gaventa to look for the same mechanisms of administration that maintain colonial domination.

Gaventa finds explanations consistent with the first dimension of power (As sometimes exercise power directly), the second dimension (Bs recognize they have unresolved grievances), and the third dimension (Bs do not appear to recognize their own objective interests). Gaventa uses Lukes's theory, but is able to get beyond Lukes's stance on objectivism and relativism. In doing so, he appears to use techniques very similar to three of our bridging devices.

Limiting Notions

Gaventa hypothesizes that the quiescence of the miner citizens in his study is the result of power. Otherwise, the glaring inequalities and life-threatening conditions in their lives would cause them at least to try to change their situation. These conditions—poor health, unsafe work requirements, low wages, inequalities, and the absence of job security—create a situation in which few would disagree that the objective (Lukes, 1974), or "real" (Connolly, 1972), interests of Bs are not being met. Due to these extreme conditions, the counterfactual test required to determine objective interest has validity. It strengthens the evidence that the third dimension of power is present. Thus, Gaventa uses concepts similar to limiting notions to counter the behavioralists' claim that the absence of Bs (re)action implies the absence of As power.

Oppositional Science

Gaventa's radical and emancipatory interests are oppositional to mainstream objectivist social science. With these oppositional assumptions (Longino, 1990), he does not assume that Bs silence implies agreement, but instead searches for its reasons. In this search, he uses traditional quantitative analysis of election results, voter participation rates, property tax records, and property ownership[9] to establish "scientific" evidence of inequalities and powerlessness. This is in contrast to the more customary explanations of apathy or agreement likely to be offered by functionalist perspectives.

Switching Rules

Gaventa uses switching rules to generate descriptive epistemology in two ways. First, Gaventa switches among epistemologies and methodologies based on the type of knowledge he pursues. He switches from historical–interpretative (hermeneutic) analysis for examining the historical and institutional roots of powerlessness to quantitative (empirical–analytic) analyses for examining the present condition of powerlessness. With his emancipatory interest and his critical theory epistemology, he bridges hermeneutic and empirical–analytic sciences.

Second, Gaventa switches among dimensions of power based on his object of inquiry: He uses a third-dimension explanation to show that managers and union and community officials (As) have exercised power to shape Bs preferences and reduce their political consciousness, a second-dimension explanation to show As have established structures and institutions that reinforce the powerlessness of Bs, and first-dimension explanations to show that As have mobilized resources to insure that Bs infrequent use of power is not effective.

Gaventa's Contributions to Substantive Theory

Gaventa has enriched our understanding of power beyond objectivism and relativism in several ways[10]:

1. *View from below.* Gaventa's theory of power includes a "view from below," that is, from the perspective of those who are targets of influence

and control. It offers new understandings about the interrelationship of power, powerlessness, and quiescence. When theorized from "below," power has a pattern, a stability, and an inevitability that are missing in views from above. In views from above elite managers, owners, and union and community officials would more likely appear as a unified legitimate opposition to discontented miners and citizens. A theory of power that looks at power as the powerless do is a subtler (Czarniawaska-Joerges, 1988) and more comprehensive theory of power.

2. *Power or authority?* From Gaventa's perspective, distinctions between power and legitimate authority are more equivocal. While company, union, and municipal officials would ordinarily be considered legitimate authorities, in Gaventa's study, they use their positions of authority to enhance sectional interests. Their legitimacy, and thus their authority, dissolves.

3. *Dimensions and their mechanisms.* Gaventa's research shows that each dimension has its own mechanisms of control. The first dimension directs attention to differences in the resources, skills, direct exchanges, and interrelationships between the powerful and the powerless. The second dimension focuses on organizational processes, institutional processes, and mechanisms and structures that maintain asymmetrical power relations. Such seemingly unbiased factors as division of labor, agendas, structures, traditions, and rules are revealed to reflect the results of previous power exchanges. The third dimension illuminates the possibility that As manufacture consensus (Burawoy, 1979) by defining (Deetz, 1992) or influencing Bs wants. Language, symbols, "rights," beliefs, and culture (Alvesson, 1991; Mumby, 1988) operate to maintain differential power in ways not entirely comprehensible to the powerless or, for that matter, to researchers using only the first dimension of power.

4. *Dimensions and their dynamics.* While each dimension has its own mechanisms, Gaventa (1980) also shows how they work together to preserve asymmetrical power. The first dimension operates until "fundamental issues of inequality" (p. 253) are identified. When a pattern of powerlessness is established, Bs are unwilling to risk further loss of resources in direct and always futile confrontations with As. As can then consolidate their power with mechanisms identified in the second dimension. Power relationships are further solidified when Bs come to believe that power differences in hierarchy, leadership, control, competition, and scarcity, are "natural" (Guess, 1981) or at least inevitable. Then, Bs tend to make choices that maintain their quiescence. When they make other choices, As are still able to rely on mechanisms from the first or second dimension.

5. *Dimensions and hierarchy.* According to Gaventa, all three power dimensions may be operating in different parts of an organizational

hierarchy. Face-to-face, first-dimension power exchanges are more likely at lower levels of the hierarchy, between adjacent levels, or between the powerless and lower-level agents of the powerful. The subtler second and third dimensions are more often exercised across nonadjacent hierarchical levels because the organizational "distance" hides the sources of power.

6. *Dimensions and contextualization.* Gaventa's study underscores the importance of a detailed knowledge of context. It is only in a context like a company town or colony that powerlessness and quiescence are likely to be so evident.

CONCLUSIONS

We argue above that our devices for creating bridging epistemologies will contribute to theory beyond objectivism and relativism. We also show how Gaventa uses techniques similar to some of our devices to do so. We end our chapter by summarizing the consequences of such activity for theory and research beyond objectivism and relativism.

1. Theorizing will be epistemological. Since there are many episte-mologies and since epistemology is always implicated in substantive theory, theorizing must be epistemological as well as substantive. The specification of theory must include the description of epistemology and the relationship between epistemology and substantive theory.

2. Theory and research will be more complex. Theory will include different local epistemologies and specify their interrelationships. Research will "test" rival epistemologies as well as rival hypotheses. It will also require diverse standards for the validation of knowledge and address the wider implications of research results.

3. Interest will drive research. Since there is no privileged epistemol-ogy, there is no methodological limit on what can be studied. Researchers can let their interests determine what they study, and their interests and the nature of the phenomenon determine how to study it.

4. Research will be recognized as a community process. Research standards represent agreements between the members of a local epistemo-logical community. When recognized as members of such communities, researchers will be required to justify the particular standards they choose.

ACKNOWLEDGMENTS

Theodore Schatzki's comments on previous drafts of this chapter have greatly improved it. We thank him and Wolfgang Natter for guiding our explorations in the philosophy of social science and for encouraging a view beyond objectivism. We also thank Mark Davis for his insightful comments on previous drafts, presented to the 1991 and 1992 Spring Management Department Research Workshops, College of Business and Economics, University of Kentucky.

NOTES

1. Both "objectivism" and "relativism" can refer to ontological, epistemological, or methodological issues in the philosophy of social science (Burrell & Morgan, 1979). Ontological issues pertain to the nature of social reality, epistemological issues to the kinds of knowledge and truth possible, and methodological issues to the procedures and tools used in seeking knowledge and truth. Issues of ontology, epistemology, and methodology are entangled: "We seem blocked from comprehending the nature of the social world (if it has any coherent nature) unless we have an epistemological path, yet an epistemological path may depend upon an ontology of both the knower and that to be known" (Hall, 1990, p. 333).

2. Burrell and Morgan's (1979) relativism is ontological and methodological, as well as epistemological. Our discussion in this chapter is limited to epistemological objectivism and relativism.

3. For example, Burrell and Morgan (1979) advocate isolation of unorthodox perspectives to protect them from eclipse by positivism. But separatism also stifles new ways of thinking (Willmott, 1990), discourages new assumptions, and magnifies some differences while suppressing others. Thus we cull from Burrell and Morgan (1979) not the call to separate nonorthodox perspectives, but the need to protect them. In this chapter, we identify a theoretical space making "room" for epistemologies to either separate (Burrell & Morgan, 1979; Jackson & Carter, 1991), pluralize (Reed, 1985), or integrate (Donaldson, 1987) themselves, protected from "trouncing" (Donaldson, 1988).

4. Our reading of Habermas (1971) is enhanced by Held (1980), Geuss (1981), and McCarthy (1985). We refer here to "early" Habermas.

5. Our reading here is assisted by Hoy (1986) and Dreyfus and Rabinow (1982).

6. Lukes's definition of objective interest is central to his arguments. "If I say something is in your interest, I imply that you have a prima facie claim to it, and if I say that 'policy x is in A's interest' this constitutes a prima facie justification for the policy" (Lukes, 1974, p. 34). This definition derives from Connolly's (1972) definition of "real" interests. Connolly's real interests are "objective" for Lukes because they can be counterfactually determined.

7. Lukes (1979) presents a explication (or revision) of his earlier model. This more recent statement tempers his initial discussion of relativism.

8. The colonial metaphor is frequently invoked in Kentucky in the media, public discussions, and analyses of the economics and political character of the central Appalachian Region.

9. Gaventa describes in detail similar research strategies that can be imple-

mented by citizens as a way to produce knowledge necessary for social change (Gaventa & Horton, 1981).

10. In this discussion, we draw heavily on Gaventa's (1980) conclusions and on Clegg's (1989a) discussion of Lukes (1974) and Gaventa (1980). For other discussions of radical perspectives on power see Clegg (1989b) and Morgan (1986).

REFERENCES

Alvesson, M. (1987). *Organization theory and technocratic consciousness*. Berlin: de Gruyter.

Alvesson, M. (1991). Organizational symbolism and ideology. *Journal of Management Studies, 28*, 207–226.

Bendix, R. (1956). *Work and authority in industry*. New York: Wiley.

Bernstein, R. J. (1983). *Beyond objectivism and relativism: Science hermeneutics and praxis*. Philadelphia: University of Pennsylvania Press.

Bunge, M. (1983). *Treatise on basic philosophy: Epistemology and methodology* (Vol. 5). Dordrecht, Holland: Reidel.

Burawoy, M. (1979). *Manufacturing consent*. Chicago: University of Chicago.

Burrell, G., & Morgan, G. (1979). *Sociological paradigms and organizational analysis*. Portsmouth, NH: Heinemann.

Butler, J. (1990). *Gender trouble: Feminism and the subversion of identity*. New York: Routledge.

Czarniawaska-Joerges, B. (1988). Power as an experiential concept. *Scandinavian Journal of Management, 4*(1/2), 31–44.

Clegg, S. R. (1989a). *Frameworks of power*. London: Sage.

Clegg, S. R. (1989b). Radical revisions: Power, discipline, and organizations. *Organization Studies, 10*, 97–115.

Connolly, W. E. (1972). On "interest" in politics. *Politics and Society, 2*, 459–477.

Deetz, S. (1992, October). *Building a communication perspective in organization studies I: Foundations*. Paper presented to the Annual Meeting of the Speech Communication Association, Chicago.

Donaldson, L. (1987). *In defence of organization theory*. Cambridge: Cambridge University Press.

Donaldson, L. (1988). In successful defence of organization theory: A routing of the critics. *Organization Studies, 9*, 28–32.

Dreyfus, H. L., & Rabinow, P. (1982). *Michel Foucault: Beyond structuralism and hermeneutics*. New York: Harvester Wheatsheaf.

Fischer, F. (1984). Ideology and organization behavior. In F. Fischer & C. Sirrani (Eds.), *Critical perspectives on bureaucratic theory* (pp. 172–190). Philadelphia: Temple University Press.

Foucault, M. (1979). *Discipline and punish*. New York: Vintage.

Foucault, M. (1980a). *The history of sexuality: Volume I. An introduction*. New York: Vintage.

Foucault, M. (1980b). *Power/knowledge: Selected interviews and other writings 1972–1977* (C. Gordon, Ed.; C. Gordon, L. Marshall, J. Mepham, & K. Soper, Trans.). New York: Pantheon.

Gaventa, J. (1980). *Power and powerlessness: Quiescence and rebellion in an Appalachian valley.* Urbana: University of Illinois Press.

Gaventa, J., & Horton, B. D. (1981). A citizen's research project in Appalachia, U.S.A. *Convergence, 14* (3), 30–40.

Geertz, C. (1989). Anti-anti-relativism. In M. Krausz (Ed.), *Relativism: Interpretation and confrontation* (pp. 12–34). Notre Dame, IN: University of Notre Dame Press.

Geuss, R. (1981). *The idea of a critical theory: Habermas and the Frankfurt school.* Cambridge: Cambridge University Press.

Giddens, A. (1976). *New rules of sociological method.* New York: Basic Books.

Gubrium, T. F., & Silverman, D. (Eds.). (1989). *The politics of field research: Sociology beyond enlightenment.* Newbury Park, CA: Sage.

Habermas, J. 1971. *Knowledge and human interest* (T. McCarthy, Trans.). Boston: Beacon Press.

Hall, J. R. (1990). Epistemology and sociohistorical inquiry. *Annual Review of Sociology, 16,* 329–351.

Hasenfeld, Y., & Chesler, M. 1989. Client empowerment in the human services: Personal and professional agenda. *Journal of Applied Behavioral Science, 25,* 499–521.

Held, D. (1980). *Introduction to critical theory.* Berkeley: University of California Press.

Hoy, D. C. (1986). Power, repression, progress: Foucault, Lukes, and the Frankfurt school. In D.C. Hoy (Ed.), *Foucault: A critical reader* (pp. 123–147). Oxford: Basil Blackwell.

Jackson, N., & Carter, P. (1991). In defense of paradigm incommensurability. *Organizational Studies, 12,* 109–127.

Krupp, S. (1961). *Patterns in organization analysis: A critical examination.* New York: Holt, Rinehart & Winston.

Laqueur, T. (1990). *Making sex: Body and gender from the Greeks to Freud.* Cambridge, MA: Harvard University Press.

Longino, H. E. (1990). *Science as social knowledge: Values and objectivity in scientific inquiry.* Princeton, NJ: Princeton University Press.

Lukes, S. (1974). *Power: A radical view.* London: Macmillan.

Lukes, S. (1977). *Essays in social theory.* New York: Columbia University Press.

Lukes, S. (1979). On relativity of power. In S. C. Brown (Ed.), *Philosophical disputes in the social sciences* (pp. 261–275). Atlanta Heights, NJ: Humanities Press.

Mannheim, K. (1936). *Ideology and utopia: An introduction to the sociology of knowledge* (L. Wirth & E. Shils, Trans.). San Diego: Harcourt Brace Jovanovich.

McCarthy, T. (1985). *The critical theory of Jürgen Habermas.* Cambridge, MA: MIT Press.

Miner, J. (1990). The role of values in defining the "goodness" of theories in organizational science. *Organization Studies, 11,* 161–178.

Morgan, G. (1983). *Beyond method: Strategies for social research.* Beverly Hills, CA: Sage.

Morgan, G. (1986). *Images of organization.* Beverly Hills, CA: Sage.

Mumby, D. (1988). *Communication and power in organizations: Discourse, ideology and domination*. Norwood, NJ: Ablex.

Orlikowski, W. (1992). The duality of technology: Rethinking the concept of technology in organizations. *Organization Science, 3*, 398–427.

Pfeffer, J. (1982). *Organizations and organization theory*. Marshfield, MA: Pitman.

Rao, M. V. H., & Pasmore, W. (1989). Knowledge and interest in organization studies: A conflict of interpretations. *Organization Studies, 10*, 225–239.

Reed, M. (1985). *Redirections in organizational analysis*. New York: Tavistock Publications.

Sjoberg, G., & Nett, R. (1968). *A methodology for social research*. New York: Harper & Row.

Steffy, B. D., & Grimes, A. J. (1986). A critical theory of organization science. *Academy of Management Review, 11*, 322–336

Sutton, R. I., & Rafaeli, A. (1988). Untangling the relationship between displayed emotions and organizational sales: The case of convenience stores. *Academy of Management Journal, 31*, 461–487.

Willmott, H. (1990). Beyond paradigmatic closure in organizational enquiry. In J. Hassard & D. Pym (Eds.). *The theory and philosophy of organizations* (pp. 44–60). London: Routledge.

Winch, P. (1977). Understanding a primitive society. In F. R. Dallmayr & T. M. McCarthy (Eds.), *Understanding and social inquiry* (pp. 159–188). Notre Dame, IN: Notre Dame University Press.

Young, E. (1989). On the meaning of the rose: Interests and multiple meanings as elements of organizational culture. *Organization Studies, 10*, 187–206.

10

Ultraobjectivity, Cross-Culturally: Interpretive Anthropology and the Arts of Rereading

JAMES A. BOON

Objective . . . *existing only in relation to a knowing subject or willing agent . . . belonging to the sensible world and being intersubjectively observable.*
Ultra- *Going beyond others, or beyond due limit: extreme, beyond what is ordinary, proper, or moderate: excessively.*
Read . . . *to discover by interpreting outward expression or signs . . . to attribute a meaning.*
Re *again, anew, back, backward.*
—WEBSTER'S NEW COLLEGIATE DICTIONARY

Règles . . . *Syn. de menstrues.*
—PETIT LAROUSSE

Menstrues . . . *Menstrua, periods, menses, catamenia; (fam.) monthlies.*
—CASSELL'S FRENCH DICTIONARY

Interpretive arts in cultural anthropology are often deemed too "subjective" when judged against standards of experimental science, whose proponents claim that its methods alone bound proper "objects" of scrutiny, susceptible of disinterested diagnoses by observers able to confirm controlled findings. A familiar countercharge by "interpretive

179

types" is that positivistic dismissal of interpretation fails its own tests: Only a loaded, reductive view of objectivity could imagine a pat distinction between objective versus subjective. By censoring evidence of concrete ambiguities actually separating its experimental repetitions, abstract reductionism dreams up a utopian realm of proper hypotheses and rigorous results.[1]

I side with this second position skeptical of narrowly controlled objectivity in cultural matters. Far from altogether disavowing "objectivity," however, I—perhaps subjectively—object to positivistic frameworks in hope of a fuller objectivity. I call the beast "ultraobjectivity," or, following *Webster's*, that which is "intersubjectively observable" in the "extreme . . . beyond what is ordinary, proper." The readiest means I know to experience such extra-ordinary ultraobjectivity is to engage in intensive rereading of worthy works, particularly cross-cultural ones.

Whatever one's discipline, efforts toward rereading may augment doubt rather than achieve certainty. Interpretive doubt becomes salutary when it encourages engagement with empirical and textual details and with intricate configurations and contradictions of social, political, and linguistic life (Boon, 1982, p. 27). Interpretive doubt thrives in the paradoxical circumstances of cross-cultural and intertemporal translation—the very conflictual circumstances where, empirically, anthropology happens. That is a fancy, rather than plain, objective fact. And if this fancy fact consigns us readers and writers (including fieldworkers) to a fate of continual countertranslation and endless rereading, then who are we—as scientists, or humanists—to regret our fate or to wish that life and its perplexing rituals, including rituals of rereading, were otherwise?[2]

Resigned to radically "unplain" circumstances, I here revisit daring moments and neglected twists in one of American anthropology's most influential works, Ruth Benedict's *Patterns of Culture* (which is likewise resigned). Benedict herself occasionally approached rituals as "readings" of experience by practitioners of distinctive cultures. I in turn propose an ultraobjectively close reading of Benedict's reading of different cultures' "readings," which readings are themselves cross-cultural, and perhaps ultraobjective to boot.

Benedict moreover merits rereading because she read other significant readers (e.g., Nietzsche); and she both read and was read by Jane Belo, who also "read" (interpreted) a much-studied culture that I too have attempted interpreting: Bali, Indonesia. Another motive for championing Benedict anew is that she (along with Jane Belo) read other controversial readers (e.g., Margaret Mead) with a certain critical distance. I show below that Benedict cited Mead's findings from Samoa in a measured, guarded, yet generous way, when working out relational schemas for comparing patterns of duress in various rites of passage. Belo, moreover, flatly challenged Mead's claims about Balinese mothers, yet remained professionally and intellectually nurtured by Mead, who was, when Belo wrote, very much around to respond.

Ruth Benedict, Jane Belo, and Margaret Mead, following Franz Boas, considered themselves to be scientists, as do I. Indeed, Benedict and Belo demonstrated more adequate ideas of argument, verification, and nuance than some of Mead's belated detractors, such as Derek Freeman or Tessel Pollmann, who imply that findings from a given culture—Samoa, Bali, and so on—can be latterly restudied and definitively disproved or confirmed (an assumption to which Mead herself was not immune).[3] Benedict and Belo, on the other hand, deemed the living Mead's work in Samoa, Bali, and elsewhere susceptible of different construals, even without contrary evidence. I beg readers of the present chapter to bear this possibility in mind, along with Benedict's apparent inklings that her own arts of interpretation resembled those of cultures that she "intersubjectively observed."

ÜBER BENEDICT

In an offbeat book entitled *Other Tribes, Other Scribes*—modeled in part on syncopations in *Patterns of Culture*, among many comparative texts—I suggested that Ruth Benedict's chapters oscillate between diversity and integration. Two subsequent articles traced possible effects of Benedict's devices on other anthropologists—including Margaret Mead, Gregory Bateson, and Jane Belo (Boon, 1985a, 1986). Clifford Geertz's *Works and Lives* (1988) has emphasized the Swiftian side of Benedict's vision, with its pervasive sense of her own culture as a contrasting case, among other "others." I wish to extend these projects by observing proclivities among "us readers" to misremember what Benedict wrote, an ultraobjective beginning point that remains pivotal throughout this exercise in rereading.[4]

I have taught *Patterns of Culture* (1934/1961), *The Chrysanthemum and the Sword* (1948), and Benedict's published letters and poems repeatedly since 1973—20 long years. A curious reader response—student and scholarly, professional and lay alike—still intrigues me. Readers in the midst of *Patterns of Culture*, proceeding from phrase to phrase, turning page by page, seem alert to the quivering quality of its style and substance. Yet, having emerged from our reading experience, we become reluctant, perhaps unable, to re-cognize that quality after the fact. *Remembering having read* Benedict, we make her arguments and writing more centered, measured, balanced—yes, more "Apollonian"—than would have been observed in the actual reading thereof. What might explain this counter-empirical fact of forgetful remembering?

One culprit may be the skewed frameworks and dichotomous slogans borrowed by Benedict from other authors, schemes that govern all too well how readers assimilate her shifting cross-cultural judgments. A key example is that Apollonian/Dionysian (read, balanced/intoxicated) formulation culled from Nietzsche's *Birth of Tragedy*, dating from the time he still championed Richard Wagner. (Having discussed the latter's importance for modernist anthropology elsewhere, I try to repress the topic here, with only partial success.[5]) Benedict stipulates that she cites early Nietzsche in order to forefront "major qualities that differentiate Pueblo culture [namely, Zuni] from those of other American Indians" (p. 79). Phrased this way, her demonstration implies differential emphases across cultures, not essential identities.

Benedict eases Nietzsche's diametric contrast onstage in a gradual and qualified way; she cites Apollonian versus Dionysian as just one philosophical or literary device to yield contrastive configurations. Its companions include *Gestalt*, *Structur*, Dilthey's idealist *Weltanschauungen*, Spengler's Apollonian and Faustian extremes (designated by Benedict "opposed interpretations of existence"), and most lyrically Edward Carpenter's tag for a hopelessly extroverted West "endlessly catching its trains" (p. 55). Benedict's suggestive array can be regarded as an "arc of configurations" of concepts of configuration. She *selects* from these possibilities Nietzsche's "eternal contradiction" (1872/1967, p. 45), engaging it heuristically to highlight dramatic variations in cultures and their rituals.

The idea of "selection" stems from Edward Sapir, whose linguistics affords another explicit frame for Benedict's book:

> It is in cultural life as it is in speech: selection is the prime necessity. (p. 23)

> The great arc along which all the possible human behaviors are distributed is far too immense and too full of contradictions for any one culture to utilize even any considerable portion of it. Selection is the first requirement. Without selection no culture could even achieve intelligibility. (p. 237; see Boon, 1982, pp. 105–107)

Benedict, too, interpretively *selects* a notion of Nietzsche's from an arc or array of themes associated with Spengler, Carpenter, Dilthey, *Structur*, *Gestalt*. She need not delve deeply into Nietzsche's work (much less

Wagner's work, into which Nietzsche's work was delving deeply). Rather, Apollonian/Dionysian serves as a positional contrast; its sides are never dialectically conjoined by Benedict, as they are in Nietzsche's *Birth of Tragedy* on its way to Wagner:

> The effects wrought by the *Dionysian* also seemed "titanic" and "barbaric" to the Apollinian Greek; while at the same time he could not conceal from himself that he, too, was inwardly related to these overthrown Titans and heroes. Indeed, he had to recognize even more than this: despite all its beauty and moderation, his entire existence rested on a hidden substratum of suffering and of knowledge, revealed to him by the Dionysian. And behold: Apollo could not live without Dionysus! The "titanic" and the "barbaric" were in the last analysis as necessary as the Apollinian. . . .
> Contradiction, the bliss born of pain, spoke out from the very heart of nature. . . . (1872/1967, p. 46)

Also Sprach Nietzsche, or early Nietzsche engulfed in Wagner's music-drama, a fulsome dialectic that Benedict never quotes thusly.

Again, Benedict restricted her use of Nietzsche's contrast in ethnographic matters, although I suspect it meant more to her personally (one might say "subjectively"; see Boon, 1985). Nevertheless, and despite the fact that Nietzsche's duality is presented as just one among many possible themes, we readers retrospectively fixate on the diametric contrast, not the multiple field from which it is selected. Benedict's work tends to be remembered as the Apollonian/Dionysian (was that Zuni/Kwakiutl?) book. This is an objective fact of readers' response—and a contradiction ("bliss born of pain?")—that I (a reader) am longing to understand ultraobjectively.

Another aspect of *Patterns of Culture* that may lead readers retrospectively to disremember it is the text's eloquence—an uncustomary attribute of anthropological prose, certainly now and even "then," when Benedict wrote. Her sentences, paragraphs, and chapters contain movements to closure that effectively transfigure the very contents conveyed. Here, for example, she rounds off a conclusion to her controversial Zuni chapter:

> Like their version of man's relation to other men, their version of man's relation to the cosmos gives no place to heroism and man's will to overcome obstacles. It has not sainthood for those who,
>
> > Fighting, fighting, fighting,
> > Die driven against the wall.

> It has its own virtues, and they are singularly consistent. The ones that are out of place they have outlawed from their universe. They have made, in one small but long-established cultural island in North America, a civilization whose forms are dictated by the typical choices of the Apollonian, all of whose delight is in formality and whose way of life is the way of measure and of sobriety. (p. 129)

By "eloquence" I refer to Benedict's own "way of measure," her prose's careful cadence of rhythmic repetitions: "of life . . . of measure . . . and of sobriety."[6]

A seemingly opposite but somehow similar kind of closure occurs at the other, Dionysian extreme of Benedict's focal case studies. Despite her insistence on an endless ambivalence of Dionysian "double aspects"—she deems them "at once death-bringers and saviors from disease" (p. 121)— readers in the main recall the dramatic negatives of the textual curtain ringing down the Kwakiutl chapter proper:

> The megalomaniac paranoid trend is a definite danger in our society. It faces us with a choice of possible attitudes. One is to brand it as abnormal and reprehensible, and is the attitude we have chosen in our civilization. The other extreme is to make it the essential attribute of ideal man, and this is the solution in the culture of the Northwest Coast. (p. 222)

My long, long years of striving to teach Benedict reveal that this arresting comparison and compound declarative sentence virtually inhibit readers from attending to matters covered in the subsequent six pages, still describing Kwakiutl, but slipped into the next chapter (or, in this case, paragraph).

"The Nature of Society" chapter is devoted to Boasian issues of variability rather than integral wholes (even *comparatively* constituted ones). Its crucial discussion plus footnotes emphasize historical disloca- tions that brought Kwakiutl from Salish lands to Vancouver Island; it outlines apparent shifts in residence and inheritance patterns and con- flicts between past circumstances and recent matrilineal adjustments. Such dimensions are the very ones that Benedict has customarily been accused of omitting by her critics. This chapter even warns against mistaking her Zuni/Kwakiutl contrast as the "Procrustean bed of some catchword characterization," but to little avail (p. 228). What readers process—or perhaps I should say, what processes readings—is that over- drawn duality that continually returns to contour closure for chapters that actually are no more "integral" than the cultures they seek to represent.

At risk of sounding suspiciously insistent, let me belabor my interpretive point. We readers of Benedict "really" encounter a manifold, dislocating text about manifold dislocating cultures. But we order our recall of that experience by means of a selective reduction of the array of devices her text unleashes; we retrospectively tidy up her topics that spill over chapter boundaries and contradict the sense of closure conveyed by the text's very prose. Readers thus commit a perhaps inevitable "misreading" (a term I borrow with trepidation from Harold Bloom or Bloomians).[7] A misreading is more, much more, than simply an inaccurate reading. Indeed, such *ex post facto* "correction" into exaggerated order of irregular experience is a process reminiscent of the achievement Benedict attributes to extreme rituals.

The form a reader's memory bestows on Benedict's chapters calls to mind those very heightened performances—Zuni prayers, Dobu sorcery, Kwakiutl Cannibal dancing—that afford interpretive entrees into comparative cross-cultural configurations, selectively. After all, if reading—or (mis)remembering having read—is not a ritual, what is it? Might we say, then, that our reading of Benedict inadvertently adds another case in point to her conviction that subtle, shifting multiplicities are converted into implicitly diametric contradictions in cultural performances? Conversely, do not Benedict's basic insights into dramatic rites clarify why we readers cannot quite deflect Apollonian/Dionysian dualities from memories of descriptions that were—ultraobjectively—not so centered on or confined by them as we seem to recall?

One aspect of Benedict's *actual* text that runs counter to her own dichotomy is quite explicit; it pertains to the way her focal cases were stitched together. *Patterns of Culture* literally decentered any Apollonian-Zuni/Dionysian-Kwakiutl diametrics when Benedict inserted the critical Dobu chapter, summarized from Reo Fortune's book. Let us try to recollect how it worked.

The Dobu of Melanesia represent a third typological extreme figured between and against Zuni on the one hand and Kwakiutl on the other (see Boon, 1982, p. 107; 1990, p. 193). Dobu sorcery and alternating matrilocality contrast with Zuni priesthood and strong matrilineality and also with Kwakiutl shamanism and transitional stage of transmitting privileges via the maternal uncle (short of outright corporate matrilineages). Furthermore, a finer weave of contrasts characterizes the Native American and the Melanesian comparisons too. Benedict occasionally surveys cultural variations among Zuni/Hopi/Navaho/Apache as well as Kwakiutl/Salish/Haida. Even in her more concentrated Dobu chapter, that culture's extreme pattern configuration of "limited good"—whereby "any man's gain is another's loss" (p. 146)–is juxtaposed to the different ethos of Trobrianders, trading partners with Dobu in the celebrated Kula ring (Benedict 1934/1961, 154–156, relying on Malinowski, 1922).

These gradations, which I would call "chromatic" in the musical sense (Boon 1986, 1989a), are little noted in the more "diatonic" recall of readers. Nor in my teaching experience does Benedict's axis of comparison between Kwakiutl and Dobu register resoundingly, despite her occasional overblown psychopathological images: Kwakiutl "paranoia" and Dobuan "jealousy" (the latter term evoking the ethos attached to marriage bonds organized as competitive relationships). Neither Benedict's scheme of multiple variations nor her unfortunate diagnostic labels for Dobu and Kwakiutl excesses dispel our apparent need to imagine that her shifting text–covering many sides of social organization and ritual practice–simply fleshes out a singular dualism, filched from a mad philosopher. Even when the occasional reader does remember past an Apollonian/Dionysian (Zuni/Kwakiutl) dichotomy to the Dobu and Kwakiutl axis, he or she fixates on the sensational, ethnocentric, psychologistic emblems.

A rereading may help momentarily remind us that Benedict's account does not fundamentally brand cultures as psychotic or even neurotic. Rather, her chapters unfold demonstrations of ritual effecting a relative semblance of coherence for cultures. She argues that cultural "integration" is ordered *like* a psychosis is ordered (p. 275). The force of the simile is paramount; any culture's "normality" is configured as a field of contradictions held together by reinforcements and replications of pattern, but also by bold opposition to alternate "normalities" implicitly resisted: Zuni/not-Apache, nor even Hopi; Dobu/not-Trobriand; Kwakiutl/not-Salish nor Haidalike (although becoming moreso). Rereading Benedict can help us remember–at least until repression sets in–that her text compares normalized cultural patterning to "complexes" deemed deviant elsewhere (see also Belo 1960, pp. 11–13).[8]

I fear that my chapter may seem to be proposing a correct reading of Benedict, rather than imagining ways to counter a repressively singular reading of Benedict, perhaps an inevitable misreading. Paradoxically, however, I can only hope to offer fleeting rereadings remembering Benedict–ones wishing to become less governed retrospectively by her eloquence or by that Apollonian/Dionysian dichotomy, but likely failing. Toward that ultraobjective end, let me review certain manifest strategies behind *Patterns of Culture* and recall actual ritual practices featured in Benedict's semithick descriptions. Again, I foreground components that become lost on readers when our memory subjects itself to the cumulative, centering effects of her (to me) laudable prose.

ENDLESSLY CATCHING HER DRIFTS

The starting point of *Patterns of Culture* was Benedict's review of American Indian vision quests, which are largely but not exclusively male. Unlike pioneering surveys by Robert Lowie and diffusionist projects by Alfred Kroeber, her study extended even to the marked *absence* of individualized ritual ordeals and ecstatic suffering. To include Zuni—significant for lacking vision quests—creates a kind of survey-plus; Benedict becomes a configurationist with a difference, willing to push comparisons across negative ethnographic examples and contrary cases (Boon, 1982, chapter 3). Apparently forgotten, if indeed even passingly noticed by readers are hints of a parallel survey of another ritual *topos*—menstruation (p. 26).[9]

Benedict announces the topic of girls' puberty with extreme cases of rites of passage, including dramatically opposed ideas and institutions of purity/pollution: first, Carrier Indians who figuratively bury alive novice menstruaters, ritually isolating them for three years; second, Apache attitudes about first menses as occasions for supernatural sources of beneficial cure. Benedict at once complicates comparisons with a paragraph on Australian boys, subjected to ordeals of subincision, one of the most elaborate genital operations known to ethnography. She rounds off this mini-survey by mentioning Mead's news from Samoa that "natural turbulence" need not accompany female adolescence, that formal ritual ordeals during processes of sexual maturation are not universal.

In my experience dramatically diverse readers, from proponents of cultural interpretation to those of sociobiology, retain from her intricate paragraphs only the relativistic point, thus obscuring how Benedict actually composed the comparison. The text multiplies empirical cases, including seemingly polar ones; she carefully inserts evidence about male ordeals when framing the striking three-way opposition of menstruation practices that set off Carrier/Apache/Samoa. Her approach entails not a washed-out relativism but intensified, manifold extremes. I have tried to emulate Benedict's interpretive devices in many writings (including the present one), only to be misremembered in turn by "objective" readers.

Benedict drew on the strongest part of Mead's Samoan study to illustrate cultures that do not endow menstruation with ritualized ordeals. However, she need not have mentioned Mead (or Samoa) at all, because the most pertinent example of a decided absence of public trauma around menses is Zuni. Although the contrast among Carrier, Apache, and Zuni is not explicitly elaborated by Benedict, its implications are dispersed throughout her book. Certain Pueblos figure importantly for lacking ritual ordeals of both vision quests and menstrual pollution-seclusion. Zuni stand out thematically ("Apollonian") and ethnographically in this double respect. The point is eventually driven home 100 pages after saluting Samoa, a bare 17 taut paragraphs from the end of her Zuni chapter:

> Their handling of menstruation is especially striking. . . . All about them are tribes who have at every encampment small houses for the menstruating woman. . . . The Pueblos not only have no menstrual huts, but they do not surround women with precautions at this time. The catamenial periods make no difference in a woman's life. (p. 120)

It is against this dramatic dearth—whether among the Samoans or the Zuni—that the Kwakiutl appear in strongest contrast. The contrast, moreover, is more than diametric; it is, I would say, downright dialectical. Unlike Zuni, Kwakiutl accentuate Dionysian excess; they also accentuate menstruation, but for male as well as female protagonists. (That particular switch is what I call the dialectical part.[10])

Benedict gathers evidence of such complex reversals in her section on Kwakiutl "Cannibal dancing"—developed from Boas's and George Hunt's materials—which documents vivid ideas of pollution under the sign of menstruation. Following an adroit allusion to the contrasting ethos of "Oceanic epicurean cannibalism," Benedict portrays Kwakiutl practices without spotlighting menstrual rites as a primary theme. But she should not really need to; objectively (perhaps ultraobjectively) the relevant details are there for the reading. Not only are first menses of daughters occasions for potlatch redistribution (p. 244), but initiates into the Cannibal Society were exorcised of their Cannibal frenzy with smoke from cedar bark stained with the "menstrual blood of four women of the highest rank." A four-month tabu imposed on the male Cannibal dancer isolated him in a polluted state, complete with techniques of mediation:

> He used special utensils for eating and they were destroyed at the end of the period. He drank always ceremonially, never taking but four mouthfuls at a time, and never touching his lips to the cup. He had to use a drinking-tube and a head-scratcher. For a shorter period he was forbidden all warm food. When the period of his seclusion was over . . . he feigned to have forgotten all the ordinary ways of life. He had to be taught to walk, to speak, to eat . . . he was still sacrosanct. He might not approach his wife for a year, nor gamble, nor do any work. Traditionally he remained aloof for four years. (p. 179)

Here Benedict neglects to indicate that these specific utensils were required in menstrual huts throughout Native American cultures, certain Pueblos excepted. Variable practices ranging across New World menstrual codes have been traced in Lévi-Strauss's *Origin of Table Manners*, which compares European ideologies of education to Amerindian ethics devoted to governing the proprieties of daughters. To quote just one summary from Lévi-Strauss's empirical demonstration during 2,200 pages of his *Mythologiques*:

> The veil lifts to reveal a vast mythological system common to both South and North America, and in which the subjection of women is the basis of the social order. We can now understand the reason for this. The human wife's parents-in-law are not content just to present her with domestic utensils and to teach her the correct way to use them. The old man also proceeds to carry out a veritable physiological shaping of his daughter-in-law. In her pristine innocence, she did not have monthly periods and gave birth suddenly and without warning. [According to the myths] the transition from nature to culture demands that the feminine organism should become periodic, since the social as well as the cosmic order would be endangered by a state of anarchy in which regular alternation of day and night, the phases of the moon, feminine menstruation, the fixed period for pregnancy and the course of the seasons did not mutually support each other.
>
> So it is as periodic creatures that [according to the myths] women are in danger of disrupting the orderly working of the universe. Their social insubordination, often referred to in the myths, is an anticipation in the form of the "reign of women" of the infinitely more serious danger of their physiological insubordination. Therefore, women have to be subjected to *règles*. (1978, pp. 221–222)

Although Lévi-Strauss has proved a dedicated rereader of Boas' (and Benedict's) work, he makes no mention in this regard of Kwakiutl variations and inversions. Yet Benedict's chapter suggests that the entire society—whether regularly or in historical crisis—would ritually phase into an extreme dialectical form. That form is the equivalent of hyperperiodicity, ultramenstrual cycles (N.B.: hyper- and ultra- both translate *über*). The striking Cannibal dancer himself is ritually treated as a superfemale—exaggeratedly secluded, too much mediated, extraregulated—but with the gender sign reversed. Perhaps we should designate this Dionysian role an *Überfrau*—ultrawoman? Still nervously remembering (and questioning) Nietzsche (whom Benedict read), I also recall that topsy-turvy ritual configurations have time and again been shown by ethnographers and historians to link cultural continuity to historical conflict and severe duress—such as the Kwakiutl themselves were doubtless living out.

Following Benedict page by page and case to case, we readers encounter dispersed images of "defamiliarized" menstruation; but again, we erase them after the fact. Insofar as I know, *Patterns of Culture* has seldom been deemed pertinent to gender distinctions figured in diverse ritual extremes, including those of the Kwakiutl. Many readers' blindness to such available insights may stem from the book's paucity of information on Northwest Coast "women's lives"–apart from techniques of salmon pressing, a detail that I sheepishly retain from my first reading of this material during early adolescence.

By "screening," so to speak, ultraobjective images of male cannibal menstruators, our reading-recall processes Benedict's contents into the equivalent of an "objective" index, a technique of labeling that irons out the "outlandish." To better understand what I mean, consider this fragment from the actual index of *Patterns of Culture* (and imagine reading said index ultraobjectively):

> Magic, Dobu . . . Zuni
> Maidu, California
> Malinowski, B.
> Manus
> Marriage (nine subentries)
> Mead, Margaret
> Medicine, Charms (Dobu) . . . Societies (Zuni)
> Menstruation, Zuni [*punkt* . . . the sole subentry]
> Mental hygiene, Western
> Mexico, Northern, religious alcohol, whirling dance
> (*See also* Aztecs)
> *Middletown.* (p. 289)

This apparently objective index omits, of all things, reference to Kwakiutl under "menstruation." Deceptive index makers (like us misremembering readers) have edited out (or expurgated) emphasis on menstrual seclusion that Benedict's text displaces to its Northwest Coast chapter and disperses there as evidence of ritual inversion. Readers and index makers alike perhaps inadvertently end by "Apollonianizing" even her description of Kwakiutl Cannibal dancing—one of the more palpable evocations of Dionysian transgression and intoxication, or ecstasy, available from the literature called anthropology.

I ask again: Does Benedict's eloquence—even when presenting hyper-menstruating men—cancel our capacity to retain what our reading "experiences"; does her eloquence effectively configure our recollection into Apollonian forms? And does the same phenomenon occur when we turn to Shasta shamanism in the final chapter?

The Shasta woman comes on stage just after Benedict's famous section on homosexuality, *berdache* transvestism, and male/female role reversals—something of a relativist manifesto for impassioned tolerance. The Shasta shaman serves, movingly, to close the parenthesis that Benedict opened with the Digger Indian chief (a Christian, by the way) whose haunting proverb reproduced in Chapter 2 also provides the book's initial epigraph and sustained feeling-tone: "Our cup is broken now." In one of the few even quasidialogic moments in *Patterns of Culture*, the Digger chief was presented speaking directly to the author:

> A Chief of the Digger Indians, as the Californians call them, talked to me a great deal about the ways of his people in the old days. . . . When he talked of the shamans who had transformed themselves into bears . . . his hands trembled and his voice broke with excitement. (p. 21)[11]

The quavering tone recurs, intensifyingly, with the Shasta woman who— although known to Benedict only through Roland Dixon's 1907 study— sounds immediate, full-voiced, and utterly personal. Neither trance nor catalepsis is ever pretty, even when "honored in the extreme" as among women in Shasta culture. Benedict, having only read this speaker in print and translation, nevertheless inscribes her possession possessingly in passages I can only fragment and paraphrase:

> The imagined voices commanding she sing or be shot.
> The dreams of grizzly bears, free falls, and swarming yellow jackets.
> The violent moaning transposed to spirit's songs, until blood oozed from her mouth.
> Seizure at the threshold of death.

Following what I trust Benedict would forgive me for calling her ultraobjective evocation of yet another *Überfrau*, she adds a blessing-like intonation and rounding-off:

> From this time on she had in her body a visible materialization of her spirit's power, an icicle-like object which in her dances thereafter she would exhibit, producing it from one part of her body and returning it to another part. From this time on she continued to validate her supernatural power by further cataleptic demonstrations and she was called upon in great emergencies of life and death for curing and for divination and for counsel. She became, in other words, by this procedure a woman of great power and importance. (p. 267)

This individual Shasta shaman may be receiving preferred treatment from Benedict, if any voice did; but the point would be hard to prove. Nor did Benedict flatly favor Zuni culture over others, as readers like to imagine. I quote her:

> Certainly, it is said, exploitation of others in personal relations and overweening claims of the ego are bad whereas absorption in group activities is good; a temper is good that seeks satisfaction neither in sadism nor in masochism and is willing to live and let live. A social order, however, which like Zuni standardizes this "good" is far from Utopian. It manifests likewise the defects of its virtues. It has no place, for instance, for dispositions we are accustomed to value highly, such as force of will or personal initiative or the disposition to take up arms against a sea of troubles. It is incorrigibly mild. (p. 246)

Benedict's judgments—even, I suspect, of Shasta—keep quivering as her prose keeps reverberating. Objective readers may dream of knowing exactly what Benedict (and Shasta shaman) meant; ultraobjective readers may realistically rest content to dwell precisely on textual and contextual specifics that provide evidence of why such knowledge is difficult to gain.

I have been asking whether we can read Benedict's readings (of other's readings—including Roland Dixon) in a way that remembers both the eloquence of her prose and the distressed descriptions that it sometimes smooths over. I desire to keep reading Benedict as she apparently read not just Zuni (in part from speaking with them) and Shasta (solely from reading of them) but others as well—including Nietzsche, Virginia Woolf, and Japanese culture. How Benedict doubtless misread Nietzsche, or more precisely the 1924 translation of *The Birth of Tragedy* at her disposal, would lead us into dialectics too contorted for a brief chapter, or perhaps even for a gargantuan book. How Benedict read Virginia Woolf would swamp us in *The Waves*, which work Benedict was perusing when writing *Patterns*.[12] How Benedict read Japanese culture, she happily tells us in tactics set forth in *The Chrysanthemum and the Sword*, a work initiated in wartime and mindful of political realities:

> The study of comparative religions has flourished only when men were secure enough in their own conviction to be unusually generous. They might be Jesuits or Arabic savants or unbelievers, but they could not be zealots. The study of comparative cultures too cannot flourish when men are so defensive about their own way of life that it appears to them to be by definition the sole solution in the world. . . .
> In studying Japan, I was the heir of many students. Descriptions of small details of life were tucked away in antiquarian papers. Unlike many Oriental people they have a great impulse to write themselves out. They wrote about the trivia of their lives as well as about their

programs of world expansion. They were amazingly frank. Of course they did not present the whole picture. No people does. . . .

    I read this literature as Darwin says he read when he was working out his theories on the origin of species, noting what I had not the means to understand. What would I need to know to understand the juxtaposition of ideas in a speech in the Diet? What could lie back of their violent condemnation of some act that seemed venial and their easy acceptance of one that seemed outrageous? I read, asking the ever-present question: What is "wrong with this picture?" What would I need to know to understand it?

    I went to movies, too. (Benedict, 1948, pp. 5, 7)

I wonder if we can read Benedict this way, along with such cultures as she inscribed (including our own), always resisting zealotry (and reductive objectivity), even during extremist historical circumstances such as those engulfing us. Can we interpret Benedict and other cultures—and can all "other" cultures interpret each other—generously yet critically, seeking what is wrong with the picture? What does a reader need to know, and I do not mean just "biographically" (e.g., Caffrey, 1989), to understand Benedict's text resulting from her reading of others? To do unto Benedict and each other that which she does unto Kwakiutl/Zuni/Dobu/Digger/Shasta/US . . . such would be my ultraobjective desire for periodic, regular cycles of rereading.

RE BELO

Meanwhile, let me conclude, as promised, with Jane Belo, if only to displace my heartfelt chapter from its author's obvious passion for, or obsession with, Ruth Benedict's writings. Jane Belo, whose personal complexities may have matched Benedict's and whose psychological frailties surpassed hers, related to Benedict and Benedict to her as each other's reader. Belo was an ethnographer *extraordinaire* of Balinese culture (see Boon, 1977, p. 56); in 1949 she published her intricate study of Bali's celebrated witch dance, *Rangda and Barong*, which Benedict had read, perhaps the very year of her death. Belo's book thanks Professor Ruth Benedict, "who patiently went over the original material and whose deep understanding of culture was an inspiration to all who knew her" (1949, p. v).[13]

    Belo's contextual account—the same one that Benedict patiently went over—takes exception with Margaret Mead's views on Balinese women, mainly mothers. Elsewhere in Belo's works, including the later *Trance in*

Bali (1960), she credits Mead (and Gregory Bateson) with showing her the light of culture and personality theory and with converting her methods to proper fieldwork techniques of clocked documentation (see Boon, 1990, p. 91). Belo thus appreciated Mead, from whom she certainly benefited during the crazy, tragic political circumstances that I attempted to revisit evocatively in "Between-the-Wars Bali" (Boon, 1986). But Belo's 1949 study sharply rejects Mead's view of Rangda as the Balinese "Mother Figure representative of the total feeling toward the mother," extended in a substitution "carried over into adulthood until the young man looks forward to marrying a girl who will turn into a witch" (Belo, 1949, p. 38). She argues instead:

> Rangda serves only as a representation of the fear aspect of the Mother Figure. There is a split in the feeling toward the mother, the destructive, witchlike, devouring, and deathly side of her represented in the Rangda, which Mead and Bateson have stressed, and the loving, beautiful, food-giving aspect of the living woman. (p. 38)

Let me go on citing, ultraobjectively and selectively, a convoluted episode later in Belo's ethnography. She has been citing, likewise, her own sequential notes from 1937 (stopwatch-timed to the week, day, hour, and minute). They run as follows:

Sindoe, April 26, 1937
It is 1:50 A.M. The girls take down the little gods from the shrine, hold them in the right hand, by the waist. They form two lines, facing the Durga shrine, and libations are poured before them. The *gamelan* is playing a delicate tinkling tune. The two lines face each other, cross and recross. . . . The *gamelan* plays the climactic music (called *batel*) as if this were the moment to go in trance, but it does not happen. . . .
The men continue with the order of the ritual, the ceremonial "crossing of spears" (*maloeang toembak*). Ketjig (who is possessed by a tiger) and I Poetoe go into trance and do the self stabbing before the Durga shrine. The small boys shout. . . . It is nine minutes past two. The girls take the little gods again. Moenet (one of the young married women, an excellent dancer) leads with the brazier . . . [and] begins a wild dance, her eyes staring. This starts them all off. Simultaneously, Ketjig begins to do *ngoerek* (self stabbing) in the center. A little plump girl, Ngales, about fourteen, falls down on her knees, her legs one to each side, crying loudly and hysterically. The girls go on dancing; one by one they give a shout and fall down crying. Ketjig falls flat on the offerings on the sand, but just lies there stiff, does not devour any of them. (p. 48)

An empirical record could hardly appear more objective. Yet Belo interrupts her self-citing description by abruptly inserting notes taken 8 months later in the same temple by Margaret Mead. Indeed, Belo cites Mead's description—whose claims she is rejecting—verbatim, from 9:00, 9:38, 10:10, 10:11, 10:19, and so on:

> Dajoe [of Brahmana caste] goes down on her knees, digging the *boeng boeng* (little god) into the ground, head down. The old priest comes and takes the *boeng boeng*. Dajoe holds her hands clasped between her knees, continues to sway. . . . Dajoe is getting more excited. . . . Ketjig gives a yell, faces each and glares into her face. . . . Second girl goes down, knees pointing out, wide apart, also digs the doll into the sand, screaming and crying. Moenet dances over her. Moenet gives the impression of being a sort of presiding genius, infinitely more advanced in the mysteries which are under foot. . . . Ngales goes down, digs her doll *into her lap* and into the sand. Priest drags Dajoe forward, in tears.
>
> 10:10 P.M. . . . Moenet . . . weaves in and out, touches the ones on the edge, gathers them into the group. (Comment) This is the most witchlike thing I have seen in Bali, the lightness, the sense of weaving a spell, catching the neophytes in a net with cool, light, impersonal Evil, is very strong. (p. 50)

Again, it is critical to note that Belo is citing Mead's "objective" description interrupted by Mead's own "subjective" comment on Balinese women's witchlikeness. But before Belo returns to her own description of eight months beforehand (Sindoe, April 27, 1937), she interjects a dissenting commentary on Mead's description plus comment. I reiterate: Belo interrupts Mead's self-interrupting notes—notes that Belo had used to interrupt her own notes that form the bulk of the evidence in her study. And the insight Belo suddenly offers into certain theories of psychological anthropology then (and even now) current is arresting:

> It is also quite clear that [Margaret Mead] sees in the little god figures something equivalent for the female to the kris (ceremonial dagger) of the male, something between a phallus and a baby. In her view, as in mine, there is an underlying principle of female fertility symbolically expressed in the little puppet-like figures. But the witchery, the threat, and the evil quality she sees surrounding this aspect of the ceremonial I tend to see rather in the Rangda manifestations and in the undifferentiated aspects of the Durga theme. (p. 51)

"Something between a phallus and a baby. . . ." Belo's memorable image could take us far into possible motives of Margaret Mead's cross-cultural readings, plus possible reasons they have prompted both appreciative and reactionary responses long after their currency (see Boon, 1985a, 1986). But my own avowed motive for interjecting here Belo's intervention—which emphasizes differences between her own reading of Balinese women and Margaret Mead's reading of Balinese women—is to savor the thought of Ruth Benedict happening upon the aphoristic "something between" during her encounter of Belo's text acknowledged in its introduction.

My reading culminates at a moment recalling the fact of Benedict's reading Belo's reading of Margaret Mead's reading of Balinese rites and extreme practices—if only to imagine a glint in Benedict's readerly eye that must have matched the quiver in her writerly prose. Cross-cultural evidence is composed of overlappings and intertextualities so richly intricate that anthropologists—as natives—can only keep trying to interpret them, ultraobjectively.

SIGN OFF

My only half-winking notion of ultraobjectivity pertains to ongoing rereading—I once designated it "reading toward the panoply"— engaged in by cultural actors and their/our investigators (Boon, 1986, 1990). In contrast to many received ideas of objectivity that imply conventions of research/restudy and proof/refutation, "ultraobjectivity" participates in the actualities (and truths) of what cultures do, including translating each other's differences. Any translator of cultures—whether he or she is willing to acknowledge the fact—is personally both culturally and historically enmeshed, ultraobjectively.[14]

Pursuing cross-cultural research as a spiraling art of rereading rather than as a singular strategy of proving is hardly a new device in the repertoire of anthropology.[15] To reiterate one last time the cycle nearest to hand, I know no more powerful insight into an objective "subjectivity" guiding Margaret Mead's work overall—in Samoa, Manus, Omaha, New Guinea, Bali—than Belo's critical insight into Mead's imagining "something between a phallus and a baby." This extreme and excessive "take"— one could even call it *ultra*—on Mead's endeavors apparently passed the muster of Benedict's perusal of the manuscript of Belo's 1949 book. That receptive reading by Benedict of Belo (and of Mead) is one reason for my continued praise of Benedict and Belo alike.

It even occurs to me that this *leitmotiv* in Mead's lifetime quest—"something between a phallus and a baby"—may help illuminate why her outsized professional example eventually has proved threatening to certain observers following in her wake and driven to refute her.[16] But to argue that point would require considering works that seem (to me) less worthy of rereading—works oblivious to fuller cultural contradictions and truths. And that "explanatory" task I resolve to leave to others, and to other brands of objectivity.

ACKNOWLEDGMENTS

I thank members of the Committee on Social Theory for generous responses, particularly Theodore Schatzki, Thomas Hakansson, John Paul Jones III, John Pickles, Jeremy Popkin, Wolfgang Natter (who mentioned Freudian "belatedness" at a timely moment), plus other participants in the seminar on "Objectivity and Its Others," and Joseph Engelberg who sent a welcome letter from an unknown biophysicist. This chapter, which ripened at Kentucky, sprang from a seed sown in 1987 at Vassar, where Judith Goldstein organized a centennial observation of Ruth Benedict's birth; celebrants who responded appreciatively included Karen Blu, Clifford Geertz, and Richard Handler. Helpful comments came from Hildred Geertz and Ernestine Friedl at Princeton University and from Robert Borofsky and Jon Anderson who read a brief version prepared for the 1988 meetings of the American Anthropological Society. Special thanks, always, to David Schneider who once gave me a copy of Belo's *Rangda and Barong* that I have been rereading ever since.

NOTES

1. On an "interpretive turn" in the social sciences or *sciences humaines* overall, see, for example, Ricoeur (1981) Rabinow and Sullivan (1979), and Skinner (1985); on anthropology in particular see Geertz (1973), Boon (1982), Clifford and Marcus (1986), and particularly Brady (1991), which samples under the refreshing rubric of "Anthropological Poetics" much "harmony and argument" in rival styles of cross-cultural interpretation, ethnographic narrative, and comparative analysis, with expert editorial guidance.

2. A useful overview of "interpretive conventions" with the accent on reading and readers is Mailloux (1982), alert to pragmatist, structuralist, post-Heideggerian, and deconstructive twists that have fueled reception study and reader-response criticism. Among abundant efforts in many disciplines to "reread" nonfiction works "as written," let me just signal Mahoney's (1982, 1987) evenhanded studies of Freud "as writer" that accentuate "the workings of the style." Mahoney places Freud's texts in a tradition of *pensée pensante*: "Typically, Freud's composition is processive, not uniformly unidirectional but still progressive amid its ebbs and floods. Its essence can be to an extent appreciated by a glance at the change from the Ciceronian to

the Baroque style in the 16th century" (1982, p. 163). Such "processive" writing engages its readers (including Freud as his own reader) in an experience of and as *reading* whose dimensions recall what Kenneth Burke (1966) designates "symbolic action." I admit to wishing to emulate rituals of writing–reading, whose analogies can be detected in many cultures and anthropologies, among other disciplines. The corpus of Claude Lévi-Strauss, for example, saturated with ethnographic evidence, is simultaneously an act of "processive" writing devised to engage readers (musically) as such (see Boon, 1972, 1982, 1985b,1986, 1989a); that this Proustian dimension of Lévi-Strauss has often fallen on deaf anthropological (and deconstructive) ears recalls the professional history of refusing such "processiveness" in Freud's writing, among that of many others.

Aspects of rituals of reading practice pertain to the concrete arts of rhetoric (see, e.g., Burke, 1970); related issues in historiography may be sampled in De Certeau (1984, 1986) and essays by La Capra (1985, 1987). An engaging, anthropological study that relates arts of reading to the social history of literary production (and Jane Austen's ethnographic gifts) is Handler and Segal (1990).

3. The vast, tangled, vivid, often livid literature swirling around the (late) Mead/(living) Freeman debate can be surveyed in Caton (1990); in my judgment this convenient collection is "loaded" (rather than "objective?") because it poses as the central issue "cultural determinism," reified into something that "theory" is either for or against. A richer sense of intensive, circumstantial paradox—pertaining to both "Samoa" and "science," in matters of "description" and "theory" alike—occurs in the reviews of Ivan Brady and in the ethnography of Brad Shore, included and referenced in the Caton volume. If this remark of mine causes readers to suspect that I side with Mead against Freeman, this very suspicion conveys the inevitability of recurring polarities produced in the name of "objectivity." What I am calling ultraobjective readings cannot simply deny such processes of polarization but must weather them; that is the epistemological, ethnographic, comparative, and interpretive point of the present chapter (see also, Boon, 1986, pp. 239–243). Pollman's piece against Mead is engaged in this chapter's final footnote.

4. For fine insights into Sapir, whose works and life so resonated with Benedict's, see Handler (1986; see also his recent essay [1990] on Benedict). For studies of diverse histories of different schools of anthropology see the series edited by George Stocking, stressing historicist, epistemological, interpretive, and political issues from the discipline's manifold pasts (e.g., Stocking, 1983, 1986).

5. I have addressed intricate connections between Wagner and Lévi-Strauss (Boon, 1989a), who writes in the history of French engagement with Wagner; I touch on "Wagner" (both Richard and Cosima) and Nietzsche as well, among many others. Prattis's recent effort (1991) to pin down Lévi-Strauss's concern with *Parsifal* (along with Jung's) ignores his arts of corpus making, attuned to relations between musical and textual form. Lévi-Strauss's attention to Wagner may appear on its surface to be a matter of parallel "synopses of mythic plots;"

but its depths and follow-through pertain to processes of composition, to myth and music *as experienced,* or perhaps as read. The very technique of myth synopsis that Prattis forefronts (1991, pp. 128–130) is continually overturned in Lévi-Strauss's Wagnerian devices of sustained, motive-driven composition (Boon, 1972, 1985b, 1989a).

6. A stylistics of "eloquence" in such anthropological authors as Frazer, Benedict, and Lowie is considered in Boon (1982, chapter 1, pp. 97–111). Similar moments in Belo's style are briefly noted in Boon (1986, p. 225). See also relevant discussions of so-called modernist anthropological textuality in Manganaro (1990). On "closure" in literary fiction as its devices affect readers' memory, see Torgovnick (1981, pp. 3–4), plus Rabinowitz (1987) and Eco (1979) from a vast literature on literature.

7. I have in mind Bloom's influential *Anxiety of Influence* (1973) and *Map of Misreading* (1975). Lacking both the expertise and the will to address ultimate consequences of Bloomian "misprision," let me again recommend Mailloux (1982) as a worthy guide for readers hoping to keep some bearings when confronting inevitabilities of misreading.

8. "Complex" in the technical sense of analytical psychology is Jung's term. I am using it more generally, as did Jane Belo when describing the "puppet complex" in Balinese aesthetics, sensibilities, selves, perhaps shadow selves, indeed life:

> The puppet complex, then, could be summed up thus: A puppet is that which represents a spirit. Plays are originally representations of nonhuman spirits. By dramatic connotation, actors and dancers are like puppets, for they behave in accordance with a spirit which is not their own. By connotation of the mystery of life and death, a baby is like a puppet, for it is mysteriously imbued with a spirit. Conversely, a puppet is like a baby, for it is small and lovable, its ways are unaccountable. Little children make the best, the most puppetlike dancers.
>
> When people went in trance, they would behave like children. They would cry, call out to father and mother, express urgent and unpredictable desires, and would not be quieted until these desires were satisfied. Being like gods, they would behave like children. In some way the gods themselves are children. (1960, pp. 11–13)

I cannot imagine a more ultraobjective ethnographic interpretation than Belo's superb summary (see also Belo, 1953, 1970).

9. An interpretive notion of *topos,* borrowed from literary history and art history, is applied to anthropological matters in Boon (1977, p. 226). A pervasive topic of *topos* (a topic of "topic") and a rubric of "ritual *cum* rhetoric" is elaborated from the comparative history of discursive practices ranging from European rhetoric to Indic "Tantrism" in Boon (1990, Chapters 1, 3, 7). A related project (Boon, 1994) begins pursuing across cultures and times ritual *topoi* of circumcision/uncircumcision with the most specific textual evidence I can muster.

10. On diverse dialectics of power and ritual associated with gender differences, see the comparative collection by Atkinson and Errington (1990) on local

politics and social structure in the cultures and histories of island Southeast Asia.

11. On "dialogic" (vs. authorial monologue) approaches in ethnographic description, see Tedlock (1982) and Clifford and Marcus (1986). The now-classic source on "dialogism" in novelistic arts and politics is Bakhtin (1981); for some links between Bakhtin and the anthropology of ritual, see Bruner (1984), and Boon (1990, chapters 3–4). Bakhtin's companion theme of carnivalization has long been foregrounded in the anthropology of ritual reversal, nowhere more persuasively than the "closing" movements (oscillating between Saturnalia and Balder) of Frazer's venerable *Golden Bough*, aptly redesignated in its French translation, *Le cycle de la rameau d'or*. "Cycle" added to Frazer's original title nicely suggests neverending rereadability.

12. For further thoughts on Benedict as writer, see Babcock (1986)—fascinating in its own right and intent on identifying. Again, for Benedict's biography, see Caffrey (1989); I (Boon, 1985a, 1986) have expressed misgivings about reading "biography" as the "life behind" any text, including ethnographies.

13. Belo's *Trance in Bali* (1960) makes key references to Benedict, including her arguments that "personality trends considered abnormal in our culture may be highly valued in another culture and therefore are considered *no longer abnormal* (p. 6); Belo also reports: "Ruth Benedict, who made the classical distinction between Apollonian and Dionysian configurations of culture, went over our material with great care and came to the conclusion that the distinction could not be applied to Balinese culture. Their customary poise and moderation resembles the Apollonian, while the outbreak into trance, approved and recognized in the culture, is nearer to the Dionysian" (Belo, 1960, p. 1). For suggestions that Bali, or any culture when closely read, deflects similar dichotomous formulations (such as Mary Douglas's "grid/group" analyses), see Boon (1983).

Jane Belo's lives and works and their intricate contexts are the subject of current research by Anne McCauley.

14. Translators across cultures "such as Bali" include such non-Balinese as Jane Belo and Margaret Mead, such Balinese as I Gusti Ngurah Bagus and I Made Badem, and such other "others" and "we's" as Ruth Benedict, I Wayan Bhadra, Gregory Bateson, and me among hosts of other others. Such a list can be drummed up for any culture—that is, for any particular "we" (including "us")—including Samoa; that list might tally Derek Freeman *as translator*, along with other non-Samoans (e.g., Mead) and other Samoans (e.g., Albert Wendt), each with contradictory credentials as such. At risk of repeating myself: It is an objective fact that multiple translators continually negotiate boundaries of "insider/outsider" cultural representations; to insistently take this objective fact into account produces ultraobjectivity.

15. For an experiment in rereading readings of Bali, including my own, which, because it foregrounds tourism, is likely to be misread as "postmodern," but is actually situated in a long-term history of cross-cultural representations, see Boon (1992); this piece, too, attempts "processive" writing (see above, n. 3).

16. Readers of Mead's *Blackberry Winter* may gather that related motives per-

vaded her "interpersonal" *recherches* as well, see Boon (1985a, 1986, pp. 240–241). Dense intricacies and occasional insinuations lacing Mead's works—both her ethnographies and popularizations—are one reason why efforts to reduce her studies to transparent, self-serving motives fail. A recent, dismissal of Mead in Bali by T. Pollmann (1990)—whose critical strategies are antithetical to the interpretive arts I am emphasizing—prompts this final, disproportionately long endnote.

Pollmann, a former reporter with *Vrij Nederland*, then Head of Public Relations at the Netherlands' Rijksdienst Monumentenzorg, has absorbed standard techniques of tabloid format. Her piece reads like second-string "investigative reporting" of nonnews, and belatedly at that. (For further thoughts about this fashion in *critique*, plus some admiring remarks about a quasiparody of such exposé style by Gita Mehta, see Boon, 1989b; a Balinese voice similar to Gita Mehta's, but unparodic, is Ibu Gedong Bagus Oka, cited by Pollmann, p. 21.) Pollmann's devices include: (1) ready and willing references to sexual preferences (e.g., Mead and her "guru" Benedict as lovers, Walter Spies's *penchant* for males); (2) smug assumptions that "informants" duped the likes of Mead (in colonialist contexts) but that "sources" today give the straight dope to investigators like herself; (3) instant reduction of complex conflicts and contradictions to packaged epithets designed to reveal the fact that the reporter is "in the know." For example, Pollmann tags Boas thusly: "Franz Boas, the godfather of modern American anthropology, is a German Jew who left his fatherland and came to America. In Germany he experienced the rise of anti-semitism. It marked him" (1990, p. 7). After a passing reference to the nature–nurture debate, eugenics, and all that, she puts Boas "on the nurture side" and drops the matter (for a fuller story, see Stocking 1974, 1979, 1983).

Pollmann ostensibly aims to expose the naiveté of various interwar connoisseurs of Balinese culture and of several brands of anthropologist: "In a way the Boasian anthropologists are the opposite of those anthropologists today who go to the Third World to change the fates of the natives. And yet they are alike: both reckon that they will have political influence at home. Both suffer from wishful thinking. Both sympathize too easily with political ideologies which change countries in police-states" (p. 9). What Pollmann wishfully thinks or sympathizes with in contrast goes unexpressed. She challenges several varieties of cross-cultural research through gambits that convert real dilemmas to slick, sarcastic copy. Preposterously— after acknowledging help from a Dutch historian here and a young American political scientist there—she claims to provide the straight dope on Balinese views. Interviews "fifty years later" with I Made Kaler—Mead and Bateson's assistant—are introduced as though his memories could coincide with events half a century ago. Pollmann declares that I Made Kaler now reveals that he "was never open with them," as though Mead (or Bateson, of all epistemologists) would have assumed the contrary (see Boon 1986). Intent on "scooping" old news, Pollmann forgets to headline that "the Balinese" might have also been unopen with that recent interviewer (a Dutch historian on whom she relies), and he with them. She leaves unexplored how intersubjectivities become translated and paraphrased (by her)–the journalist's stock in trade (see Malcolm, 1989).

Pollmann achieves "reflexivity" and testy critique about *them* (e.g., Mead and Bateson) and their profession, but not about herself and hers; and she presumes to speak *for* I Made Kaler. An equally testy counter-critique must address whether that patronizing style Pollmann so quickly points up in colonialist-era descriptions is an object of "denial" in her own. Regardless, her rhetoric of reportage censors evidence of complexity and tags as "symptoms" sexual preferences, political persuasions, and perhaps nationalities and *zeitgeists* as well (see Boon, 1986, 1994). Against such "objectivity"–whether directed at "natives" observed or "observers" observed–I promote the arts of rereading, devoted to rich contradictions of Balinese and Balinists alike. (*Re*reading, by the way, produces the "first" evidence of anything, including "Bali," that can be argued; see Boon, 1977, pp. 66–69).

This terminal note, however, has interrupted rereading Benedict and Belo (and Mead) to read against Pollmann. In doing so, whose puppet (or, in Balinese terms, puppet, child, and god [see above, n.8]) am I? What forces govern my lapse into an analysis that confronts and dismisses Pollmann, as she confronted and dismissed Mead, rather than leaving that objectionable task to other objectivities? How can my long note and the closing paragraph of the essay that it "counterpoints" manifestly contradict each other's stated desires and resolve? For an answer to this (rhetorical) question, do not ask me (an interpretive type); rather ask someone like Pollmann herself (as this endnote has imagined her), or like Pollmann's imagined Balinese. Yes, ask "them," if such transparent, consistent, and undialectical "natives" or "reporters" exist, to be investigated and diagnosed–which I salutarily, and at risk of self-contradiction, doubt . . . ultraobjectively.

REFERENCES

Atkinson, J., & Errington, S. (Eds.). (1990). *Power and difference: Gender in Island Southeast Asia*. Stanford: Stanford University Press.

Babcock, B. (1986). *Not in the absolute singular: Re-reading Ruth Benedict*. Paper distributed for Wenner–Gren Conference, *Daughters of the Desert*.

Bakhtin, M. (1981). *The dialogic imagination* (M. Holquist & C. Emerson, Trans.). Austin: University of Texas Press.

Belo, J. (1949). *Bali: Rangda and Barong*. Monographs of the American Ethnological Society. Seattle: University of Washington Press.

Belo, J. (1953). *Bali: Temple festival*. Seattle: University of Washington Press.

Belo, J. (1960). *Trance in Bali*. New York: Columbia University Press.

Belo, J. (Ed.). (1970). *Traditional Balinese culture*. New York: Columbia University Press.

Benedict, R. (1948). *The chrysanthemum and the sword*. Boston: Houghton Mifflin.

Benedict, R. (1961). *Patterns of culture.* New York: Houghton Mifflin. (Original work published 1934)

Bloom, H. (1973). *The anxiety of influence.* New York: Oxford University Press.

Bloom, H. (1975). *A map of misreading.* New York: Oxford University Press.

Boon, J. A. (1972). *From symbolism to structuralism: Lévi-Strauss in a literary tradition.* New York: Harper & Row.

Boon, J. A. (1977). *The anthropological romance of Bali, 1597–1972: Dynamic perspectives in marriage and caste, politics and religion.* New York: Cambridge University Press.

Boon, J. A. (1982). *Other tribes, other scribes: Symbolic anthropology in the comparative study of cultures, histories, religions, and texts.* New York: Cambridge University Press.

Boon, J. A. (1983, Spring). America: Fringe benefits. *Raritan,* pp. 97–121.

Boon, J. A. (1985a). Mead's mediations: Some semiotics from the Sepik, by way of Bateson, on to Bali. In R. Parmentier & B. Mertz (Eds.), *Semiotics, self, and society* (pp. 333–357). New York: Academic Press.

Boon, J. A. (1985b). Claude Lévi-Strauss. In Q. Skinner, (Ed.), *The return of grand theory* (pp. 159–176). Cambridge: Cambridge University Press.

Boon, J. A. (1986). Between-the-wars Bali: Rereading the relics. In G. Stocking (Ed.), *History of anthropology* (Vol. 4, pp. 218–247). Madison: University of Wisconsin Press.

Boon, J. A. (1989a). Lévi-Strauss, Wagner, Romanticism: A reading-back. In G. Stocking (Ed.), *History of anthropology* (Vol. 6, pp. 124–168). Madison: University of Wisconsin Press.

Boon, J. A. (1989b). Against coping across cultures: Some semiotics of self-help rebuffed. In G. Urban & B. Lee, (Eds.), *Semiotics, self, and society: Essays in honor of Milton Singer* (pp. 153–170). The Hague: Mouton.

Boon, J. A. (1990). *Affinities and extremes: Crisscrossing the bittersweet ethnology of East Indies history, Hindu-Balinese culture, and Indo-European allure.* Chicago: University of Chicago Press.

Boon, J. A. (1992). Cosmopolitan moments: Echoey confessions of an ethnographer-tourist. In D. Segal & H. Liebersohn, (Eds.), *Crossing cultures* (pp. 226–253). Phoenix: University of Arizona Press.

Boon, J. A. (1994). Circumscribing circumcision/uncircumcision: An essay amidst the history of difficult description. In S. Schwartz (Ed.), *Implicit understanding* (pp. 556–585). New York: Cambridge University Press.

Brady, I. (Ed.). (1991). *Anthropological poetics.* Savage, MD: Rowman & Littlefield.

Bruner, E. (Ed.). (1984). *Text, play and story: The construction and reconstruction of self and society.* Prospect Heights: Waveland Press.

Burke, K. (1966). *Language as symbolic action.* Berkeley: University of California Press.

Burke, K. (1970). *The rhetoric of religion.* Berkeley: University of California Press.

Caffrey, M. M. (1989). *Stranger in this land.* Austin: University of Texas Press.

Caton, H. (Ed.). (1990). *The Samoa reader: Anthropologists take stock.* Lanham, MD: University Press of America.

Clifford, J., & Mareus, G. (Eds.). (1986). *Writing culture*. Berkeley: University of California Press

De Certeau, M. (1984). *The practice of everyday life* (S.F. Rendall, Trans.). Berkeley: University of California Press.

De Certeau, M. (1986). *Heterologies: Discourse on the other* (B. Massumi, Trans.). Minneapolis: University of Minneapolis Press.

Dixon, R. B. (1907). The Shasta. *Bulletin of the American Museum of Natural History, 17*, 381–498.

Eco, U. (1979). *The role of the reader*. Bloomington: University of Indiana Press.

Geertz, C. (1973). *The interpretation of cultures*. New York: Basic Books.

Geertz, C. (1988). *Works and lives: The anthropologist as author*. Stanford: Stanford University Press.

Handler, R. (1986). Vigorous male and aspiring female: Poetry, personality and culture in Edward Sapir and Ruth Benedict. In G. Stocking (Ed.), *Malinowski, Rivers, Benedict, and others: History of anthropology* (Vol. 4, pp. 127–155). Madison: University of Wisconsin Press.

Handler, R. (1990). Ruth Benedict and the modernist sensibility. In M. Manganaro (Ed.), *Modernist anthropology* (pp. 163–180). Princeton, New Jersey: Princeton University Press.

Handler, R. & Segal, D. (1990). *Jane Austin and the fiction of culture*. Tucson: University of Arizona Press.

LaCapra, D. (1985). *History and criticism*. Ithaca: Cornell University Press.

LaCapra, D. (1987). *History, politics, and the novel*. Ithaca: Cornell University Press.

Lévi-Strauss, C. (1978). *The origin of table manners*. (J. Weightman & D. Weightman, Trans). Chicago: University of Chicago Press.

Mahony, P. J. (1982). *Freud as a writer*. New York: International Universities Press.

Mahony, P. J. (1987). *Freud as a writer* (expanded ed.). New Haven: Yale University Press.

Mailloux, S. (1982). *Interpretive conventions: The reader in the study of American fiction*. Ithaca: Cornell University Press.

Malcolm, J. (1989, March 13, 20). Reflections (journalism), Parts I and II. *The New Yorker*.

Malinowski, B. (1922). *Argonauts of the Western Pacific*. London: Routledge & Kegan Paul.

Manganaro, M. (Ed.). (1990). *Modernist anthropology*. Princeton: Princeton University Press.

Nietzsche, F. (1967). *The birth of tragedy and the case of Wagner* (W. Kaufmann, Trans.). New York: Vintage. (Original work published 1872)

Pollmann, T. (1990). Margaret Mead's Balinese: The fitting symbols of the American dream. *Indonesia, 49*, 1–35.

Prattis, J. I. (1991). "Parsifal" and semiotic structuralism. In I. Brady (Ed.), *Anthropological poetics* (pp. 111–131). Savage, MD: Rowman & Littlefield.

Rabinow, P., & Sullivan, W. (Eds.). (1979). *Interpretive social science*. Berkeley: University of California Press.

Rabinowitz, P. J. (1987). *Before reading: Narrative conventions and the politics of interpretation*. Ithaca: Cornell University Press.

Ricoeur, P. (1981). *Hermeneutics and the human sciences* (J. B. Thompson, Trans.). Cambridge: Cambridge University Press.

Skinner, Q. (Ed.). (1985). *The return of grand theory in the human sciences*. Cambridge: Cambridge University Press.

Stocking, G. (1974). *The shaping of American anthropology: A Franz Boas reader*. New York: Basic Books.

Stocking, G. (1979). Anthropology as Kulturkampf: Science and politics in the career of Franz Boas. In *The uses of anthropology* (Special Publications 11). Washington, DC: American Anthropological Association.

Stocking, G. (Ed.). (1983). *Observers observed: History of anthropology* (Vol. 1). Madison: University of Wisconsin Press.

Stocking, G. (Ed.) (1986). *Malinowski, Rivers, Benedict, and others: History of anthropology* (Vol. 4). Madison: University of Wisconsin Press.

Tedlock, D. (1982). *The spoken word and the work of interpretation*. Philadelphia: University of Pennsylvania Press.

Torgovnick, M. (1981). *Closure in the novel*. Princeton: Princeton University Press.

Index